BEYOND THE
INVISIBLE HAND

BEYOND
THE INVISIBLE HAND

GROUNDWORK
FOR A NEW
ECONOMICS

Kaushik Basu

PRINCETON UNIVERSITY PRESS   PRINCETON AND OXFORD

Published by Princeton University Press, 41 William Street,
Princeton, New Jersey 08540

In the United Kingdom: Princeton University Press, 6 Oxford Street,
Woodstock, Oxfordshire OX20 1TW

press.princeton.edu

Library of Congress Cataloging-in-Publication Data

Basu, Kaushik.
Beyond the invisible hand : groundwork for a new economics / Kaushik Basu.
p.   cm.
Includes bibliographical references and index.
ISBN: 978-0-691-13716-2 (hardcover : alk. paper)
1. Economics. 2. Economic policy. I. Title.
HB71 .B37 2010
330.1—dc22
2010012135

British Library Cataloging-in-Publication Data is available

This book has been composed in Goudy

Printed on acid-free paper. ∞

Printed in the United States of America

1   3   5   7   9   10   8   6   4   2

To the memory of my father,

Keshab Chandra Basu (1905–86)

CONTENTS

PREFACE

In economics, there is a substantial literature that demonstrates how a free market has several attractive qualities. As an if-then proposition this is certainly valid. Free markets can serve socially useful functions, even though those social ends may not have been contemplated by the individuals who constitute society. Or as economists would put it, a free market equilibrium can be socially efficient even though it is a product of individuals each pursuing their narrow self-interest. There are theorems that establish this with precision and all the artillery of modern economic theory.

Where a large body of professionals—lobbyists, lawyers, politicians, and influential economic journalists—that draws on the old-fashioned economics literature errs is in its failure to recognize that while the textbook conceptualization of the free market may have all those qualities, such a free market does not and probably cannot exist in reality. Furthermore, one cannot make even the 'limiting claim' that approaching the extreme case of a fully free market will take us toward some kind of social ideal. The free market proposition is a powerful intellectual achievement and one of great aesthetic appeal, but its rampant misuse has had huge implications for the world—in particular, in the way we craft policy, think about globalization, and dismiss dissent.

This book is an attempt to give form to the dissenting voice. It is founded in the belief that while the dissent against globalization and corporatization that we hear on the streets and from unruly protesters may be inarticulate and even inconsistent, it is an expression of a genuine and plausible critique of contemporary economics along with its disproportionate influence on the world of policymaking.

I have written this book without the usual trappings and garden implements of contemporary economics—algebra, calculus, geometry, and in particularly unrepentant cases, topology. In so doing, my hope is to reach out to the uninitiated. At the same time, this is a monograph meant for professional economists, with the aim being to cause them some discomfiture. But being acquainted with the crust of unquestioning opinion that most experts tend to create around themselves, I am reconciled that my main hope of winning over people must rest largely in the camp of the uninitiated. This is not to deny that among contemporary economists, especially those on the front line, there are individuals who have taken up positions and methodologies similar to the ones advocated in the pages that follow, but they constitute a minority.

The book is primarily a critique of mainstream economics, and it promotes a particular perspective for the positive analysis of society and economics. It comments on normative economics, but such remarks are few and far between.

A large part of modern economic theory is driven by the research of mathematical economists. This has meant that ideas that might have been important, but were not mathematically hard enough, got left by the wayside. This is understandable (not to be confused with commendable); scientific journals do not want to publish papers that are not analytically challenging, and the lure of complexity is an enduring force. This quest for complication has hurt the discipline of economics. Simple truths escaped our attention in the stampede to discover complicated truths or, worse, complicate truths.

There is a tale, though the author is unknown, of Sherlock Homes and Dr. Watson on a sleuthing trip in rural England feeling tired and deciding to pitch a tent in an open field. In the middle of the night Holmes nudged Watson: "Look at the sky, and tell me what you can deduce?" Watson rubbed his eyes, and staring at the wondrous heavens, said, "Living in London one does not realize that there are so many stars in the sky. Well, since there are so many stars, we can deduce that there are many planetary systems. If there are many planetary systems, we can safely conclude that there are several planets which are like the earth. And if there are several such planets, there must be a few with intelligent life on them. So I *deduce* that there is intelligent life out there in the universe." Holmes looked at him with exasperation and replied, "Someone stole our tent."

Watson's mistake is rampant in economics. My decision to eschew formalism is not merely to reach a larger audience but also to avoid the pitfall of unnecessary complication. It is a self-disciplining device and stems from the belief that *some* of the most important ideas in the social sciences are also simple. My profession's predisposition to Watson's mistake has kept these ideas away from us.

Beyond the Invisible Hand is in some ways a sequel to my earlier *Prelude to Political Economy: A Study of the Political and Social Foundations of Economics*. But I have written it so that it can be read on its own. In fact, one needs nothing but a rudimentary knowledge of economics and a little proclivity for deductive reasoning to be able to read this book. I have recounted some basic concepts of economics from scratch. These occur in chapter 2, and the trained economist is advised to speed-read through this chapter. I also summarize a few ideas that occur in my *Prelude to Political Economy* so as to make this book readable on its own. One central precept that this book shares with *Prelude* is the idea that the economy must be viewed as embedded in society and politics. I go further here and argue that to do this successfully, we must be prepared in places to break away from the shackles of 'methodological individualism.' Not to do so can be a serious handicap and is the source of the conservatism that marks so much of economics. Minimally, we must make room for social norms and identity, both for how they affect the economy and how the economy molds them. Done properly, this can radically alter the way we do economics and craft policies.

The importance of norms is evident from the trivial, quotidian contexts of life. I grew up in a traditional Bengali household in Calcutta (now known as 'Kolkata'), where when elders spoke in the presence of children about a relative's extramarital transgressions, they lowered their voices. But they lowered their voices even more when discussing how a relative had started playing the stock market. I grew up taking the norms implied by this behavior for granted, unaware that there are societies where the decibel levels accompanying these two discussions would be reversed.

To think of such norms and shared beliefs, and the social pressures that they place on individuals, as trivial or inconsequential to the functioning of an economy would be a grave mistake. On the other hand, taking account of these properly is an extremely difficult job—one that raises intricate analytic issues and compels us to follow uncharted lines of thought, since economics has for so long been so firmly rooted in individualism. Hence, although this book addresses the layperson, it is not meant to be bedside reading. Readers have to sit up and *work* their way through it.

Once we scrutinize the foundational assumptions of mainstream economics, fault lines show up that are deep, and run through both the positive and normative parts of the discipline. As we reconstruct parts of economics so as to avoid these tectonic flaws, it becomes evident that several radical political agendas that are dismissed out of hand by mainstream economists as flawed are compatible with coherent economic theory. Thus, the analysis that I undertake here has significant implications for normative thought and political activism. Evidently the challenge that confronts this book is huge, and I am fully reconciled that given the limitations of my experience and, more so, my ability, I shall be able to shed light on only some small parts of this large arena. As the Catholic nun and art critic Sister Wendy wryly observes, in the context of discussing David Hockney's painting of Peter in the nude heaving himself out of Nick's pool, "Artists can only paint things that are central to themselves. ... It would be useless for Hockney to decide, for the loftiest political reasons, to paint something like dole queues in Bradford in the rain, because intention is not enough to carry a work to a triumphant conclusion."[1]

It must be evident by now that this is an ambitious book. It hopes to cater to the interests of the layperson, concerned with everyday issues of economics, politics, and society. At the same time, it aspires to make professional economists and social scientists reconsider some of the foundational assumptions of their discipline. But let me say no more. To raise the reader's expectation in advance is to court disappointment. I know this from experience. I had just finished my PhD and returned to India when my mother, with her unwavering urge to help less-fortunate children and equally absolute belief in my abilities to deliver on that, persuaded the principal of a school for poor children, just outside Calcutta, to invite me to speak. Over tea before the lecture, my mother told the principal how brilliant and famous I was. We then went to the classroom, a cavernous hall with some fifty rowdy children in their early teens. The principal began by saying how they were lucky to have me speak to them, that I was dedicated to spreading education in India, and that I was an economist committed to change. He went on and on, describing me more than once as "this famous economist." I puzzled about the length and content of the introduction, but did not realize that the poor man was playing for time while waiting for that lightbulb moment. It never came. He eventually had no choice; he turned to me and asked, "Excuse me, what is your name?" The children were poor but not unintelligent. The class broke out in a roar. I gave one of the worst lectures of my career.

Let me just say that my hope is that while what this book manages to achieve and shed light on may be limited by the author's own limitations (and I am only too aware of their severity), it will open up an important agendum that will draw in the more talented and technically skilled. This can lead, in the long run, to a revitalized economics, and through that, policies and activism that result in a better world.

My intellectual indebtedness in taking on this project is large. Over the years I have been influenced deeply by the writings of and conversations with George Akerlof, Kenneth Arrow, Prasanta Pattanaik, Ariel Rubinstein, Amartya Sen, Joseph Stiglitz, and Jörgen Weibull. Traces of this influence will no doubt be visible in what I have written. Some of these conversations occurred in locales that were in themselves memorable. I must in particular thank Rubinstein for his choice of the Arab café in Jaffa where we conversed at length. I like places where ordinary citizens go, and so one gets to glimpse life in its mundaneness. This was one such place.

The other memorable conversation backdrop was on January 10, 2007, with Stiglitz and Anya Schiffrin in the Calcutta Coffee House, famous as the hotbed of revolution during India's freedom fight and a favorite watering hole for left-wing student activists in the late 1960s. On this occasion, however, the intake of coffee and the flow of conversation were interrupted halfway by the flash of cameras, as the local media got wind of Stiglitz being there.

With Weibull I have conversed and worked in many locales, but my favorite is in southern Sweden, in Maglehem, a small village in the Skaane region, built around the decrepit Blaaherremoella, or the Blue Herron Mill. I stayed on different occasions in Jorgen's beautifully reconstructed old country home and a few miles away at the rustic inn, Drakamollan. In that northern setting, with gurgling brooks, sloping sunlight, grazing horses, old thatch-roofed cottages, and a paucity of human beings (this may not be an entirely correct observation, and may well have something to do with the fact that I was born and spent the first years of my life in one of the most people-intensive parts of our globe—north Calcutta), I felt surprisingly at home. It was a perfect setting in which to parley, argue, and do research.

Sen was my adviser when I did my PhD at the London School of Economics. I have succeeded in holding him to that role over the years, though, and have sought his advice on a variety of research questions. I have always been fascinated by his rapier-like intellect, and ability for deductive reasoning on everyday matters that I have not seen bettered by anybody else. In fall semester 2005, an unusual opportunity arose of lecturing *with* him to graduate students at Harvard University on social choice and welfare. It was intellectually a fascinating experience, and I used the lectures to raise some of the questions that I subsequently developed and wrote up for this book.

By leaving it at this, I do injustice to many other locales and individuals—to conversations with S. Subramanian (Subbu) in his home in Chennai in the shadows of Saint Thomas's Mount, with Karla Hoff in College Town Bagels in Ithaca, New York—but the list is too long to complete.

There has been help from many economists and other social scientists, without which the book would not be what it is. For discussions on related topics, and in some cases, reading and commenting on the manuscript or specific chapters, I am grateful to Masa Aoki, Abhijit Banerjee, Pranab Bardhan, Alaka Basu, Karna Basu, Avner Ben-Ner, Larry Blume, Sherry Colb, Michael Dorf, Patrick Emerson, Amanda Felkey, Jayant Vivek Ganguli, Garance Genicot, Hirak Ghosh, Herb Gintis, John Gray, Richard Hall, Yujiro Hayami, Robert Hockett, Carsten Herrmann-Pillath, Karla Hoff, Hyejin Ku, Luis-Felipe López-Calva, Annemie Maertens, Mukul Majumdar, Richard Miller, Tapan Mitra, Karl Ove Moene, Puran Mongia, Victor Nee, Machiko Nissanke, Patrick Nolen, Karine Nyborg, Ted O'Donoghue, Stephan Panther, Wilson Perez, Jean-Philippe Platteau, Peter Railton, John Roemer, Eduardo Saavedra,

Neelam Sethi, Rajiv Sethi, Tony Shorrocks, Alice Sindzingre, Nirvikar Singh, Rohini Somanathan, S. Subramanian, Richard Swedberg, Erik Thorbecke, Eduardo Zambrano, and Homa Zarghamee.

The bulk of the actual writing occurred at Cornell University. When I arrived at Cornell in the mid-1990s, given the university's formidable reputation, I had expected to find intellectual excellence and organizational dynamism. What I had not expected yet found in equal measure was warmth. Colleagues, spread across departments, provided support and friendship almost immediately on our arrival on campus. The Katzensteins—Mary and Peter— Shelley Feldman, Isaac Kramnick and Miriam Brody, and Erik and Charla Thorbecke were among our first friends, and have remained a major resource for fraternizing and intellectual camaraderie. While still in India, I had written a review in the *Times of India* of the biography of Harold Laski, paying scant attention to the names of the authors, Kramnick and Barry Sheerman. It was a mixed review without the precautions that one takes when one expects to meet the author. Soon after I arrived at Cornell, Kramnick phoned me to say that he was a professor in the government department and was surprised to learn that the reviewer of his book had just joined Cornell. I was equally surprised to learn that the reviewee was among my new colleagues. We met for lunch and had a nonstop conversation, about Laski, politics—in the world and the university—and much more. Later, Hunter and Elizabeth Rawlings also became part of this interdisciplinary circle of friends that my wife and I have had on campus and cherished.

One month's intense work on the manuscript was done in summer 2008, in Siena, at the beautiful Santa Chiara Scuola Superiore, part of the University of Siena, where I was invited by Ugo Pagano and Lorenzo Sacconi to the newly created visiting professorship in economics and ethics. Here I got what I needed to be able to cut myself off in a hermetic manner, and I was lucky that I got this in beautiful Tuscany, amid so many reminders of medieval scholarship and science. I am also grateful to Francesca Mattioli for providing unstinting assistance during my stay in Siena.

For excellent secretarial support during the writing of this book I am grateful to my assistant, Amy Moesch. For reading through the manuscript in the final stages and commenting on it I am grateful to my research assistant, Shuang Zhang. At Princeton University Press, my editor, Seth Ditchik, has taken an interest in the content of this book way beyond what I could have asked for, commenting on it and making suggestions through its history of production. I also appreciate the comments of three anonymous referees, all of whom put the fact of their anonymity to good use. One referee, Steven

Medema, whose identity was later revealed to me, made detailed comments that proved invaluable for the last round of revisions.

I have been lucky in finding in Alaka and our children, Karna and Diksha, conversation, laughter, and on occasion and with a lot of persuasion, readers for parts of the manuscript.

My father, Keshab Chandra Basu, was a remarkable person. Born into a large and poor family, his early years were filled with struggle. After several years on a meager and irregular income from coaching school students, when he became a lawyer and began practicing out of a cubbyhole in north Calcutta with no contacts in the world of business or law, it must have seemed like an impossible uphill climb. He would subsequently become one of the city's premier lawyers and also the city's mayor.

For me, as a child, more fascinating than this personal history were my father's seemingly flawless powers of deductive reasoning, and his magical ability to simultaneously read and listen to someone speak. He would grow impatient with his new clients, who not knowing about this ability of his, stopped speaking when I entered his chamber and gave him my school report card to read.

I got a real glimpse of his intellect when late in his life, I started school geometry and did poorly in the first exam. My father was disappointed because he thought geometry was nothing but common sense. That was the only time he took a direct interest in my studies; for a month he taught me euclidean geometry, quickly glancing through a few pages of my schoolbook, and then going over the theorems and riders with complete fluency, as if he had been doing nothing but teaching geometry all his life.

I was born late in my father's life. He was forty-seven years old at the time of my birth and busy professionally. Hence, I had less interaction with him than I might have otherwise. Nevertheless, I owe lots of happy memories and my early intellectual awakening to him, and dedicate this book to his memory.

BEYOND THE INVISIBLE HAND

CHAPTER 1

In Praise of Dissent

Discontent and Discourse

By most counts, the world is a better place today than it was in ancient times. First and foremost, we have the comforts that come from our greater collective wealth. But even apart from that, we do not live in perpetual fear that another nation's marauding army will come and take away our land and belongings. When we return home from dining out, we do not expect to find that strangers have broken in and occupied our homes. The physically weak do not have to be reconciled to being economically destitute. There are numerous rights of individuals and nations that are presently treated as fundamental and inviolable. We do not have to be on constant guard to defend these rights by force or guile. Others recognize the rights and usually respect them, and when they do not, the community or the state usually enforces them.

It would be a tortuous claim to say that we are not, on average, more fortunate than our ancestors. It will be argued in this book, however, that we are not *as* fortunate as may appear at first sight. The fact that the exploitation of the twenty-first century occurs within the laws and norms of the twenty-first century should not make us oblivious to it. Even in ancient times, what appear to us today as brutal, confrontational behaviors and morally indefensible conquests were more often than not justified using the morals, norms, and practices of the times. When Plato or, closer to our time, Thomas More wrote about a utopian society in which all men were treated well and with dignity, it did not even occur to them that there might be something wrong in leaving women and slaves out of this scheme. When during the seventeenth, eighteenth, and nineteenth centuries Native Americans were systematically separated from their land, occasionally by force but frequently by what on the face of it looked like voluntary transactions—elaborate contracts that the Native Americans usually did not understand, since prior to the arrival of the Europeans they had neither experience of land trade nor written contracts[1]—they were being exploited quite ruthlessly, as their subsequent impoverishment suggests. But it was widely believed that what was happening was lawful and morally justified (Banner 2005, especially 52–53; see also Robertson 2005).

Some accounts of these "voluntary" treaties and contracts are tragic, such as when in 1755 in South Carolina more than five hundred Cherokee met with a similar number of settlers. South Carolina Governor James Glen convened the meeting. Gifts were exchanged, and meals were served in silver bowls and cups. The Cherokee were pleased, and declared that the tribe wished to give "all their Lands to the King of Great Britain … for they acknowledge him to be the owner of all their Lands and Waters" (Banner 2005, 59). The settlers sensed that this was a metaphoric use of language, just a way of being nice to outsiders.[2] This was especially clear when the Cherokee refused to take any payment for their offer. But the offer was too good for the settlers to allow qualms about metaphoric speech to get in the way. To make it into a contract, the settlers persuaded the Cherokee to take a small payment, which they accepted out of politeness. Little did the Cherokee realize that they were about to lose all their land.

At one level, deals like the above one were voluntary, but the question must arise about the meaning and significance of voluntary contracts between two parties when one of them does not understand what a land sale means because it has not had any experience of that in its history. Many of the settlers considered the deals to be fair, and so did many of the natives, though of course there were settlers who were out to take ruthless advantage of the simplicity of the natives. When Christopher Columbus and his crew landed in what is now the United States (Bahamas), the Arawaks ran to greet them with food and gifts. They had no idea that Columbus viewed the whole situation as an opportunity. In Columbus's own words, "They brought us parrots and balls of cotton … and many other things…. They do not bear arms and do not know them for I showed them a sword, they took it by the edge and cut themselves." And having noted the simplicity of these people, he went on to observe that "they would make fine servants. With fifty men we could subjugate them all and make them do whatever we want" (Zinn 2003, 1).

Likewise today, when we see the rule of law prevail, property rights as defined by our courts respected, and blatant military conquests decrease in number, we feel that what we see happening in the marketplace and our conference rooms where treaties and agreements are signed is the outcome of fair play. We know that people get cheated in markets and that individuals do get exploited, but overall, when we play by the rules of the market and do not snatch and rob, we believe we are on the right path. Some do get impoverished and some get rich. Well, we tell ourselves, this has to happen, does it not? Would trying to halt this not impede progress and economic growth? We have seen—for instance, in the Soviet Union—what happens when other systems are attempted. But history, such as the cases just discussed, should alert us that even today, there may well be other kinds of unfair contracts and treaties taking place. After all, the exchanges that happen in reality are not just of apples, haircuts, guns, and butter with money, as our textbooks suggest, but complex deals involving long stretches of the future and complicated rights. It is likely that groups are being outwitted in novel ways that will become clear to us only in retrospect.

It is arguable that if we measure inequality simply by the income gap between the richest and poorest segments of society, then the present-day world has inequality at a level that has never occurred in human history.[3] This is because the poorest people's condition has remained much the same from ancient times. Their lives are nasty, brutish, and short—to use an abbreviated version of Thomas Hobbes's famous description of life in the state of nature; the poorest people barely get enough to survive. Their well-being is usually determined by the biological subsistence needs of human beings. Even poorer people will not be around to be counted. Wealth, on the other hand, has no natural ceiling. The richest people today can do things that neither Genghis Khan nor Nero could even dream of.

It can be shown by some simple back-of-the-envelope calculations that the ten richest people in the contemporary world together earn the same income as is earned by the entire population—close to forty million people—of Tanzania (Basu 2006b). Given that Tanzania has its own share of millionaires and the super rich, it is obvious that if we leave such people out and compare the ten richest people with the poorest people in the world, we would find a gap that should be mind-boggling. What is shocking is that it does not boggle our minds. We usually do not think about these matters, and when we do, for the most part we treat the inequality and poverty as inevitable concomitants of the market system—that grand, invisible machine that coordinates millions of participants in this huge global system, creates efficiency, and helps the world grow richer.

Intracorporation inequality has been rising exponentially. In the United States, the average pay of the CEOs of large corporations used to be forty times that of the average production worker in 1980. Ten years later the ratio had climbed to eighty-five, and at the start of the twenty-first century the ratio had risen to four hundred.[4] We have been persuaded to believe that a CEO who earns ten million dollars a year (not an implausible figure when the stock options are added to the base salary) needs that as *incentive* for their high-skilled job. The presumption is that in case the pay per unit of time for all executives was halved, so that the above CEOs now earned five million dollars a year, they would say, "With such low compensation I will not work hard anymore." It is a sign of our remarkable gullibility and complacency that we buy such arguments.[5] I have tried to demonstrate by constructing a formal model (Basu 2010a) how through the clever design of salaries and benefits, it is possible to create a situation whereby pay can vastly exceed productivity. Quite apart from the inequity of this, it creates a world prone to financial crashes, as witnessed during 2007–9.

The complacency that prevails in our societies in the face of such inequity is not altogether spontaneous, though. It is propped up by a large number of people who benefit from the system. These people are a minority of the world's population, but one that matters; it consists of those who have a voice and can make themselves heard, either by paying to have their opinion fed into our laws and regulatory systems, or by being better networked and better embedded in the citadels of power.

This is known to all but the most gullible. Yet the complacency also has another prop. It is made possible by legions of economists, plying their daily trades—writing their monthly columns, publishing their annual papers, and putting out their decadal books. This has created a 'central opinion': a body of intellectual material that describes how a modern economy functions, and assures us that as a system, the current world economic order, founded on individual selfishness and the 'invisible hand' of the free market, is right or, at any rate, the best among what is feasible. It may not always function as it should but as an ideal, it is the right one to pursue and uphold.

When I distance myself from mainstream economics, I am aware that there are contemporary economists who share my concerns and would have no problem with my critiques. I am happily reconciled to the fact that the book's novelty value will be limited for them. Nevertheless aided by a majority of practicing economists and economic journalists, the profession's central tendency remains wedded to the view that the current world economic order as supported by the market economy of the industrialized nations is the only viable one not just for now but also in all conceivable futures. Our only task is to implement reforms to keep the existing system well oiled and humming.

Occasionally, this complacency gets ruffled. Bewildered by the depth of poverty and riches like never seen before, some people—including some who may themselves be privileged but have the courage to question—feel troubled. They wonder, Are we being duped into thinking that we have hit on the ideal system, our only task being to keep the system functioning smoothly? Anger builds up among these people, and it occasionally erupts in violence or unruly protests, in Saigon, Santiago, Seattle, or the streets of Washington, DC.

When those who have long been trod on and those who have empa-thy for them eventually decide to protest, their actions are often seen as the 'rampages' of 'marauding mobs.' But the inchoate suspicion that these protest-ers have felt about the existing world economic order is not entirely without justification. They may have failed to articulate their point of view, and their suspicions may have found expressions that appear pathological to the out-sider, but their feelings hide an important truth that can be given intellectual foundations.

That is the reason for this book. Exploitation, conquest, and property grabbing are alive and well. The manner in which these practices occur has changed. Just as the modern world tries to plug the loopholes of blatant ex-ploitation, and strives to halt plunder and egregious violations of basic human rights, human beings and governments discover newer and less obvious ways of exploiting the simple, the innocent, and the less materialistic. Whole na-tions, groups, and masses of people are being continuously outwitted and im-poverished, not, or rather rarely, through wars and direct confrontation, but through complex financial maneuvers, the discovery of loopholes in the law, and the new opportunities that economic globalization opens up and the lag-ging process of social and political globalization leaves vulnerable to plunder. The decimated economies of sub-Saharan Africa, parts of Central and South America and Asia, and even some regions of Europe bear testimony to this.

One does not always have to go to faraway poor countries to discover the exploited or the outwitted. Even rich nations have large numbers of poor people and the destitute, who sleep in the streets (Jencks 1994; O'Flaherty 1996). As I write this, over forty million people in the United States live with no medical insurance, and close to 10 percent of the nation's labor force is unemployed.

Some of these poor people are no doubt less productive than the rich. But one can argue that being less productive should not be deemed reason to be cast into destitution and extreme poverty. Just as most of us would agree that being handicapped should not be a reason for being denied access to cinemas, restaurants, and shopping complexes, and hence we have laws that require public places to have special provisions for the handicapped, it could be contended that being less productive should not be a reason for suffering food deprivation and being denied medical help.

Even if we dismiss this line and go with the neoclassic assertion that it is fine for people to earn according to their productivity (and that is what makes an economy function efficiently), the truth is that the poor people of rich nations are not invariably or even typically the less productive ones. There is, for instance, overwhelming evidence that being born into wealth helps one to be wealthy. Human capital acquired by going to elite schools and real capital transmitted from one generation to another through the legal protection of inheritance enables people *born into* advantage or disadvantage to remain that way, akin to what happens in caste-based societies. Further, people often fail to earn what would be prescribed by their productivity because they are outwitted of their wealth through the use of ever-more sophisticated financial contracts and exchanges.[6] This can create an 'undeserving underclass' in rich countries.

All this is kept from coming to a boil through a continuous ideological barrage of written and other media articulation of two myths: that an industrialized nation's markets are free, and that free markets are fair. The legions of economists who dismiss the protesters in the streets of Seattle, Cancun, and Washington, DC, out of court are like those missionaries who accompanied the occupying armies of yesteryears, pacifying rebellion through comforting words, and ignoring the demurrers as misguided and befuddled. As Albert Einstein (1949, 9) wrote in the inaugural issue of *Monthly Review*, "The priests, in control of education, made the class division of society into a permanent institution and created a system of values by which the people were thenceforth, to a large extent unconsciously, guided in their social behavior."

It is not being suggested that all this is happening through some conspiracy of the powerful and the rich. The world has fewer conspiracies than most people believe. There are conspiracies to be sure, but the force of unwitting atomistic action is usually far greater than we realize and in the end becomes the overwhelming force. And this is the force that is difficult to understand and needs serious intellectual inquiry to master. Adam Smith was right about this, and we must hold on to this wisdom even when we reject what in this book I refer to as Smith's myth. What has to be kept in mind is that the absence of a conspiracy does not invariably make the equilibrium that prevails in society benign.

There is another view of the invisible hand that shares with Smith the idea that systems can run on their own steam, with no ultimate authority in charge, but the outcome is more malevolent and, on occasion, chilling. This is the vision of Franz Kafka, as immortalized in his unfinished novel, *The Trial*. Joseph K is caught in a surreal world where he is charged with a crime that he has not committed, and he does not fully understand the basis of the charge. He runs from pillar to post, from minion to minor bureaucrat, to find out what the charge is and who has handed it down, so that he can appeal his innocence. But in the society that K inhabits, there *is* no central authority or person to appeal to. All individuals in this labyrinthine world go about their limited daily chores, and this gives rise to forces that transcend each individual. In some ways, Kafka's view of our society is more pertinent than Smith's. It is true that Smith had scientific precision in his writing, while Kafka had all the ambiguities of a litterateur. Yet in social analysis, there is at times a need for the latter, and for meanings and messages to be conveyed through a deliberate use of ambiguity.

The state of our thinking on the global economic order that breeds complacency has intellectual roots that are deep and need to be excised carefully. That is the aim of this book. It is written in praise of dissent.

I should warn my readers at the outset, however, that many of them will be disappointed by this book, for it offers no panacea and has little of the edge of optimism one finds in revolutionary tracts. The aim is simply to hold a light up to society, and show that social and economic processes are not what we make them out to be. They are more venal than what the textbooks of economics suggest. The world is poised on a dangerous ledge. There is a risk that we will go headlong into a mean, materialistic future. What may disappoint some readers is my view that maybe, that *is* our future. Unlike most radical monographs, this book offers no compelling reason to believe that we will be able to avert this dismal predicament. At the same time, I hope that clarity in seeing the world as it actually is may enable us to think of ways to steer clear from such a future. I do offer some prescriptions and suggest new policy initiatives, but am aware that these may not measure up to the task. My central aim here is to lend clarity and be relentless about that, with the hope that someone more capable will provide the solution.

Another disappointment for some readers will be the eclectic methodology that is used here. For one, I critique mainstream economics but use many of its methods of analysis. For some it may seem that a natural instrument for a radical critique of the mainstream is Marxian economics. But the poor record of Marxian methods to dislodge neoclassical economics is a good warning sign. While I find Karl Marx's utopian constructions and normative yearnings attractive, as scientific method Marxian economics has little appeal to me. The search for, and more alarmingly, discovery of, empirical regularities over large swathes of human history is inevitably flawed. While I believe in determinism, which implies that the future that stretches in front of us is foretold, and as unalterable and free of chance as the history that lies behind us, I see no way that we can ever discover the trend that will unfold over the long run.[7] There may well be laws that an economy follows in the long run, yet claims of discovery of those laws appear to me, for the most part, delusional. It is one thing for something to exist, and quite another for it to be discovered or even be discoverable.

Moreover, while many contemporary Marxist thinkers have laudable normative aims—of a society that is more equitable and free from poverty—and rightly refuse to accept the present distribution of wealth and income as fair, their positive analysis has been marred by a precommitment to certain set ideas about how society works. True radical thought requires us to be more open to new facts and newly discovered ways of reasoning. My strategy in this book is to pick the best available methods of reasoning, unmindful of where they come from. It so happens that much of the method used here has its roots in Smith's work. The fact that so much of mainstream economics can be laid to waste using its own instruments of analysis makes the critique that much more compelling.

To sum up, there is a large body of opinion that treats the current economic order, based on the pursuit of individual self-interest and untrammeled free markets, as the only viable one. It is argued in this book that all economic systems rely on social norms and beliefs. Much of the economics profession has taken the norms of capitalism so much for granted that these have, over time, become invisible and created the illusion of there being no norms. In truth, capitalism would collapse without its attendant norms.

This suggests that a more equitable and fair society than the one we currently inhabit is viable. There can be structures of norms and institutions that bring individual behavior into alignment with such a society. The design of such a system, and an understanding of its attendant norms and institutions, will not be an easy task both because this entails venturing into totally new areas of research and because those with a vested interest in the present system—that is, those who control most of the wealth of the world—will resist change and sabotage attempts to create a more equitable society. The aim of this book is to lay out the intellectual road map for this challenging project and develop a grammar for dissent.

This program of research and action gives rise to an important conundrum. It recognizes that piecemeal efforts for change and the adoption of idealistic policies, *as if* we already inhabit a utopian world, may well make matters worse. The failure to recognize this is a common mistake that some radicals have made. As long as we continue under the present system, we may have to live with conventional policies. For this reason, the message here must not be confused with the argument for a large government that some have proposed. A large government, in the current economic order, is a sitting duck. Large corporations and vested interests know that capturing this is a single-window access to profits. It is for this reason that many private firms consider the state to be the best business partner; they can, in the present system, fleece it for their own gains. The big versus small government debate is a misleading one, and it detracts from the larger aim of a more equitable world. The latter will be met with resistance from those who have vested interests in the current regime, and to ensure that in the name of creating a better world we do not simply create another regime with a new oligarchy of interests will require a huge amount of intellectual effort.

What we have to realize is that prescribing standard (but intelligent) economic policies for the current regime and working toward a regime change are not inconsistent objectives. Indeed, both these underlie the project that is this book.

Smith's Myth

The central opinion of economics has its origins in Smith's remarkable discovery that the order that we see in the world needs no central coordinator. The bread arriving on our dining table, the baker being supplied wheat by the farmer, and the farmer getting their seeds and fertilizer from the merchant can all be explained with no reference to a central coordinator or some benevolent conspiracy. Or to draw from Smith's most quoted line ([1776] 1937, 14), "It is not from the benevolence of the butcher, the brewer or the baker, that we expect our dinner, but from their regard to their own interest."[8] Each individual serving his or her own interest can keep an economy brimming with activity and thus growing. An outsider viewing a modern economy, with goods changing hands and workers toiling away to produce goods in which they themselves have no interest, may be tempted to think that there is an outside agency or divine will that organizes this huge machinery. But Smith argued that this is not the case; the market is like an invisible hand that can guide producers and have goods delivered where they are most needed.[9]

The same view of the central opinion in mainstream economics was described more eloquently by the British Marxist economist Joan Robinson (1979, 43), in a commencement speech at the University of Maine in May 1977: "The philosophy of orthodox economics is that the pursuit of self-interest will lead to the benefit of society. By this means the moral problem is abolished. The moral problem is concerned with the conflict between individual interest and the interest of society. And this doctrine tells us that there is no conflict, we can all pursue our self-interest with a good conscience.... This doctrine is attributed to Adam Smith."

In case Smith's discovery seems obvious to us now, it is sobering to recall that the theory of the invisible hand would remain a conjecture for close to two centuries after the appearance of his classic, *An Inquiry into the Nature and Causes of the Wealth of Nations*, despite the copious writings by Smith himself and his successors in political economy. It took a considerable machinery of mathematical economics, and the research of Kenneth Arrow, Gerard Debreu, Lionel Mackenzie and others, for it to be given formal shape and proof. It was well into the twentieth century that the conditions under which a competitive equilibrium exists and is optimal were formally demonstrated. That is, it was formally proved that, given some condition, all individuals pursuing their respective self-interest leads society to an optimal state. This has come to be known as the First Fundamental Theorem of Welfare Economics and is the formal statement of the invisible hand conjecture. I shall here refer to the Fundamental Theorem more colloquially as the 'Invisible Hand Theorem.' The terms used in the theorem, such as competition and optimality, belong to the jargon of modern economics, and as such have technical meanings. These are clarified in chapter 2, where the theorem is elaborated on.

This stateless, godless view of the world, as Smith's theorem implied, shook the foundations of social thought in the eighteenth and nineteenth centuries.[10] It was a truly great idea.[11] But as with so many great ideas, some people worked to subvert it and others worked to modify its popular understanding to serve their own interests. In any case, it soon became the dominant idea, and from then on Smith's *The Wealth of Nations* became the new orthodoxy.

As with religious texts, masses of people latched on to the orthodoxy with no further thought and no desire to question it, and without even the desire to read Smith further for fear that his ifs, buts, and provisos (and there were many of those in Smith's writings) might dilute their conviction.[12] Smith's great insight gradually ossified into a hard and unbending doctrine, which is referred to here as Smith's myth. The "myth" referred not to what Smith wrote but rather to the way that his writings have come to be interpreted in popular perception. Regrettably, all the qualifiers and the warnings that Smith had sounded fell by the wayside. It is surprising to most contemporary economists who have not read *The Wealth of Nations* to learn that the invisible hand theory is not as central to Smith as it is made out to be.[13] Smith was much more critically concerned about economies of scale in the labor market, and the consequences of increasing returns for an economy's growth and overall development. In fact, in the original index of his book there was no entry for invisible hand—this was later added by an editor when another edition appeared after Smith's death.

It was not just Smith; several classical economists, notably John Stuart Mill and John McCulloch, took a more sophisticated view of the role of the market than the orthodoxy suggested. When some of these economists, including Smith, critiqued the state, part of the critique was an attack on mercantilism, and in particular, stemmed from the apprehension that the state would be captured by the merchant class and thus be subservient only to its interest (see O'Brien 1975).

In spite of these exceptions, the orthodoxy thrived. In debates in the nineteenth century on setting statutory limits on the hours of work, people would flag Smith. If workers offered themselves for fourteen hours of work each day and entrepreneurs were willing to pay them for that, why should the state get into it? The invisible hand of the market would ensure that this 'natural state' was optimal. If women agreed to work for a wage less than what men got and firms were willing to hire women and men on those terms, why should the state get into it? If poor people offered themselves to a landlord to work as slaves and the landlord found the offer acceptable, then should the market not be left free to allow such a contract? These questions are not academic constructs but were instead matters of actual policy and debate. For instance, in 1859, the state of Louisiana declared voluntary slavery or what is often called 'waranteeism' to be legal.[14] That is, individuals were granted the right to become slaves. The law was, some would say, discriminatory because it granted this generous right only to persons of color.

It was argued that the state's involvement in all these matters would violate Smith's doctrine and be socially suboptimal. The fallacy in this assertion will be discussed in chapter 7.

So deep was this conviction that when the Invisible Hand Theorem was formally established in the mid-twentieth century, most economists treated this as a mathematical vindication of the belief. Even today, many economists equate the Invisible Hand Theorem with the normative proposition that we should leave individuals free to pursue their own selfish ends without any restraint. David Hume's famous warning about the fallacy of trying to get to normative propositions from purely positive axioms has been wantonly overlooked. The usual qualifiers—such as, there must be no negative externality associated with a person's own pursuits—are of course recognized by economists. But little beyond these minor caveats is acknowledged.

The Lay of the Land

Since so much of the central opinion in economics relies on the Fundamental Theorem or, more accurately, misunderstanding the Fundamental Theorem, it is important for the reader to invest some effort to understand it. Hence, the next chapter begins with this and shows how much of contemporary popular thinking on economic policymaking is rooted in this theorem—or again, to state this more carefully, in a misreading of this theorem. This chapter covers little fresh ground for trained economists, so they may wish to skip or skim through it. (But be warned that there are more people who think of themselves as trained economists than there actually are trained economists.)

There are many well-known critiques of why the theorem must not be taken to the real world too hastily for application. Those standard critiques are not of much concern to the present book; they are invoked only rarely. But for reasons of completeness and also to spare the subsequent chapters of interruptions to explain what is known, these critiques are also discussed in chapter 2.

The project of this monograph begins after that. The ultimate aim is ambitious: to show that the wisdom that was given to us by Smith has ossified into an ideology, which has hurt our understanding of how economies function, why some economies fail, and the role of markets and policy interventions. And these revisions, in turn, urge us to discard our complacency about the current world economic order. The conservative's dismissal of all other systems as 'incentive incompatible' and therefore not viable is a ruse, often unwittingly carried out, to sustain the vested interests of the current order. I will have occasion later in the book to study the true implications and meaning of incentive compatibility. The last chapters of this book will argue that global democracy is on the retreat and being continuously subverted by the powerful, and thanks to the marginalization of large sections of the world that is occurring concurrently with globalization, the world is headed into uncharted political waters, marked by turbulence. At an intuitive level, this is known by the laity. Yet this awareness has not transformed into policy, because of the economists' *modeled* world in which the market always delivers. As long as interventions are kept to a minimum, and the externalities are corrected with taxes and subsidies, the system is fair, all workers earning what is their marginal productivity. The fact that state-of-the-art journal papers have moved away from such a world has little effect on this 'central tendency' of the profession, and its penumbra of journalists, technocrats, and international civil servants. Moreover, the journal papers tend to marginalize themselves by being obsessed with the technical and mathematical criticisms.

There are more fundamental criticisms possible, which enable us to view the dismal conclusions of this book as compatible with and even a consequence of economic theory, thereby making it unnecessary to go into a denial of reality. And so the interim chapters—from 3 to 8—attempt to criticize and reconstruct the central model of economics. Chapter 3 discusses some deep flaws in our understanding and interpretation of the Invisible Hand Theorem. These criticisms are mathematically easy but conceptually hard. They suggest new axioms for economic theorizing. Chapters 4 to 7 demonstrate how these revised axioms result in an altered view as well as a deeper understanding of how an economy functions and the role of policy interventions. In addition, these chapters maintain that economic theory needs to move away from its unquestioning adherence to methodological individualism. Chapter 8 carries these arguments over to the domain of globalization and international policy, and sets the ground for an analysis of global democracy and its erosion in chapter 9. The last chapter is a speculative one on how we could try to alter the current economic order, ranging from minor, relatively easy policy interventions to more radical and futuristic suggestions.

Before venturing into all of this, I want to sound a warning on understanding. What does it mean to *understand* how an economy works? It is important to answer this question, since much of this book is meant to be a contribution to our 'understanding' of how an economy functions, and how it interacts with society and politics, and it is hoped that the learning will occur at a level deeper than getting to know facts and mastering theorems.

On Understanding

When I say the aim of this book is to create a deeper understanding of how an economy functions, I mean this in a somewhat unusual sense. There are at least two different senses in which we popularly use the term understanding. When people say that they "understand general equilibrium theory or Brouwer's fixed point theorem," and when they say that they "understand music or human psychology," in both cases they are referring to cognitive processes in the brain, leading to some acquisition of information, but in different ways. The former refers to a 'technical understanding,' an ability to reproduce what one understands, and maybe even extend and modify what one understands. On the other hand, when people say that they understand music, this refers to an 'intuitive understanding.'[15] This understanding is difficult to demonstrate to an outsider. (This is one reason that it is safe to claim that you understand music or art even if you do not.) But in some ways it is a deeper understanding. Consider a mentally challenged child. The trained psychologist will understand the child, but the child's parent or sibling, with no training in psychology, may also make the same claim. However, the former's understanding will be closer to what is called technical understanding above, and the latter's understanding will be more intuitive. In many cases, the latter will have a better sense of what the child seeks and how the child will respond to certain stimuli. The parents or siblings may not be able to explain how they get to this understanding and so may not be able to impart this understanding to another person, but most people who have dealt with such situations will easily agree that parents or siblings do have a kind of understanding that is different and in some ways deeper than that of the professional psychologist. It should be stressed here that it is not as if intuitive understanding cannot be enhanced through training. It can, and further, it can be more potent when combined with some technical understanding. People can learn to intuit better.

In most formal disciplines, we rely primarily on professionals with their technical knowledge. How good or bad this knowledge is depends on the discipline. For an automobile engineer, a good technical understanding may be adequate, or virtually so. My view is that in economics, the need for intuitive understanding is much greater than most economists would have you believe. Good economic policy requires a 'feel' for things over and above the knowledge of theorems and regression coefficients, just as one cannot be a good entrepreneur or a skilled driver merely by learning the techniques of management and innovation, or learning how the hand and foot movements of a driver translate into the maneuverings of a car. Though this may sound paradoxical, there are formal reasons for the need for intuitive understanding. It is an important part of this project to explain why this may be so.

For a full comprehension of this book, it is crucial to understand the material presented here *intuitively*. Hence, the style of writing in this book differs greatly from the standard text in economics. *Beyond the Invisible Hand* does not merely catalog results but also tries to construct a viewpoint by using reasoning, citing real-world examples, and most important, urging introspection. Moreover, in understanding what is presented here, there is some unlearning involved. People who have learned a lot of theory develop an incapacity to view the world as it really is. This does not have to happen—some of the most enlightened contemporary writers are also fine theorists—but it often does.[16] Textbook assumptions and axioms tend to crowd out other forms of learning, especially that which we learn from our daily experience. In some cases people who have learned a lot of theory do try to also learn from real life, but thanks to the distortion in their lenses caused by excessive learning, what they see merely confirms the presumptions that they have already formed.

This is not surprising in light of the research that has occurred on "confirmatory bias" (see Rabin and Shrag 1999)—that is, the propensity in human beings endowed with some initial opinion to find confirmation of that view in new information that is provided to them. Two persons with right-wing and left-wing views, respectively, exposed to the same set of new world events, would typically find reason to be even more convinced of their right and left wingness. In a fascinating experiment on this (Bruner and Potter 1964), a group of persons was shown a picture on a screen that was severely blurred and then gradually brought into focus, though it was never brought into full focus. At the end of the experiment, the people were asked to guess what the picture was. Some of the participants were allowed to see the screen from the beginning (the stage of severe blur) and some from a little later on (when the picture was less blurred). Interestingly, the former group (those who got to see what the latter saw *and more*, since they started watching from an earlier time) got the right answer less frequently. One-quarter of them were right, and of those who started viewing from the less-blurred stage, half got it right. The most plausible explanation has to do with confirmatory bias. Those who started watching from an earlier stage formed opinions based on little information, and then what they saw later merely confirmed the initial opinions.

It is not as if modern theoretical economics teaches us something wrong, for most of these books teach us if-then propositions—*if* all human beings are rational, if they are subject to the law of diminishing marginal utility, and so on, *then* X, Y, Z will follow, where X could be, for instance, "free trade enhances national income." Having lived in the world of those "ifs," all but the clearest minds tend to confuse that world with the real one they inhabit.[17] And the "thens," which are *parts* of the if-then propositions, become parts of their reality. In some ways it is like a magic show. A good magician in principle shows you everything, but keeps your attention focused on the few things that they want you to see. After a while, what the magician wants you to see becomes your world, and you are ready for illusion.

Much of this book is an attempt to clear the illusions that we have come to acquire through repeated reference to doctrinaire claims, the blinkered observation of the 'facts' of economics, and the segueing of textbook models into our beliefs about reality.

CHAPTER 2

The Theory of the Invisible Hand

Competition and Social Welfare

Smith's novel theory was that the free market system is like an invisible hand that can unobtrusively coordinate the behavior of a multitude of individuals, interested only in maximizing their own selfish utility, so as to bring about efficiency and a socially optimal outcome. Smith did not put it in those words, but he discussed this basic *idea* in several places in his classic book. For instance, he pointed out how in making economic decisions, each person "intends only his own gain, and he is in this, as in many other cases, led by an invisible hand to promote an end which was no part of his intention" ([1776] 1937, 423). Smith provided arguments to establish this, but never really managed to give a hard proof. As a result, his observations and also the statement above gave rise to plenty of ambiguities. What did "efficiency" mean? And how do we define a "socially optimal" outcome? It was more than a century and a half later, through gradual improvements in the techniques of economic analysis and formalizations—thanks to the work of Leon Walras, Vilfredo Pareto, Arrow, and Debreu—that Smith's conjecture was formally established as the First Fundamental Theorem of Welfare Economics, which again, being a mouthful for repeated references, will be called the Invisible Hand Theorem here.

Let me turn to some terms, which are routine for economists, but need to be explained before I can accurately spell out what the Invisible Hand Theorem says. What is ideal or optimal for an *individual* may not be too hard for us to understand, especially if we go along with the widely used assumption of 'consumer's sovereignty'—namely, that each person knows what is best for the person. But *social* optimality is another matter, and clearly we can take conflicting stances on this. Here is a suggestion that was first articulated by the Italian engineer turned sociologist-cum-economist Vilfredo Pareto. Suppose we are considering a country with n persons. If this were India, n would be 1.1 billion. Now consider two alternative full descriptions of India, x and y. Thus, x could be the way India actually is, and y is the way that India would be if it removed all tariffs and quotas and went for a system of complete free trade. These full descriptions of course include details of how well-off individuals are. Typically, for large populations, we would find some people better off in state x and some better off in y (and some may be indifferent between the two). If this happens, how do we say which society is socially superior? This can be a matter of dispute, depending on how we weight one person's loss against another's gain. If it so happened that in x at least one person is better off than in y and nobody is better off in y than in x, however, then Pareto would urge us—and most of us would agree—that as a society, x is better than y. In the jargon of economic theory, x is described as "Pareto superior" to y.

To recapitulate, of two alternative social states, x and y, we shall say that x is *Pareto superior* to y if at least one person is better off in x than in y and everybody is at least as well-off in x as in y. Given two states x and y, if everybody is indifferent between x and y, we will say that x and y are 'Pareto indifferent.' Of two states, x and y, if neither is Pareto superior to the other, and nor are they Pareto indifferent, then we say that they are 'Pareto noncomparable.'

It must by now be evident that in making Pareto comparisons, even though I began by saying that we need to have full descriptions of the states involved, what we really need is information about how well-off individuals are in these states. Just to get the above definitions straight, let us consider an example. Suppose we are considering a country with two persons. Each person's level of happiness will be represented by a real number—the amount of 'utility' that the person gets. If we believe that how well-off a person is depends on the person's income, then instead of utilities we could simply write down the person's income in dollar terms. In the present context, how we interpret utilities does not matter. All I am saying is that in case there are just two persons alive, then a possible society can be represented by two numbers, the first one being the utility enjoyed by person 1, and the second number being the utility enjoyed by person 2. Now consider a country, currently in social state x, that is described as follows:

$$x = (90, \ 99)$$

In this society, person 1 gets 90 'utils,' and person 2 gets 99 utils. If you are a believer in income alone fully representing happiness, then where I mention utilities, you can simply read dollars. Suppose there are two other ways of organizing this country, which would lead to societies or social states y and z, respectively, as follows:

$$y = (99, \ 99)$$
$$z = (0, \ 100)$$

The reader should feel satisfied that y is Pareto superior to x, y is Pareto noncomparable to z, and x and z are Pareto noncomparable to each other.

Let me now define 'Pareto optimality.' Among a collection of possible social states, we describe a particular state as *Pareto optimal* if there does not exist any other state that is Pareto superior to it.[1] Suppose we are considering the collection of states consisting of x, y, and z. You can check that among these, there are two Pareto optimal states, y and z. In modern economic theory, the term Pareto optimality is used interchangeably with "efficiency." So when it is said that a society is efficient, it is meant that it is optimal in the sense of Pareto. This usurpation of the ordinary English term, efficiency, by economists is worth keeping in mind, especially since I will use the term Pareto optimal interchangeably with efficient or, to be extra careful, Pareto efficient.

Next, we need to understand the meaning of a 'competitive economy' and its 'equilibrium.' Basically a *competitive economy* is one in which no individual can alter the prices prevailing in the market by the individual's own behavior. Each single person or agent is considered to be too small for that. Hence, my decision to buy or sell more bread cannot alter the market price of bread. This is not to deny that if a whole bunch of people decide to buy more bread, then the price of bread will rise, and if a group of sellers decide to sell more, the price will fall. It is simply that each *single agent* treats the prevailing market prices as unchangeable. This is described, in brief, by saying that every individual in a competitive economy is a 'price taker.'

A 'rational,' self-interested individual or agent is basically someone who looks at the prevailing prices, and then decides how much to buy or sell so as to maximize the person's own utility, well-being, happiness, or preference. In specialized branches of economics, these terms are treated as having different shades of meanings, but in the present context there is no need to fuss over these distinctions. I will do some hairsplitting on these in chapter 6.

Consider the problem faced by a consumer. The consumer has some income, which would typically be determined by the prevailing price of labor (meaning salary) along with any other nonlabor income or wealth that he or she may have, and the consumer faces the prevailing market prices. Given these prices, consider all the bundles of goods that cost less than or equal to the consumer's income. Clearly these are the bundles that are feasible for the consumer. Thus, the consumer may be able to buy a car and food, or a television, refrigerator and food, but cannot buy both these bundles. The collection of all such bundles that can be afforded within the budget is called the consumer's 'budget set.' A rational consumer is a person who chooses a bundle from within the budget set so as to attain the highest possible utility.

In a fuller description of a competitive exchange economy, we do not distinguish between a consumer and a supplier. Each person is assumed to own some initial bundle of goods, and, on seeing what the prices are, they decide how much of which ones they would like to buy more of and how much of which ones they would like to sell off.

Now consider an arbitrary list of prices for all goods available on the market. Let individuals choose how much each person would like to buy or sell of each good on the basis of these prices. Check if for each good the total demand (that is, the demand from all individuals) is equal to the total supply of that good. If not, then we do not have an equilibrium. We would then expect the price to rise or fall depending on whether there is an excess demand or supply. Once we find a price vector such that the total demand equals the total supply for each good, so that there is no pressure for prices to change, we have found a 'competitive equilibrium' or simply an 'equilibrium.' More specifically, a list of prices—one for each good—that results in the total demand for each good being equal to the total supply, is referred to as an equilibrium. Once such prices are achieved there is no pressure for the prices to change; hence the use of the term equilibrium.

With this in mind, the Invisible Hand Theorem can be described as follows:

If we have a competitive economy, where all individuals choose freely according to their respective rational self-interest, then (given a few technical conditions) the equilibrium that will arise will be Pareto optimal.

With a little bit of investment in algebra, this result can be proved as rigorously as any theorem in mathematics or axiomatic geometry.

It is easy to let the brevity of this claim distract us from recognizing its importance; this is a theorem that leaves us with a lot to ponder.[2] This formalization of Smith was a major breakthrough in economics.[3] Most important, it clarified situations where it would not be valid—something that we could not have understood from Smith's informal and largely descriptive statements. We know now that in situations where some individuals are powerful enough to be able to alter the market price, we cannot assume that the invisible hand will function effectively. If individuals can cut intertemporal deals with other people, stretching into infinity, asking each successive generation, for instance, to make some sacrifice for their elders, then the theorem breaks down again (Shell 1971).

The main significance for the world of policy has been the way that this theorem has been misunderstood and misused. First and foremost, a point that is not always appreciated is that like all theorems in mathematics, it does not really say anything testable about the real world or anything that would allow us to make any predictions. Instead, it establishes the equivalence between two definitions: equilibrium and optimality. In that sense it is no different from the Pythagoras theorem, which gives us an equivalence between two sides of a right-angled triangle and the third side. In itself it does not give us any insight into the future or any practical guidance about policy. Pythagoras, when he was not doing mathematics, was in fact notoriously lacking in practical sense. He promoted a religious cult that had as its founding principles the need to give up eating beans and offer total subservience—on this he did show some sense—to the head of the cult, which happened to be Pythagoras himself. According to Bertrand Russell, the cult came apart because some disciples could not resist beans and cheated.[4] The Pythagoras theorem is, nevertheless, useful; and so is the Invisible Hand Theorem.

One criticism of the Invisible Hand Theorem that in my view is invalid, is to dismiss it on the grounds that it is a mathematical truism with no predictive power. Relatedly, some commentators say that it is of no use unless it is first established empirically. It is not clear to me what it means to check the empirical validity of a proposition such as this. This makes as much sense as checking the validity of Pythagoras's theorem empirically before taking it as valid. Presumably this would entail going around with a measuring tape, checking if Pythagoras's claim was valid in reality. But if we did find it to be not exactly valid, what would it show? To me this would show nothing more than the eccentricity of the measuring tape. And if the theorem did turn out to be empirically valid, there would still be no way of knowing if the relation would hold in the case of untested triangles. If we relied on knowledge only after empirical testing, then clearly we should have no faith in the Pythagoras theorem for untested triangles.

Empirical economics is extremely important, but there are times when the call for it is taken to absurd lengths, and the attempt to dismiss theoretical work for being just that is a harmful propensity. If this criticism were prevalent and effective in the time of Pythagoras and Euclid, we would not have had modern geometry.

The critique of the invisible hand claim cannot be of the theorem itself, which was an outstanding mathematical achievement in the social sciences and has contributed greatly to enriching our thinking about the economy. Its critique has to be aimed at its use in real life.

The Standard Critiques

To take the Invisible Hand Theorem to the real world and enhance our understanding of it necessarily entails a leap of imagination. And this is where most of the problems creep in. It is not for nothing that economics is known as a discipline where whenever one wants to refer to the real economy, one is expected to say "real-world economy." The default—that is, a reference to an "economy" without a qualifying adjective—is presumed to be a reference to the theoretical, textbook model of an economy.

Many of the problems and limitations of taking the theorem to the real world are well known in the literature (Arrow and Hahn 1971; Hahn 1985). First, the qualifier "given a few technical conditions" in the statement of the theorem is often overlooked by market fundamentalists eager not to allow any impediment in their zeal for unhindered markets and vanishing governments. But good theorists have been aware of these conditions; in fact, one achievement of formalizing Smith's wisdom into a theorem is that it spells out where the result does not apply and what precisely are the technical conditions that need to be satisfied for a competitive equilibrium to be demonstrably Pareto optimal. Let me not dwell on these technical conditions, however, but instead elaborate on two, more general warnings against taking the theorem to the real world with too much alacrity.

For one, the Invisible Hand Theorem is a result that applies to a competitive economy, in which each individual is tiny and inconsequential, often referred to as 'atoms' in the economy. If, on the contrary, individual agents are larger and able to singly affect the well-being of others—such persons are referred to as strategic agents—then this result may cease to hold.

This point has been driven home firmly by the rise of game theory in the latter half of the twentieth century. In game-theoretic models of economics, individuals are typically strategic agents and the outcome of individual rationality is frequently not socially optimal. The Prisoner's Dilemma is arguably the most famous illustration of this. But game theory is replete with such examples. The Traveler's Dilemma game supplies a similar result (Basu 1994b). Reinhart Selten's (1978) Chain Store game, Robert Rosenthal's (1981) Centipede, and much else reinforce the same point. Of course, economists know this, as do many market-fundamentalist commentators and conservative policy buffs. But somehow they treat the large body of game-theoretic literature as pathology and competitive market models as the norm. Among those who realize that there is no basis for this presumption other than one's prejudice, the dominant view is nevertheless that the competitive economy is the ideal that we may not currently have but one that we should aspire toward. For such people, all we need is the free market, coupled with a well-designed antitrust policy to promote competition.

There is a technical difficulty with the assumption in competitive analysis that each individual's action has no impact on other people's welfare, but the behavior of a large number of people can affect the well-being of others.

It seems at first sight that if the latter is true, then if a series of individuals takes some action, there has to be some point where one more person's action affects the well-being of others. This is reminiscent of the 'heap paradox' of the fourth-century BC Greek philosopher Eubulides, who argued that since the addition of one more grain to some existing grains can never alter what was not a heap into a heap, we can never create a heap of grains starting from nothing. Standard competitive equilibrium has gotten around this problem by assuming that there is an infinite number of individuals.[5] I will not pursue this here but will return to some similar issues in chapter 7, where I show how this relates to Derek Parfit's 'moral mathematics' (1984).

The other criticism that pours cold water on the policy usefulness of the Invisible Hand Theorem has to do with the notion of Pareto optimality. A point that has been made by some of the finest minds in the profession is that there is little ethical appeal in the idea of Pareto optimality as a sufficient condition for what society ought to achieve (Bergson 1938; Samuelson 1947; Arrow 1951; Varian 1975; Sen 1997).

To elaborate on this, return to the above example of a two-person country that has the option of being any of three possible kinds: x, y, and z. We have already seen that of these, y and z are Pareto optimal. So if we agreed that it is sufficient to get to a Pareto optimal outcome, we should be satisfied with whether this country reached state y or z. But many of us would argue that while y and z may both be Pareto optimal (as they indeed are, by definition), there is something distinctly better about y than z, since one person gets zero utility in z, even while the other enjoys 100 utils, whereas in y both get 99 utils. If we consider the (99, 99) outcome superior to (0, 100)—and I expect most of my readers would (I would be alarmed at the readership I was attracting if that were not the case), then the Invisible Hand Theorem offers little comfort because it merely assures us that competition will lead to *some* Pareto optimal outcome. In other words, competition may well take this country to the morally less attractive outcome—namely, (0, 100). The theorem loses some of its luster once this is recognized. Clearly, a Pareto optimal or an efficient outcome can be a pretty obnoxious thing.

It should be emphasized that this is not a critique of the theorem but rather of its interpretation by conservative commentators or "theological free marketers," as Robert Solow calls them. The point I make above can also be made in the context of general equilibrium theory. In competitive general equilibrium analysis, which particular Pareto optimal or efficient outcome an economy settles into depends on the initial endowments of the individuals or the initial distribution of wealth. As Solow (2006) put it recently, "So the free market outcome is no 'better' than its starting distribution of wealth. It can be described as socially desirable only if the allocation of initial endowments was socially desirable. The theological free marketeer likes to omit that proviso. A good student should not."

In response to this, many economists have proposed rejecting Pareto optimality as a sufficiency condition, but retaining it as a necessary condition. In other words, for us to consider an outcome attractive or acceptable, it must be Pareto optimal (*among the set of alternatives available*), although the fact of an outcome being Pareto optimal is by no means reason enough for it to be considered acceptable. This is often called a 'Pareto inclusive' welfare judgment. I find this attractive and for the most part uphold this normative axiom in this book. As we shall see in chapter 7, though, trying to hold on to this can lead us into some intricate questions of ethics and deductive logic.[6]

Just to clarify before moving on, suppose you have to choose from among x, y, and z. If you are using a Pareto-inclusive welfare criterion, then you must not choose x. This is fully compatible with your choosing y and considering z obnoxious, and you can even take the view that you would sooner choose x than z. That is, if your choice was confined to x and z, it would be reasonable (and compatible with having a Pareto-inclusive welfare criterion) to choose x. On the other hand, if you are committed to simply Pareto optimality—that is, you consider Pareto optimality to be sufficient for choosing a state—then you would not mind selecting y or z, when all three are available.

The above discussion is reason enough not to be enamored with the Invisible Hand Theorem. In making this observation, I should immediately add that this must not be taken as a call for unrestrained government intervention in markets. Governments too often intervene in ways that make matters worse and to enable the powerful to corner additional gains from the market, as the classical economists knew when they attacked mercantilism. Both interventions and noninterventions have too often been left to the ideological whims of believers. They need to be founded on analysis and reason, and not on faith.

There are criticisms of the theorem other than the ones discussed in this section—ones that are deeper than these and less well known—that open up new questions and urge us to take a more sophisticated view of economic theory, and via that, a more sophisticated view of the world than the one espoused by the believers in Smith's myth and those who may not be believers in it but fear that they have too much to lose personally by the world's jettisoning of this myth. That is the subject matter of chapter 3, and the remainder of the book fans out from the critique outlined next.

CHAPTER 3

The Limits of Orthodoxy

The Dual Interpretation

To stay away from the familiar criticisms of the Invisible Hand Theorem, let us shed for now whatever objections we may have to the idea of Pareto optimality and pretend that a Pareto optimal outcome is sufficient for the outcome to be considered good. Let us also assume that individuals are atomistic and not strategic, so the competitive model is a valid depiction of reality. With these distractions out of the way, the Invisible Hand Theorem seems to become the gospel according to market fundamentalists eager to banish the state and allow individuals to pursue their own self-interest, unhindered.

But does the Invisible Hand Theorem really permit such a conclusion, even allowing for the above qualifiers? The answer is no. The theorem is actually a mathematical truism and, as we saw in the last chapter, has no normative content. If we are going to interpret it beyond its literal meaning so as to derive real-world policy wisdom, it is equally easy to derive the opposite conclusion, or what I call the "dual interpretation."

Think for a moment why the theorem is treated as a celebration of individual selfishness. The optimality result is predicated on individuals having the freedom to maximize their own selfish interest. To see this, recall that in this model, each person is left free to choose any bundle from their 'budget set'—that is, the collection of all bundles of goods and services that are feasible, given the limits of the person's income or budget. What the Invisible Hand Theorem showed is that the claim of society achieving optimality on its own works when all persons in this society are given the option to choose freely what to consume, given nothing but the restrictions of their income. If, on the other hand, government places restrictions, such as banning consumers from buying a certain product or placing a tax on some item, which shrinks the options open to the consumer, then it is no longer guaranteed that society will reach the optimum outcome in equilibrium. Hence, it does seem that it is allowing individuals the unfettered freedom to choose that gives us the optimality result.

Note that in this model, the full freedom to choose means the freedom to choose any bundle of goods from the person's budget set. But if we think outside the model, it is evident that human beings can do many things other than choosing a consumption bundle. They can abuse and steal; they can threaten, slander, and spread rumors; they can tear at their hair and wring their hands; they can ostracize people or embrace them; they can be good-humored or bad; they can love their neighbors and do them a good turn at every opportunity or hate them. Hence, in reality, human beings choose not just from budget sets but also from the many other things that they can do. If they do choose some of these actions, would society still achieve efficiency? The answer is not obvious anymore; standard economics does not have any theory to guide us once we expand the range of behavior in this way. There are some actions that clearly seem to thwart optimality. If a person inflicts physical violence on another in order to make that person part with some of their goods, the outcome is socially suboptimal.[1]

Hence, if we start with the true set of actions available to a person (all elements in the budget set *plus* the many other kinds of behavior that the person can indulge in) and then think of the Invisible Hand Theorem, we reach a different perspective.

The Invisible Hand Theorem can then be restated as follows:

If we have a competitive economy, where the freedom of individuals is restricted so that they are not allowed to choose from all the alternative actions available to them but instead are simply allowed to choose a point from their budget set, then (given a few technical conditions, as before) the resultant equilibrium will be Pareto optimal.

As mentioned above, this is what I call the dual interpretation. It is exactly the same theorem that we encountered in the last chapter, but stated this way it seems to be not a celebration of individual freedom but in fact its opposite: it appears to emphasize the need to place restrictions on individual choice. Hence, the central opinion in economics and its adulatory periphery—namely, that a complete free market is the ideal to pursue—does not have the theoretical foundation popularly assumed. Smith did not prove this nor did it get established by the subsequent rise of mathematical economics. Its foundation is a myth—one that has had reverberating implications for the way we view economic policymaking in the world, and our hopes or rather lack thereof of a better and fairer economic order.

This is not to say that we may not have other reasons for propagating a free market, yet these are founded on hunch, intuition, partial reasoning, and conjecture. These are not matters that should be dismissed out of hand, as discussed in chapter 1. There are legions of governments that have harmed the economy by trying to overcontrol markets while frustrating individual enterprise and initiative. What I am asking for here is that the reasons for freeing the market should be seen for what they are. Viewed in this way, even when we promote the free market, we are aware that we may need to temper it with the hand of the state, since it is not the all-encompassing theorem that many economists made it out to be.

Let me clarify that the principal appeal of the Invisible Hand Theorem, especially as a bulwark for conservative thought, resides in the popular belief that a competitive economy with maximal individual freedom guarantees social optimality. On closer scrutiny, however, the freedom that is ensured is only the freedom to choose from within one's budget set. If one 'expands' the 'opportunity set' beyond the budget set, to include the freedom to do the many other things that we can do in reality, then the resulting outcome is no longer necessarily optimal.[2] It is at least not known to be so. Hence, if we start from these larger, real-life feasible sets of individuals and want to get to the Invisible Hand Theorem, we would have to say that if somehow each individual's freedom could be restricted so as to permit individuals to do nothing but choose from their budget sets, then we would be sure of attaining social optimality. Viewed in this entirely legitimate way, the theorem no longer provides a case against government intervention. This is true even if we rule out the standard conditions under which we conventionally justify government intervention, such as the presence of externalities, increasing returns to scale, or the existence of multiple equilibria.

Further, these extramodel behaviors and actions are often matters of trade and exchange. Beyond the world of prices, wages, and market-based transactions, which is the bread and butter of economic theory, there is the wide world of barter. It is true that we do not barter meat for grain or corn for sheepskin anymore, but it is a myth that the world of barter has been replaced by the market. There is barter occurring all the time, everywhere, at times openly but often through nods and winks.[3] X offers to help Y get admittance to an exclusive club, and keeps this in a mental log and expects Y to help X secure a business deal at a later date. The chiefs of a company may help secure a political office for a friend, and then expect that just in case that friend happens to destroy a nation, the contract to rebuild it will go to their company. Journalists who tow the government line often are privy to breaking news. An economist who helps vested interests remain entrenched gets plum 'research support' from the same vested interests. Indeed, when one thinks objectively about this it becomes clear that barter is the norm rather than the exception. Crony capitalism is all about barter. What the wealthy know and the nonwealthy typically do not know is that you rarely get rich by simply selling or buying products and services at the market price. Not all, but most of the rich got there by mastering the art of barter through nods and winks as well as the extensive use of the exchange of favors—activities that we were told had ended in the medieval age. Once we recognize the occurrence of barter along-side standard market exchange and trade, there is no telling what happens to the Invisible Hand Theorem. It is no longer clear, even in the pristine world of economic models or what Ronald Coase (1991) referred to as "blackboard economics," if leaving it all to selfish maximization and the free market leads society to an optimal outcome.

Before moving on, it is worthwhile to add a terminological clarification. I am using the term 'selfish' behavior interchangeably with 'self-interested' behavior, in keeping with the common practice in mainstream economics—in particular, general equilibrium theory and game theory (see, for instance, Thaler 1992; Bowles 2004). Yet as will become evident, this is one area where language turns out to be especially constraining. Language is also inadequate for the range of motivations that prompt human action, from the completely self-centered one, concerned solely with one's own bread and butter, through shades of more enlightened self-interested behavior that accommodates more than one's own material gains, to the virtually selfless one. Some authors have tried to cut through this by distinguishing between terms such as selfishness and self-interestedness (Medema 2009), and there are also excellent dissections of the very idea of 'interest' (Swedberg 2005). In the pages that follow, and especially chapters 5 and 6, we will encounter different motivations for human action and choice; I will elaborate on them at that point.

The classical writers were (and even unclassical ones, I like to believe, are) aware of the multiplicity of human motivations and the fact that people are not impelled solely by self-interest. But this must not be confused with the fact that Smith's discovery is exciting precisely because it shows that (admittedly in a somewhat rarefied setting) *even if* human beings were completely selfish, society would achieve optimality, or in the more colorful language of Duncan Foley (2006, 2), "By being selfish within the rules of capitalist property relations, Smith promises, we are actually being good to our fellow human beings."

Evolving Feasible Set

A fundamental step in broadening the scope of economics is to recognize that the feasible set of actions open to individuals is much larger than our models make it out to be. We saw above that a consumer can do much more than choose bundles of goods. Likewise in the theory of oligopoly, a firm or its entrepreneur is supposed to choose how much quantity it will sell, as per the model of Augustin Cournot, or what price it will charge, as per the formulation of Joseph Bertrand. There are more sophisticated models where firms can do more, such as choose a quantity *and then* choose a price (Kreps and Scheinkman 1983; Benoit and Krishna 1987). But all these do not come close to what firms can do in reality, which includes hit the entrepreneurs of other firms on the head (after dusk), spread rumors about the products of their competitors, plant stories about malpractice in other firms, conceal part of the price information about their products from consumers (Ellison 2005; Gabaix and Laibson 2006), misinform consumers about the risks associated with their own products, offer bribes to journalists who threaten to expose this misinformation, and do away with journalists who do not accept the bribe.

There are models that allow for larger sets of actions open to firms or consumers. Yet what is rarely done is to recognize that the set of actions open to economic agents go far beyond what the textbook model suggests, and includes many 'noneconomic actions,' such as violence and invective speech. This recognition also means that we have to treat the normative prescriptions that seem to emerge from these models with a great deal of caution, and use them in practice with a good dose of practical intuition. The two other failings of much of the standard literature is the nonrecognition of the fact that in most situations, the set of feasible actions open to an agent is evolving—since people 'discover' new actions that they were earlier unaware of, and more fundamentally, the actions available to a person may be so large and complex as to not even constitute a set. As we now know, there is no such thing as a set of everything. This is a philosophical matter, and related to well-known discussions in logic on the meaning of a set, but I will ignore it here.

In one narrow sense the evolution and enlargement of the feasible set of actions through time is allowed for in the existing literature. Technological innovation is nothing but discovering new actions. Earlier I used chemical x and chemical y separately. If we suddenly discover that mixing the two can generate energy, then the act of mixing x and y, which was never considered before, becomes a part of the set of actions that one might choose from. But beyond technological innovation, we seldom allow for the fact that the full feasible set may be unknown to the individual, that over time they discover newer and newer possible actions, and so their feasible set expands. This happens in all kinds of ways in reality. Entrepreneurs trying to maximize profit do not, as our textbook says, spend all their time looking for the most profit-generating strategy from the set of feasible strategies. A part of their time is spent on discovering new strategies that they and others may have been unaware of hitherto.

A decade or two ago, cricketers were generally not financially well off. They played cricket, gave pleasure to millions of viewers, and earned a meager income. In India it was routine for the nation's top cricketers—including some of the eleven who played on the national team—to work as clerks in banks or government offices to supplement their cricketing income. In contrast, leading cricketers today are millionaires. This happened not because the cricketers themselves began doing something differently but rather because some entrepreneurs discovered how to tap the pleasures of the millions of viewers and make money for themselves, and then the players began earning a share of this collection. Other entrepreneurs discovered that having a cricketer wear a particular brand-name cap or shirt, or endorse a product, meant a higher demand for that brand name. A new market then developed whereby firms would offer to pay cricketers a fee for wearing their products. Soon the 'endorsement income' of the cricketers started piling up, as did the profits of companies advertising their goods.[4]

One area, outside of economics, where the discovery of new actions and strategies has had important consequences for our lives pertains to democracy. It is frequently pointed out that for a democracy to function well, the citizens need to learn how to participate in a democracy, since democracy is not just about voting but also includes a variety of other forms of civil participation. This is seen as the reason why new democracies often flounder. Citizens not used to the system may go about casting their votes diligently, but fail to participate in decision- making in other ways, such as debate and discussion. While this is true, it misses out on the fact that just as citizens learn how to function in a democracy, governments also learn, and the latter can have a subversive effect. Basically, governments learn how to allow citizens to express their opinion and then do as they please regardless of the public.

Hence, democratic governments may not be quite as democratic as they appear at first sight. Autocratic governments or military leaders in charge of running a state stop people from expressing opinions that are critical of what the leaders wish to do. Democratic governments allow the expression of contrary opinions and this is of course laudable; but it has to be kept in mind that over time, they learn to 'manage' these opinions, to ensure that they do not translate into action. I have described this elsewhere as the *elé belé* phenomenon.[5] This does not mean that an autocracy, a monarchy, or a dictatorship is better than a democracy but simply that democracies are not as democratic as we may think.

Consider the case of George W. Bush's war on Iraq. Never before had there been so much opposition in the United States to a war *before* it occurred. There were student protests on a number of university campuses. The AFL-

CIO took an explicit position against the war. Ordinary citizens, troubled by the dubious morality of a preemptive attack that would kill thousands of civilians, spoke out against the war repeatedly. This aspect of the United States, similar to India, the United Kingdom, and several other nations, is admirable: there is little effort to muzzle the freedom to criticize government, as would happen in scores of dictatorial countries around the world. What is not so nice, however, is that these democracies are becoming increasingly adept at not allowing the freely expressed opinion to control and restrain what the government does. It is fascinating to see how mature democracies manage and, in many cases, even shape opinion. Every time Hans Blix commented on the UN inspection of Iraq, it was interesting to listen to members of the Bush administration paraphrase him. The paraphrasing consisted of subtly changing the comments to suit the U.S. government's case for war. The hope was that by repeating the altered comments sufficiently often, mass opinion would favor the war.[6]

In India political analysts have puzzled over the fact that civil society, across the board, was critical of the handling of communal violence in Gujarat in 2002 by the state government under the stewardship of its chief minister, which led to a massacre of ordinary Muslim citizens, and yet this had no effect on the subsequent behavior of the government. The media, especially the English-language ones, were vocal about the shameful failure of the state government to punish the perpetrators of the carnage. But evidently such free expression of opinion is not enough to restrain a mature democratic government. We clearly cannot allow democracy to lull us into complacency.

From a historical point of view, the more dramatic example of the evolving feasible set is the rise of colonialism. In ancient times, one nation established control over another by sending large occupying armies, often led by the king or emperor, to overwhelm some hapless region or country. Colonialism was the discovery that you can occupy another nation by using only a few people from your own country, simply by creating the right incentives among the people of the land you seek to control so that they effectively control themselves.

The Portuguese conqueror Alphonso d'Albuquerque took a major step toward this when he set up his viceroyalty in Goa in 1512–15. Intelligent and by then battle hardened, he realized that confrontation and direct occupation could at times be outdone by the careful crafting of strategy whereby he could rule over large masses of indigenous people with few of his own. The technique was improved and mastered by the British, who would then go on to rule India with an impossibly small British force.

This process has by no means come to an end. Nations are forever discovering ways of controlling other nations by making use of the latter's own citizens. Hence, economic control and even extortion can be affected by an ever-smaller loss of lives and energy on the part of the controlling nation. This realization that the true feasible set is seldom known but evolves has large implications for the way we view the world. It weans us away from the rather static view of political economy that we have otherwise been used to. This theme gets picked up in different ways later in this book.

Evolving Preference

The other constancy that deserves to be challenged is that of human preference. On this, fortunately, there is some recognition in the economics literature—mostly recently but also in some earlier writings, notably those of Thorstein Veblen (1899) and Harvey Leibenstein (1950).[7] The full implications of endogenous preferences remain unexplored, though, perhaps because the mainstream economists' peripheral vision makes them aware that this is a Pandora's box that can destabilize their worldview more than is good for their job.[8]

Some of the most untenable assumptions in economics are the ones that are not even written as axioms but instead are built into the woodwork of the discipline. Take the description of the competitive equilibrium model discussed in chapter 2 or any mainstream microeconomics text. It is standard for this to begin by saying that "each consumer's preference for goods and services is assumed to satisfy certain axioms." One such axiom, for instance, is that of 'transitivity,' which says that if a person considers some alternative, x, to be at least as good as y, and considers y to be as at least as good as z, then the person must consider x to be at least as good as z. Another axiom is that of 'vector dominance' or, more colloquially, 'more is preferred to less.' This says that if one bundle of goods has more of everything than another bundle, then this bundle must be preferred to the other bundle. This is not to deny that there have been advances in economic theory that have made it possible to construct niche models that can do without one or more of these standard axioms.

All axioms have been subjected to criticism in the literature. Take, for instance, the transitivity axiom. It seems to be perfectly reasonable to assume that most people cannot tell the difference between zero grains of sugar in their coffee and one grain of sugar; and between one grain and two grains; and more generally, between n grains and n + 1 grains. But of course someone may prefer one spoon of sugar to no sugar. By the above assumption, any consumer will find zero grains to be at least as good as one grain (since no one can tell the difference between these) and one grain to be at least as good as two grains, and hence, by transitivity, find zero to be at least as good as two. By repeated use of this argument, the person should find zero to be at least as good as one spoon of sugar. But this is not true; transitivity is therefore violated by this person. For this reason, many authors have questioned the transitivity assumption.[9] And as we shall see in chapter 7, this has implications for an analysis of the correct form of state intervention.

The vector dominance axiom is also frequently criticized. Most of us recognize that greed, especially an entirely self-centered greed, is not as generic to human beings as the social sciences make it out to be. The social scientist's discomfort concerning the lack of greed is summed up humorously by Norman Rush (1991) in the opening pages of his novel *Mating*. Having discussed how whites in Africa always "want more," Rush goes on to observe, "The average black African has the opposite problem: he or she doesn't want enough. A whole profession called Rural Animation exists devoted to making villagers want more and work harder to get it" (5).

The strongest assumptions in consumer theory, however, have gone virtually unchallenged simply because not being stated as axioms, they have gone unnoticed. Consider again the sentence above that was placed in quotes and captures the way that textbooks view consumers. To repeat: "Each consumer's preference for goods and services is assumed to satisfy certain axioms."

A huge assumption slips in as soon as we make this assertion and even before any axiom is posited. This is the assumption that each consumer has a preference relation over bundles of goods and services.[10] In addition, in standard analysis this is presumed to be an unchanging preference. Tucked away in the woodwork of our models, these assumptions—that each person has a utility function, and that this is unchanging—go unexamined, but if we do examine them, we will find that they are strong assumptions and quite unacceptable in lots of contexts. Often, we have no well-defined preferences, and make choices from a vague and ill-defined idea of what we want.[11] This leads to vacillation and changes in our ordering over different goods. Waitstaff in restaurants know this even if scholars do not.

When we do have preferences, these often change depending on what others do and on what kind of equilibrium comes into existence. Our sartorial preference may depend on what film stars or pop divas wear. I have seen little girls dressed like Britney Spears, which I refuse to put down to coincidence.

This has been known for a long time. Veblen (1899), who thanks to his all-pervading sense of alienation could subject the world around him to objective scrutiny of the kind that anthropologists bring to bear on distant, primitive peoples or zoologists apply to primates, wrote witheringly on the subject.[12] What is not always appreciated is that this 'endogeneity' of preference not only allows us to create more sophisticated models but also may be quite destructive of the foundations of standard analysis. What is being suggested here is that a person's preference may depend on what the equilibrium outcome of the economy looks like. This immediately means that the methodological, individualistic assumption that one can begin by first describing the individuals and then going on to describe the society that they will create is untenable, since the society they create may in turn alter the way that the individuals are characterized—for instance, their preferences. This can lead to unusual implications. For one, it can easily lead to the nonexistence of any equilibrium, which would leave much of our analysis in a vacuum. It could also lead to multiple equilibria, opening up interesting new questions concerning government intervention. Both the nonexistence of equilibria and the possibility of multiple ones are easy to see.

Suppose each person's preference for jeans depends on how many others wear jeans. In particular, assume that there is 'snob value' in this (Leibenstein 1950). That is, the fewer the people who wear jeans, the greater the value of jeans. Let me make this a bit extreme and assume that each person is willing to wear jeans if, and only if, 10 percent or fewer people wear jeans. Otherwise, each person feels, this fashion is too plebian to indulge in. Notice that the market for jeans can now not have any equilibrium. If 10 percent or less than 10 percent of people wear jeans, then everyone will want to wear jeans. So 10 percent or fewer people wearing jeans is a situation that cannot persist. If, on the other hand, more than 10 percent of people wear jeans, then no one will want to wear jeans. So we can never have an equilibrium with more than 10 percent of people wearing jeans either.

Suppose next that people have a herd mentality.[13] If more people wear jeans, then each person's urge to wear jeans increases. It is easy to fill in the blanks and see that in some specific constructions, both no one wearing jeans and everybody wearing jeans can constitute equilibria. The argument is spelled out in greater detail below. Later in the book, I will return to more complex and socially relevant situations where this kind of equilibrium problems can arise.

Social Norms and Culture

The standard model of economics, as the description in the previous section makes clear, functions as if social norms, culture, and collective beliefs do not matter. These features of life are not denied but they are treated rather like the candles on a cake, or as superficial window dressing that makes no substantial difference to the substance of economics. This is admittedly changing; there is a growing literature on how norms interact with economics, though its influence still remains largely on the fringes.[14]

I would argue, however, that social norms and culture not only matter, in many situations they are more important than standard economic variables, such as tax rates and fiscal deficits, in determining how efficiently an economy will function and how rapid a growth an economy will achieve.[15] To understand this we must recognize that all human beings are socialized (in different ways no doubt) so as not to act in certain ways or forego personal gain for reasons of conformity with social norms. Some actions or nonactions are so instinctive that the word 'choice' becomes a misnomer. When we get into a bus, we choose whether to grab the window seat or be seated in the aisle, whether to take the incoming cell phone call or switch the phone off, whether to get up for the old person clearly having difficulty standing or keep sitting while feigning to be riveted by the scene outside the window. But we typically do not choose between stealing the wallet bulging out of a copassenger's pocket and not stealing it. We just do not think about it. By "we" I do not mean everybody, for there are of course pickpockets. Yet for most people, social programming is such that they do not even consider that choice, since emptying out other people's pockets is treated by them as beyond the alternatives they would consider. Some economists like to think of all choices as a result of deliberate cogitation. For them, our 'choice' of not picking other people's pockets is simply a consequence of a cost-benefit analysis that shows that the expected benefit of stealing a copassenger's wallet exceeds the expected costs, given by the probability of getting caught multiplied by the fine or the pain of being thrashed by irate passengers. Such a view is a classic case of "trained incapacity," which makes us believe that all choices are deliberate, and makes us miss out on the truth, which is that lots of options are not taken by us simply because we do not even consider them. Much of our social norms take exactly this form. They demarcate the domain within which we think and choose rationally, and so, equivalently, they specify actions that we do not even consider or are collectively programmed to evaluate in a certain way.[16]

How varied and instinctive these collective beliefs can be was driven home to me some years ago, when I called a pest-control agent to our apartment in Delhi to banish termites. A cheerful man arrived, armed with canisters and receptacles containing various chemicals along witha big syringe. Every time he sprayed, a mist settled on everything. I asked him if all this hard work would actually get rid of the pests. As he pressed on the syringe and squirted another round of some chemical, he smiled comfortingly and said,

"Sir, have no worry. This is very strong stuff. It is totally banned in the United States." I thanked him for his effort, while edging out of the room.

How well an economy does depends on what our collective beliefs are, what options people choose instinctively, without thought, and what actions people do not even consider. If you belong to a society where, after you have collected a small sum of money from a person in order to deliver some goods to them a week later, you do not even think if you should deliver those goods, you just do it, then this helps economic efficiency and development. People in such a society will be able to cut deals and effect exchanges freely, and such actions are at the base of an economy's progress. A society where rational choice extends to the decision about whether to supply the goods that you have told someone you will supply is likely to do much worse.[17] Either there will have to be expensive third-party enforcement, involving the courts and police, or lots of potentially fruitful transactions will not take place. The norm of trust and trusting behavior as a crucial ingredient for economic progress has been written about for a while, within economics but mostly beyond (see, for instance, Landa 1995; Fukuyama 1996), and I will return to this subject in chapter 6.

Social norms vary across societies. In some societies, cutting ahead of people in a line is fair game, and in other societies it is not. In India, not to cut ahead in a line that has gaps between people is like in the United States not to raise prices when the market will bear the rise—it is treated as an opportunity for gain that one would be foolish to forego.

In North American suburbs, there is increasingly no effort to defend the boundaries of one's property by building a wall or fence. This does not lead to encroachment, as would happen in many societies.[18] It is interesting to see the number of ways in which people leave themselves vulnerable to exploitation by others, but do not get exploited. The art is to know what is considered "not a done thing" in a particular society (for a discussion of group-specific norms, see Landa 1995), and one can keep those flanks safely open. In U.S. suburban societies, it is not done to encroach on other people's property, and so it is safe to leave one's property unfenced.[19] To an outsider this seems quite a utopian arrangement. There are no expensive boundary walls, which also can be eyesores, and at the same time, there are no fights and running to the courts.

Some of these socially valuable norms can create vulnerabilities, however. I have elsewhere (Basu 1995) called them 'normative loopholes': vulnerabilities vis-à-vis other societies that arise from the fact of having some of these norms, which are useful props for society's everyday functioning. It is possible that the lack of the sense of personal property that the native people of United States had concerning land helped them to function effectively, but this became their weakness when the settlers arrived and made claims on their land.[20] It is like the loss of some antibodies that happen through the prolonged lack of exposure to certain germs. This makes us healthier, but also vulnerable to illness when the germs suddenly arrive. The gradual development of useful norms and the concurrent normative loopholes could have important clues as to why powerful and long-settled civilizations crumble and eventually make way for others.

Nevertheless, all this means that societies can come to acquire norms of the kind discussed above—ones that make us hold our self-interests in abeyance—and these can persist over long stretches of time. This should make us aware that there is no reason why we cannot in the future have societies where people curb their self-interest *in other ways* and so make more utopian social systems viable. Maybe we can have a society where people work hard even though there is a ceiling on how much each person can earn or, by law, everyone gets the same income, whether or not they work. I know this sounds implausible, and if in today's world someone tries to start a society of this kind it will be an immediate disaster. This is the reason why so many utopian revolutions have ultimately come to grief. But once we look around us and take stock of the numerous ways in which we, thanks to our contemporary social norms, forego greater income opportunities, we will see that there is no reason to rule out, a priori, other norms coming into play in the future that make other kinds of—and especially, better—societies possible.

Some may argue that what I am describing as cases of foregoing some individual advantage is not really that because those individuals have different preferences, and so it is in their utility-maximizing interest to forego those things. But this is a purely semantic point, with which I have no disagreement except to note that this kind of a definition of utility is tautological and devoid of content.[21]

Where these norms come from remains an ill-understood question. Many of these self-imposed restrictions on behavior are built into our psyche or consciousness by example or training from the time of our childhood, and come under the rubric of culture, social norms, or collective consciousness. They become so ingrained in us that we may be unaware of them, and hence even for the outside analyst they are not always visible. One learns to detect these norms from the cadences of language. There are, for instance, subtle differences in the use of language between societies that are instinctively respectful of contracts and those that are not, and one may need an anthropologist's antenna to pick up on these. When the moneylender comes to collect the overdue loan, an entirely plausible response of the borrower in a noncontractual society is, "If I give you the money, how will I pay for my thatch roof?"

Contrast this to what the recalcitrant borrower's response would be in a contractual society: "I know I am supposed to pay you, but last year has been an especially bad one." And there will also be clear differences in speech in the lender's response in the two societies. If by some freak accident a borrower were to give the response involving the roof in a contractual society, one can see what the lender would say: "That's your problem. You should have thought of that when you took the loan." Whereas in parts of rural India that are stubbornly noncontractual, I can easily see a lender responding to such an answer by saying, "But why do you want a thatch roof? You can nowadays get cheap plastic-based material that can be used for roofing."

While this may seem like a tangent to my readers who live in contractual environments, I can assure you that this is a normal dialogue in a noncontractual society, illustrating that these differences can become completely part of the fabric of life. This is the same reason why when we travel from one cultural zone to another, we may need to have aspects of life explained to us that the locals take for granted. In the New York–based play *Queen's Boulevard*, an Indian merchant with a marked Indian accent explains a slew of rules for easy assimilation into North American life, including, "When at a 7-11, don't take Sierra Mist Free without paying for it. . . . It is free from sugar, not free to take."

How societies employ *culture* to constrain individual behavior can make all the difference to how well societies function. Much more important than enshrining property rights in the laws is to have the respect for property built into our values. One can then save on policing costs and economize on law courts. As we will see in chapter 4, social norms can be as binding on individuals as the law. Just as a poorly designed law can damage an economy's prospects of development, a growth-unfriendly social norm can do so too. Economists have long recognized the salience of laws. A law banning imports can cripple an economy. A law that requires that workers should not work for more than four hours a day will do the same. But as we will see in the next chapter, these same outcomes can occur via social norms with no use of the law. Hence, if laws are important in causing and thwarting economic development, so are social norms. Our lack of attention to social norms is a big caveat.

Unfortunately, our understanding of where norms come from, how they acquire stability, and why and when they wither away is still quite rudimentary. One reason for this must be the economist's belief that norms do not matter. This is a research gap that will need to be plugged if we are to understand the economy better. I will demonstrate here and in later chapters some initial steps that we can take in incorporating the role of law and culture into the study of economy, but these must be recognized as no more than first steps in a large, open territory.

It is critical to begin by recognizing that the moral goodness of norms and the growth friendliness of norms are separate matters. People in industrially advanced nations by and large adhere to the norm "thou shalt not steal" (at least not in blatant and petty ways). In poor countries people take a more relaxed view on this matter. Through their own complex histories, these countries have failed to endow their individuals with the social norm "thou shalt not steal." I use the word 'failed' with unease because I see nothing morally special about this norm. If the person you are stealing from has gotten their wealth through improper means, or if the person refuses to give any of their ample wealth to the poor and malnourished, it is not clear that it would be *morally* wrong to steal from them. As Thomas Aquinas ([1265–74] 1911, II–II:66.7) wrote in his thirteenth-century classic *Summa Theologica*, demonstrating that some of our most radical ideas have origins in theological writings, "In cases of need, all things are common property, so that there would seem to be no sin in taking another's property, for need has made it common. . . . [I]f the need be so manifest and urgent that it is evident that the present need must be remedied by whatever means be at hand, then it is lawful for a man to succor his own need by means of another's property, by taking it either openly or secretly."[22]

But this does not change the fact that "thou shalt not steal" is a norm that makes economic life more efficient, helps growth and development, and thus, to that extent we should try to encourage society to adopt this norm.[23]

This is a mistake that some radicals have made. They have tried to be true to *morally* defensible norms, failing to realize that this may be neither necessary nor sufficient to make an economy function well, and for development to occur. For the latter, we have to teach people to adhere to *growth-friendly* norms. Of course, given people's propensity for moral living, it may be worthwhile deluding people into believing that norms like "thou shalt not steal" are moral. Successful growth is often a by-product of such illusions.

While we have to wait for research to yield us a better understanding of where norms come from, and when and why they wither away, before we can say much about how to craft policy to take advantage of this, some important policy insights can be gleaned from what we already know about norms. In common parlance, we frequently talk about how things happen because of culture. We say how in some society, the culture of hard work has broken down or how the "work culture" is excellent; we speak about the "culture of crime"; and we complain about the bureaucratic culture of some office. Is this meaningful talk? The answer is yes. Let me illustrate this in the context of a real-life problem that is currently plaguing India—that of teacher absenteeism in government-run schools.[24]

A recent study (Kremer et al. 2005) shows that at any point in time, during regular work hours 24 percent of the teachers in government-run primary schools are not present on the school premises.[25] This high level of teacher truancy ends up being a big drain on government resources and causes poor school outcomes. When economists talk about correcting this, the attention is invariably on incentives—how to penalize a truant teacher or how to financially reward a diligent one. This misses out on the fact that large amounts of our behavior in reality have little to do with economic incentives. In good universities, professors teach regularly, even when the penalty for not doing so is negligible. Clearly this has something to do with the culture of work.

One way to model this is to recognize that in deciding whether to play truant or not, one cost that is significant but often ignored in traditional economics is a subjective moral cost. This can come from social stigma or social norms, or be an internal moral cost—I feel bad if I do not do what I am supposed to do. Even without knowing much about this kind of moral cost one thing that we can assert is that this cost will be smaller in societies where lots of teachers play truant—I feel bad for being truant, but not *that* bad because "everybody does it"—and higher in societies where few are truant—by being truant I stand out. Once this happens, we can get multiple equilibria. If teachers expect lots of teachers to be absent, the moral cost of truancy is low and so lots of teachers choose to be truant; if few teachers are truant, the moral cost of truancy is high and for that reason most teachers choose not to be truant. This society can get caught in a high- or low-truancy equilibrium. Therefore, two otherwise-identical societies can exhibit different kinds of behavior, as in the teacher truancy analysis above. This also suggests that a society can change its behavior without there being any fundamental changes. These kinds of shifts in behavior do happen. People who are known to be lazy or unpunctual can seemingly change their behavior suddenly and without any fundamental cause (Basu and Weibull 2003).

If we learned how social norms can be changed, we could effect changes in behavior deliberately.[26] But we may be able to effect changes even without learning this. If in India for some years teachers were monitored for truancy and fined, this could alter behavior (purely because of the financial incentive). Once the change happens and truancy goes down, however, the social cost of truancy would go up, and *even if the fine for truancy were removed*, truancy could continue to be low. Hence, the monitoring cost does not have to be borne permanently, as would appear in a norms-free model. After the monitoring is done for a while, social mechanisms for sustaining the good behavior could kick in and hold the desirable outcome in place without the need for policing.

Before closing this section and at the risk of digression, I want to comment on one general methodological assumption that underlies much of this
book. It must be evident from the last few paragraphs that I am assuming that
innate human differences are much smaller than they appear at first glance,
and differences between large groups of people, such as races, religions, or
nationalities, are even smaller. In fact, for the most part, when speaking about
large groups—for instance, groups with different social norms and culture—I
treat them as *ex ante* identical. This perspective permeates much of the book
and may seem confusing at first blush. So let me elaborate.

When we look around us, we find lots of differences across people and
groups. It is often remarked how the Japanese are trustworthy, Latinos are fun
loving, Buddhists are kind, the French are romantic, Americans believe that
the French *believe* that they are romantic, the British have room to work on
their taste buds, Brazilians are unpunctual.... I think it is judicious to stop before I make more enemies of large swathes of humanity. Some of these beliefs
are myths, but some are true. People do differ in their tastes, norms, cultures,
and behaviors.

The assumption that runs through this book is that most of these differences are 'equilibrium differences' rather than 'innate differences,' or more
minimally, the innate differences are larger than equilibrium differences. That
is, in terms of innate preferences, talents, and disadvantages, we human beings
are similar. But we respond to our environment and other human beings, and
begin to display behaviors that may be different. So ex post—that is, after society has settled into an equilibrium—we appear to be different. These height-
ened differences may be referred to as equilibrium differences because they are
not innate but instead involve our response to our situation.

This is close to how Smith viewed the world. "The difference of natural
talents in different men, is in reality, much less than we are aware of.... The
difference between the most dissimilar characters, between a philosopher and
a common street porter, for example, seems to arise not so much from nature,
as from habit, custom and education" (Smith [1776] 1937, 15).

This point was driven home to me powerfully when I was doing some research with Weibull (Basu and Weibull 2003) on societal differences in relation to punctuality. There is, we quickly learned, a substantial literature in
social psychology and sociology on punctuality. This literature notes that punctuality differs not only across individuals but also across societies and nations.
North Americans are more punctual than South Americans, the Japanese are
hyperpunctual (maybe to the point of inefficiency), and there is extensive data
to show that Brazilian wristwatches are not as well coordinated as North American ones (Levine, West, and Reis 1980). Using a bit of linguistic anthropology

and no data, I concluded that Indians also have poorly coordinated watches. Around the time that we were working on our paper, on a trip to India, as soon as I got out of the New Delhi airport, a gentleman asked me, "Excuse me, sir, what is the time by your watch?" And I realized that we did not need data. The routine use of the qualifier "by your watch," when asking for time in India, is surely a sign of society's recognition that time is watch dependent.

Most of the existing literature seemed to put down the societal differences in punctuality to deeply rooted factors, like the region's ecology, the society's religious beliefs, or deep-seated cultural factors. While there can be no denial that these things matter, we nevertheless concluded that how punctual a person chooses to be depends largely on how punctual others with whom they have to interact are. This immediately opens up the possibility of multiple equilibria. Two innately identical societies can get caught in different equilibria—one where everybody is punctual, and the other where everybody is tardy.

The fundamental similarity of large groups of human beings is, admittedly, an assumption of convenience. After all, if we consider the group of tall people and the group of short people, the two groups will not have the same profile of heights. So group similarity is not something that would happen across *all* groups. But for groups such as nationalities, races, and religions, especially when we take a historical view, I find it a good approximation to treat their basic traits as similar, and certainly more similar than they would appear from the overt behavior of the members of the groups.

A Comment on Incentive Compatibility

One of the major contributions of modern economics is the study of incentive compatibility and mechanism design. As we have seen, and as thoughtful economists have long warned, contrary to the myth inspired by the Invisible Hand Theorem, free markets frequently do not bring individual incentives into alignment with social interests. We may need to consciously design how individuals are rewarded and punished for different kinds of behavior so as to make what is socially desirable consistent with individual aspirations. This has spawned an elegant literature and is among the most socially useful contributions that economics has made to the design of policy.[27] It has vastly improved our ability to design auctions, and given us new insights into pricing strategy and organizational behavior.[28]

I have some personal, if trivial, experience of designing optimal behavior that makes critical use of other people's rationality. One is required to leave one's footwear outside when entering Indian temples. This, in turn, results in a high incidence of stolen shoes and sandals, robbing those who have gone in to pray or admire the statuary of mental peace. I devised a system for countering this problem. Since most temples have more than one entrance, my technique is to take off a shoe, place it in the pile of footwear outside a door, hobble over to another door, and leave the other shoe in the pile there. The chances are now remote that my shoes will be stolen. Thieves operate under a severe time constraint and are aware that a single shoe does not command a high market price.

I used this technique successfully for some time and then published it in a popular Indian newspaper in order to make a social contribution. Few newspaper articles of mine generated as many grateful letters and emails as this one (evidently, thieves either do not read newspapers or do not believe in wasting precious time sending hate mail).

Nevertheless, despite these advantages, it is possible to take our concern for individual incentive compatibility to extremes, where, devoid of common sense and intuition, they begin to hurt instead of help the design of good policy. This is a recurring theme of this book. The flaw in taking this to a polar extreme is best understood in light of the above discussion on social norms and culture, and hence the brief intrusion of this subsection.

In many countries bureaucrats do not do their jobs. They slack off, take up illegal second jobs, and accept bribes. The growing data on "doing business" from different countries, compiled by the World Bank, show how these bureaucratic inefficiencies can become impediments to growth and development. I have already commented on how teachers in state-run primary schools in India play truant from school, inflicting huge costs to society in terms of illiteracy and lack of education, not to mention the fiscal burden.

The response of the incentive-incompatibility literature to these phenomena is to point out that they are caused by the poor design of incentives for the bureaucrats and teachers, as mentioned previously. The only way to solve this problem is to design a system of pay, rewards, and fines that bring the interests of these agents into line with what society wishes to achieve. The word I object to is "only." By placing the blame for malfunctioning public administration on the lack of incentive-compatible compensation for bureaucrats, we tend to minimize, if not eliminate, the role of personal integrity.[29] As observed in the previous section, life gives us lots of opportunities for small gains that we routinely forego. Which particular opportunities for personal gain are foregone largely depends on the prevalent social norms, and these vary from society to society. Economic prosperity is made possible by us having appropriate norms.[30]

Bureaucrats who work diligently in one of South Korea's successful state-owned enterprises may do so in part for personal career advancement, but also because such diligence is an innate component of their social norms.[31] In India's leading institutes of higher education, there is as little monitoring of a professor's teaching as there is of the teacher's teaching in state-run primary schools or a professor's teaching in a U.S. university. Yet professors in these institutes continue to teach diligently. To put this down purely to self-interested behavior is to miss out on some essential ingredients of human nature, and then to design policy based entirely on such a presumption is to doom policy to failure.

The absurdity of expecting a socially efficient society in which all human beings are guided by their individual rationalities—a fully incentive-compatible system—becomes clear if we move on from schoolteachers and bureaucrats in state-run institutions to magistrates and judges. In such a system a judge gives the just verdict *only because*, among the set of all available verdicts, the one that is in the judge's own self-interest *happens* to be the just one. Surely, no successful society relies on such totally selfish judges. There can probably be no incentive-compatible system that guarantees this.

Finally, consider taxes. The free-rider problem here is huge. Whether or not you pay up your taxes, the benefits you get from the government are largely the same. Through monitoring and fines one can try to bring individual incentives into alignment with tax compliance, but it is difficult to do so fully. Paying taxes is often not an incentive-compatible activity. In keeping with textbook theory, tax violation is common in India; in violation of textbook theory, tax violation is rare in Norway. This shows the value of standard theory and also the need for caution in using it indiscriminately.

Successful societies rely on individual honesty and integrity, appropriate codes of behavior, the ability to communicate, and the possession of economy-friendly social norms much more than economists have been willing to concede.[32] In the crafting of good policy, we are right to search for better systems of incentives, but wrong to ignore that we also need a certain fabric of social norms, culture, and personal integrity. We need to divert some of our research energies from the study of how to steer fully selfish individuals to socially optimal behavior to understanding ways in which our norms are formed and how we can learn the codes of socially desirable behavior.

On Methodological Individualism

Underlying much of orthodox economics, based on rational choice, as described in chapter 2, is a common philosophical method: 'methodological individualism.' This method has much to commend itself as an underlying approach. Yet an unbending adherence to it becomes a hindrance, as we saw in the previous section. The right approach is to use it in a measured manner and be prepared to step out of its confines where needed. To understand how we should do so, we need to step back and reassess what methodological individualism is all about.

Methodological individualism is a doctrine in the social sciences according to which a proper explanation of every social regularity or phenomenon is founded in individual motivations and behavior, even though some of these may be "as if" assumptions (Friedman 1953). In other words, according to this methodology, individual human beings are the foundation from which we must build *up* in order to understand the functioning of society, economy, and polity. We may not in all our research succeed in doing so, but to committed methodological individualists such research must be viewed as interim, waiting to be completed, and ideally be accompanied by a slight feeling of inadequacy on the part of the researcher.[33]

Social scientists, outside of economics, typically think of economists as being the most ardent methodological individualists; and on the rare occasions when economists have joined this debate, they have tended to agree with them. The difference is that noneconomists mean this as criticism, whereas economists take it as praise.

At first sight this characterization of economics seems right. As discussed earlier, textbooks of economics almost invariably begin by specifying individual utility functions or preferences, and asserting that human beings are rational in the sense of behaving to maximize their utilities. They then build up from this to explain market phenomena, claims about social welfare, and discussions of national economic growth. There are macroeconomic models where economists are unable to build all the way up from individual behavior and instead use aggregate behavior descriptions as the starting point. But these models are almost always accompanied by effort to 'complete' them with proper microfoundations, and the profession regards these models as somewhat awaiting the definitive work.

That economics may not actually be quite as methodologically individualistic as generally presumed by both the discipline's admirers and its demurrers is a matter to which I shall return later. What is interesting to note here is that the debate on methodological individualism has been surprisingly cantankerous—spawning enemies and intrigues. Some social scientists swore by it. Others castigated it as an instrument of exploitation and the maintenance of the status quo. Concepts and categorizations have multiplied over the years, adding to the brew of confusion.

One cause of the controversy is the confounding of positive and normative social science. To some commentators, methodological individualism implies that it is fine to leave it all to individuals and by implication it amounts to an argument against government intervention. Friedrich von Hayek and James Buchanan, for instance, have taken this line, as have some sociologists, who felt that the conservatism of traditional economics was founded on its adherence to this method. This happens because of a logical error, or a failure to appreciate Hume's law—namely, that a normative proposition cannot be derived from a purely positive analysis. Arrow (1994) has rightly criticized the tendency in some writers to treat methodological individualism and "normative individualism" as inextricably linked. Similarly, Marxists often link methodological individualism automatically to certain ethical implications. It is possible, as spelled out by John Roemer (1981) and Jon Elster (1982), that this is not a valid link. In what follows, I treat the two as separate and methodological individualism as having no automatic normative implication.

The term methodological individualism was used for the first time in the English language in 1909 by Joseph Schumpeter, translating his own prior German use. But this method had been *practiced* from much earlier, going at least as far back as Smith's ([1776] 1937) classic, and had been described as a deliberate methodology, although without the term being used, by Carl Menger ([1883] 1986). It was written about later, and expounded on by Max Weber, and published posthumously (Weber [1922] 1968).

From the perspective of economics, it seems reasonable to treat Menger as the first proponent of methodological individualism. He certainly did it vociferously, dismissing the German historical school of economists and their methods as outdated as well as flawed. He advanced the idea of 'spontaneous order' in society, which sprung from atomistic individual behavior, reminiscent of Smith's invisible hand and the efficiency of markets that was an outcome of rational, self-interested behavior on the part of individuals.

A distinction is frequently drawn in philosophy between methodological individualism and 'atomism.' The latter is treated as a more extreme version of individualism, in which it is possible to characterize each individual fully without reference to society and then explain social behavior by simply imagining such individuals being brought together under one society. Since the proponents of these ideas did not define terms with that much care, I shall stay away from drawing fine distinctions and treat these neighboring terms as all representing the broad *idea* of methodological individualism. Moreover, concepts like these are probably innately indefinable. They are understood through a combination of approximate definitions and repeated use.

It is useful in expositions like this to consider the polar opposite of the method under consideration. This is captured by the concept of 'methodological holism,' developed (without endorsement) by the philosopher John Watkins. Methodological holism refers to the belief that there are "macroscopic laws that are *sui generis* and apply to the system as an organic whole" (Watkins 1952, 187), and the behavior of its components are then deduced from it. In economics, this would imply beginning our analysis by stating the laws of an aggregate economy, and maybe the behavior of prices and industries, and from there deducing how individuals behave and what motivates them. Stated in these terms, it immediately becomes clear that economics is situated near the methodological individualist end of the spectrum.

After a flurry of these early writings, interest in this subject flagged. Social scientists, especially economists, continued to do research without trying to explicitly articulate the method that they were using. Many researchers, particularly economists, began to feel that the problem of methodological individualism was either trivial or resolved in their favor. A couple of engaging essays from the early 1990s onward (notably Bhargava 1993; Arrow 1994; Davis 2003) broke the gathering insouciance of the economists. Rajeev Bhargava summarized various points of view on the subject and then challenged the orthodoxy, especially within economics. He argued that in describing society or an economy, we are compelled to use concepts, which are *irreducibly social*. The reason why the assertion that certain beliefs and concepts are inextricably social is unlikely to stir a hornet's nest is that though many economists claim to be rigid adherents of methodological individualism, they do use—and always have—social concepts and categories. Arrow convincingly takes this stance. He points out how a variable such as price in a competitive model is an irreducibly social concept. Each individual takes the price as a given, but the price that comes to prevail is an outcome of the choices made by *all* the individuals. So economists constructing equilibrium models who claim to be hardened methodological individualists are actually not, in the sense that they use some concepts that are irreducibly social. Knowingly or not, they follow a method that uses social categories.

There are more contentious claims that one can make about the role of social concepts in economics. One of these relates to the *permissibility* of a certain class of propositions in social science, such as this one: "The landlord will undertake action A, *because* it is in the landlord's *class* interest to do so." (Action A, for example, could be "refuse to hire a servant who has fled another landlord's employment and offers to work for this landlord for a low wage.") Let me call this proposition P.

The bone of contention between neoclassical and traditional Marxist economists is frequently pegged on the permissibility of such propositions. There are many neoclassical economists and some political scientists (especially those belonging to the positive political economy school) who believe that P is not permissible. There is also a small group of writers who maintain that Marxism is compatible with methodological individualism, and that class and other aggregate behavior should ideally be built from individual motivations and preferences (Roemer 1981; Elster 1982).

In any case, whether or not proposition P is wrong, mainstream economics certainly considers it to be so. If economists were to use an axiom like proposition P, they would usually want to first satisfy themselves why it might be in the landlord's *self*-interest to behave in a way that is in their *class* interest. This does not negate the use of beliefs as well as other concepts and variables that are irreducibly social. It is not clear if a researcher who does both (that is, resists explaining individual behavior solely in terms of its ability to serve group or class interests, but uses concepts and beliefs that are inherently social) is a methodological individualist or not. This is a definitional matter and of no great consequence. The important and contestable question is whether assumptions like proposition P should or should not be used.

I believe that if economics is to deal with reality better, it has to allow for the use of such assumptions. I will return to this contentious claim at the end of this section. Here, I want to mention two important but less fundamental ways in which modern economics has moved further away from methodological individualism than the fact of using irreducibly social concepts, such as prices, even without using propositions like P. First, most models of economics make use of the idea of 'rules of the game.' In Cournot duopoly, firms choose quantities and then wait for prices to form. In Bertrand oligopoly, firms set prices and then wait to sell what the market demands from them. In most real-life situations, these rules evolve over time, through intrinsically social processes. We may not fully understand what these social processes are, but few individuals will deny their existence. Arrow has emphasized this, along with the significance of '*social* knowledge.'

Second, as already mentioned, there is an increasing recognition in economics that individual preferences are endogenous. These preferences evolve over time and may be responsive to what happens in society at large. As Veblen (1899) recognized—around the same time that neoclassical economics was taking shape—human preferences for certain objects often depend on who else is consuming those objects. If a film star wears a brand-name shirt, you may be willing to pay more for that brand-name shirt. If the elite like a particular wine, then there are people who will *get* themselves to like that wine, and moreover, there are people who will then treat these people as belonging to the elite because of their taste in wines. In other words, people frequently use goods to associate themselves with other people who use those goods (Frank 1985; Basu 1989). These are obvious matters (though they were sidelined during Veblen's time), and any economist whose ability to think is not damaged by excessive textbook education will recognize that these kinds of preference endogeneity are true. What is remarkable about Schumpeter is that he understood (admittedly in a somewhat inchoate way) that this recognition might cut into the methodological individualism of economics. Schumpeter (1909, 219) observed that given the human tendency to conform to society, "there will be a tendency to give [each individual's] utility curves shapes similar to those of other members of the community."

To see how this can ruffle methodological individualism, let me return to a similar example concerning endogenous preference noted above and suppose that each person likes to wear jeans if more than 60 percent of society wears jeans. Or more precisely, if over 60 percent of society wears jeans, each person is willing to pay for jeans more than the marginal cost of producing jeans; otherwise they are willing to pay less. This society will have two possible equilibria: one in which no one wears jeans, and another (however revolting it may be to visualize this) in which everyone wears jeans. There is circularity in models of this kind between society's behavior and each individual's preference. Once we recognize this, there is no reason to start our analysis by characterizing the individual. We may still do so through force of habit. But we could equally begin by considering a social behavior postulate, such as, for instance, that 50 percent of people wear jeans. Then we could work out how much each individual prefers to wear jeans (and so how much they are willing to pay for their jeans) and check if the initial social postulate is sustainable. If it is, then we have found an equilibrium. If not (as in the above example), then the behavior is not one that will prevail in equilibrium. This method is neither one of methodological individualism nor methodological holism. It is therefore evident that as economics becomes more sophisticated, it is moving away from pure individualism toward this kind of a hybrid methodology.

I now believe that we need to go further and recognize that descriptions like proposition P are a part of reality. Individuals do often act in the interest of what they consider to be their group. Moreover, not only do we not need to explain such acts from individualistic foundations, it may actually be erroneous to do so. To act in one's group interest is usually innate.[34] I will refer to this as the 'public good urge.' Once people are persuaded that a particular behavior, if undertaken by all individuals in the group, is good for the group, they have a tendency to undertake that behavior. A person would tend do so even though doing so alone may have little positive impact on society and may inflict a cost on the person. Hence, the public good urge is not rooted in self interest; it has to be treated as a primitive. Stated in this manner there are some ambiguities. What does one's group refer to? After all, each human being belongs to many different groups. Surely this urge is not unequivocal but rather gets nurtured by the sight of others giving in to this urge and gets dampened if others are freeloading. How we resolve these questions will influence our understanding of how societies function. But the recognition of the general idea of the public good urge is important for designing good policies, and understanding the success and failure of nations and communities.

A major failing of neoclassical economics has been its inability to recognize that an individual is generally prepared to take some personal losses to serve the interest of the group or community to which the individual belongs. This recognition drives a wedge between a person's utility function (that which measures the person's welfare) and the maximand (that which the person seeks to maximize). It opens up the possibility of identity-based behavior, which is germane to so much of reality, yet has eluded economics because of the economist's commitment to methodological individualism. Chapter 6 will develop on this theme and illustrate the scope for new analysis once we broaden our methodology.

On Knowledge

Picking up on a theme touched on at the end of chapter 1, I want to warn the reader of a general flaw in the way we have tried to acquire and use knowledge in mainstream economics. Far too much of the human quest for knowledge is marred by the belief that we have found that knowledge. Our pursuit of scientific knowledge should be marked by hesitation and a preparedness to retreat, to concede ground to skepticism. In addition, we need to recognize that intuition and nonscientifically acquired information play a crucial role in our understanding of the world. Even as we try to assemble the 'hard facts' of the world, to abandon altogether the 'soft' sources of our understanding of society and the economy—our intuitive knowledge, as I called it earlier—we court failure. Here I spell out my reasons for taking such a line, and then leave the skepticisms and doubts unsaid but present in the rest of the book.

I am not concerned here with economic *theory*, since the knowledge that this gives us is not knowledge about the world but rather logical equivalences. For instance, it tells us things such as if starting with a huge right-angled triangle marked on an open field, Eve appropriates for herself two squares, each of which treats one of the two shorter sides of the triangle as one side, and Adam does the same with the long side of the triangle, then the area of the land owned by Adam will be the same as that owned by Eve. This is of course one kind of knowledge, but what I am interested in here is critiquing knowledge that goes beyond logical equivalences. Let me therefore begin by considering what may be the best-founded empirical claims available in economics. These usually come from controlled experiments or regression analysis with carefully selected 'instruments.'[35]

One reason for the popularity of this method is the precision of its findings, yet also because once a result is discovered by this method, we fully understand what it is that has been discovered. Let me consider here one particularly elegant paper written in this mode (Chattopadhyay and Duflo 2004). One of the results reported in this paper is that in West Bengal, India, having a woman serve as the head of a panchayat (a village council) has made a difference in terms of what the *panchayat* does; it leads, for instance, to the better provisioning of water in the village.

In a lot of empirical research, there is the risk that causality may be the reverse of what is being claimed. For example, suppose that in areas with poor water supply, women (whose traditional job is to fend for the household's water) are so preoccupied with the task of fetching water that they cannot participate in local panchayat politics. This could easily create the impression that if women participate in panchayat politics then *this leads to* the better provisioning of water. In this case the deduction would be wrong; the causality runs the other way around. What is remarkable about the new empirical development economics is that by using the fact of an exogenous randomization, it gets around this problem. There are many misconceptions about this method of scientifically acquired knowledge that need to be countered, however.

First, it must be recognized that this method does not help us predict the future. Suppose a researcher, studying the effect of aspirin, administers a low dose of the medicine (150 milligrams, say) to a random sample of people found walking in the streets of Delhi and discovers that if a person with a headache takes aspirin, they typically (meaning, say, in 90 percent of the cases) benefit from it. Let me call this the "research result" (RR). Now suppose you are asked what would have been the effect of giving aspirin to a random selection of people in Delhi who were lying down with a headache. Based on the RR, could you say that they would have benefited from it? The answer should be no, since this sample does not belong to the population on which the original study was done.

Let me now consider how we might be able to use the RR for forecasting. If the next year we give aspirin to the people of Delhi who are walking around, could we expect that those with a headache would benefit from this? Strictly speaking, the answer is no. The people of next year's Delhi are not the population from which the RR was derived. To use the RR and predict the future is like doing a study of the effects of administering aspirin to people who are walking and then presuming that it will apply to those who are lying down. If we are fussy about proper randomization for our study and take the view that we should not accept the wisdom of samples drawn in a biased manner or from the wrong population, we should also take the view that we cannot say anything about the future. This, in turn, means that we cannot make policy prescriptions since they are always recommendations for the future.

One could try to counter this by arguing that between yesterday and tomorrow, there is no fundamental difference, and so there is no reason to expect a relation that was true yesterday to be untrue tomorrow. But the difference between yesterday and tomorrow is not just a matter of time. Between yesterday and tomorrow there can be war and pestilence; between 8/11 and 10/11 was 9/11.

One may respond to this by saying that wars and pestilence do not make any difference to the human physical constitution, and so we would expect the aspirin result to carry over from yesteryear to the future. This is reasonable, but in making this argument we are conceding a role to intuition. We are combining our statistical finding with our prior 'knowledge' that for matters of health, knowledge acquired from one population can be carried over to another. We may hesitate to do this about the role of women in panchayats, but feel confident about aspirin. This brings us to precisely the point I would endorse. These statistical findings are not useless for prediction but instead have to be combined with unscientific intuition for them to be considered useful. We cannot reject the unscientific *and* claim that our method has predictive power.

Our intuition or unscientific judgment comes in gradations. Before aspirin is tried on anyone, we may have no faith in aspirin; but once we know it has worked on people last year, we then have more faith in it next year. And the faith grows inductively. For that matter, the fact that it has worked on people who were walking may make us inclined to believe somewhat that it will work on people lying down, for we may have a prior intuition that a person's posture has no connection to a drug's efficacy. But note that there is nothing objective about these beliefs. What we so often take to be features of the world are actually propensities of the mind.

Let me move on from prediction to yet another problem of knowledge. Suppose you know of the RR (and assume this holds over time). You are walking down a street in Delhi with a headache, wondering if you will benefit from taking aspirin. The answer depends on whether you can be thought of as a random draw of a person from the walking population of Delhi. The answer has to be no. There are many things that you know about yourself with no equivalent knowledge about others. Hence, you cannot deduce any policy lesson for yourself from the research result. This is rather worrying. It means that whenever I want to use a research finding (based on properly controlled experiments) for *my* own treatment, strictly speaking there is little reason for me to have faith in the result, since I am not a random draw from the population. This relates to the discussion above. When it comes to decisions about oneself or one's acquaintances, there may be good reason not to rely on otherwise-scientific evidence and rely instead on one's intuitive knowledge.

Despite my own inclination toward skepticism, I am aware that one must not have an unbending adherence to it (that would be a contradiction anyway for a skeptic). One possible mistake that both the skeptic and the practitioner of the new empirical method in development economics have to guard against is that of denying that there may be multiple modes of acquiring knowledge.

To understand this, consider the number of things that we learn from poorly controlled experiments or, for that matter, no experiments. A growing child learns that a frown implies displeasure and a smile approval, that a slap hurts and a massage soothes (especially a neck massage), that when persons cry, they are sad, and when they laugh, they are happy. Suppose a girl's father stops the girl each time she makes an inference, by asking whether she is sure that she is making the deduction from a proper random sample and not merely from her experience with those she happens to bump into in her everyday life. Suppose the father asks the child to discard any knowledge not picked up from properly randomized experiments. Surely this child will turn out to be an ill-informed adult. The fact of the matter is that the knowledge that we human beings carry in our heads is disproportionately from wrongly conducted experiments and biased samples. The knowledge that we have from scientifically conducted studies—things such as that eighty milligrams of aspirin a day can cut the risk of a heart attack by half and oatmeal reduces cholesterol—are a tiny fraction of what we know.[36]

This is indeed a puzzle: How *do* we know so much given the atrociously biased methods we use through life to collect information? There are three responses. One is to try to show how, even if each person uses a biased sample, by the act of pooling our individual information, as we human beings do through conversation and other forms of communication, the biases tend to cancel out. This would be an interesting research problem in probability and information theory.

If this theoretical exercise turns out to be futile (and until such a result is proved, it seems reasonable to proceed as if it were not true), then there are two possible positions that we can take. One is to claim that we human beings actually know very little. Much of our knowledge is chimera—a mere illusion of knowledge. Many religious traditions and also some irreligious philosophers take such a view. There is a long Greek tradition of this. The most famous is the fourth century BC philosopher Pyrrho. Pyrrho did not write down any of his philosophy because he was skeptical about its value (of course, he could have been equally skeptical about the value of not writing and have written a lot, like Bertrand Russell, also a skeptic, did). It is believed that he went with Alexander's army to India and returned humbled, because in India he had met sadhus, who not only did not write but did not even speak.

Legend has it that Pyrrho heard one of his teachers asking for help after falling into a ditch, but he walked away calmly because he could not be sure that the teacher would be better off outside the ditch than in it. The teacher in this case happened to be Anaxarchus, a philosopher who held many similar views to those of Pyrrho. After Anaxarchus was heaved out of the ditch safely by others, his greatest praise was for Pyrrho, whom he had seen walk past the ditch with complete sangfroid (Laertius 1925).

To counter these extreme versions, the second century BC Greek philosopher Carneades stressed that behaviorally, a skeptic need not be any different from a nonskeptic.[37] It may be recalled, however, that Carneades caused some comical problems by arguing one day in favor of justice and another day against it, since he felt committed to neither perspective. In fact, the Greek physician and philosopher Sextus Empiricus (second century AD) held that the main consequence of skepticism was the tranquillity of mind achieved by resigning oneself to the futility of the quest for knowledge.

This brings me to the third response based on an evolutionary view of knowledge. It begins with the admission that we do not know how we know things, but if it is the case that a person's knowledge or the facility for acquiring knowledge is inheritable, then the people who have wrong beliefs or knowledge (those, for instance, who think that the frown on the face of the person approaching them menacingly, knife in hand, indicates friendliness) would perish in the long run. Hence, the people we see around us know that an apple released in the air will fall downward and know that the knife being plunged into a person will kill them. The fact of these people being around means that they and their ancestors have survived the weeding process of evolution. The ones who knew the wrong things or did not have the facility for learning correctly from nature are not around anymore. By this theory, there is no right way to acquire knowledge. Nature is too idiosyncratic for that. Some minds are synchronized with this idiosyncratic nature, and some minds are not. The people we see around us, by virtue of the fact that they exist, have minds that are in reasonable synchrony with nature.

My belief about the puzzle of knowledge lies somewhere between the skeptical and evolutionary claims. I have faith in our intuition. Two correctly done empirical findings may have the property that one resonates with our intuition—we simply feel that if it was true in the past, it has a reasonable chance of being true in the future—and the other does not. My inclination would be to go along with the intuition (while admitting that intuitions can go haywire). The same is true with theoretically derived results. Some *feel* right; some do not. I would be tempted to give in to the feeling. Hence, the issue is not between theory and empirics.[38] We need to do both, and then use our intuition to select the propositions we want to live by and base our policy recommendations on those.

Economists have a propensity to find a lack of evidence of causality in other people's research. We complain about how other people's empirical papers demonstrate correlation but not causality. This is fine, as long as we realize that there is no real way to demonstrate causality, whether it be in other people's papers or one's own. Indeed, there may be reason to doubt that there *is* anything objective in nature called causality.

Causality lies in the eyes of the beholder. We human beings have it hardwired in us to *think* in terms of causality. This can be a useful feature of our mind. It allows us to be more sure-footed than we would be if we could not live *as if* causality existed.[39] And as we saw earlier, there is reason to believe that what our mind takes to be causal is dependable because it has come to be reasonably well synchronized with the way nature actually works, thanks to thousands of years of human evolution.

To sum up, scientific knowledge has to be combined with intuition and a shot of skepticism for it to be useful. One quality of religious fanatics that I appreciate is their suspicion of scientific knowledge. Their blunder is that they shed this skepticism totally when it comes to the other form of knowledge that they are certain about and that rightly earns them opprobrium. Conversely, for people who put faith in science it is worth remembering that the sanguineness that we feel about *our* beliefs could easily slide into the sanguineness of the religious fundamentalist. It is important to always let in that chink of doubt and be prepared to admit that the science of today that we take to be the font of knowledge may be no different from Aristotle's 'science' or, worse, religion.[40]

CHAPTER 4

The Economy according to Law

Kafka's Invisible Hand

"Someone must have slandered Josef K., for one morning, without having done anything truly wrong, he was arrested" (Kafka 1998, 3). Thus begins one of the great novels of the twentieth century: Franz Kafka's *The Trial*.

There was something oddly mysterious about the men who came to arrest K.

"What sort of men were they? What were they talking about? What office did they represent? After all, K. lived in a state governed by law, there was universal peace, all statutes were in force; who dared assault him in his own lodgings?" (6).

That morning, arrested by taciturn, emotionless characters, wearing fitted black jackets, Josef K. was charged, though of what he would never find out. From then on, his life would be a journey through a labyrinthine court of faceless minions doing their chores and carrying out orders, though from whom would never be clear. Maybe there *was* no one in charge, and he was a victim of forces beyond any individual's control? The forces would be oppressive and real enough for him, but their origins would remain a mystery. Maybe they *had* no origin?

This chilling, surreal tension that arises out of nowhere and segues into the mundane, quotidian lives of ordinary citizens persists until the last scene of *The Trial*, in which Josef K. is finally executed in an abandoned and desolate stone quarry.

"[K.'s] gaze fell upon the top story of the building adjoining the quarry. Like a light flickering on, the casements of a window flew open, a human figure, faint and insubstantial at that distance and height, leaned far out abruptly, and stretched both arms out even further. Who was it? A friend? A good person? Someone who cared? Someone who wanted to help? Was it just one person? Was it everyone?" (230–31).

Tragedies and deaths tend to "obliterate the dailiness of life," to use Joan Dideon's eloquent phrase (2005, 27). What is masterly about Kafka is how in violating this tradition, he cloaks his tragedy in dailiness. The distant window, silhouetting a human form that could be one person or every person, reinforces our sense of everdayness and thereby heightens the atmosphere of repressed anxiety.

As if to drive home the point of his allegory, Kafka died without completing *The Trial*. The only reason we can read it today is because his friend Max Brod chose to disregard Kafka's "last request" made in a letter to "Dearest Max" to make sure that all his unpublished writings be "burned unread."[1]

Brod justified this act of 'letting down' a friend on the ground that Kafka, in entrusting Brod as the sole person responsible for destroying the manuscripts, was making sure that the manuscripts would not be destroyed since having known Brod well, he must have known that Brod would never destroy them.

Let me leave this intriguing piece of posthumous game theory aside. The reason I bring Kafka into a discourse on economics is because he gives us the other side of the invisible hand. He brings to life an invisible hand that, unlike the one described by Smith and so ubiquitous in modern economics texts, is malevolent. His style is of course different from that of Smith. He is not analytic and deductive in the way that Smith is. Yet it is a sign of Kafka's genius that he creates a theory of society and polity as powerful as that of Smith. He concurs with Smith about the forces that can be unleashed through atomistic individual actions, with no centralized authority, but broadens our canvas of understanding by making us aware that while these can be forces of efficiency, organization, and benevolence, they can equally be those of oppression and malignancy.

Kafka's invisible hand is not as far removed from our contemporary world as one may imagine. There are, first of all, recent writers, like José Saramago, who have created similar imageries of faceless bureaucracies, of which all individuals, including the ones who seem to run them, are victims.[2] Moreover, one of Kafka's own compatriots, Václav Havel, has described faceless totalitarian societies, where the malign power of the *system* transcends *every individual* in those societies. I have elsewhere argued that Havel's portrait comes close to contemporary game-theoretic models of power (Basu 1986, 2000), and provides a bridge between Kafka's literary imagination and modern social science.

In this chapter and again later, I will try to show that if one takes this larger view of the invisible hand, which can be good or bad, one gets an understanding of society, polity, and economics that is much deeper than the one propagated by traditional social science. This, in turn, opens up a view of policymaking and the state that is radically different from the traditional perspective, and a more convincing depiction of reality.

Law's Economy: The Standard View

The main instrument used by governments to influence economic policy is the law or, more generally, legally backed policy interventions. Therefore, a correct understanding of the role of law in an economy is crucial for crafting effective policies and steering an economy to success. Likewise, to understand why some economies fail and some succeed, it is important to understand the manner in which the law and government policy interventions interact with the economy.[3]

Consider first the question at the heart of the discipline of law and economics: How exactly does a law influence economic outcomes? The standard answer to this is quite straightforward: A new law alters the returns that individuals expect for certain actions, and thus influences the choices that individuals make, thereby altering the outcome that finally comes to prevail. As an illustration, consider a country in which there is no legally specified speed limit. You are contemplating driving at eighty-five mph (as opposed to sixty-five mph, and suppose for simplicity's sake that those are the only two speeds at which your cruise control can be set) and trying to decide whether it is worthwhile to go so fast. You will presumably calculate the probability of skidding at that speed and the cost of injury from a skid; the expected cost of collision with another car; and the wear and tear on your car engine caused by the high speed. Balancing these costs, you will calculate the time saved on travel and the extra value of those additional minutes; the joy you get from your belief that onlookers think of you as some kind of a James Bond character (even though in truth, most onlookers will think of you as someone with limited mental faculties); and so on. And if the total benefit outweighs the total cost, you will set your cruise control so as to travel at eighty-five mph.

Now suppose a new law is announced that sets the speed limit at sixty-five mph; so the new law is that anybody caught driving at speeds above that will be fined a hundred dollars. Evidently, the drivers' cost-benefit calculations will change. They will now have to add the additional expected cost of the fine (that is, the probability of getting caught multiplied by the fine) into the costs of driving at eighty-five mph. Some drivers—to wit, those for whom the benefit of driving at eighty-five mph was only slightly greater than the cost before the new law came into effect—would now decide against driving at eighty-five.

TABLE 1
Prisoner's Dilemma Game

		Player 2	
		A	**B**
	A	8, 8	0, 9
Player 1	**B**	9, 0	1, 1

This is the standard paradigm behind the substantial literature on law and economics. And indeed this paradigm can be used to do many things, like trying to calculate how altering the size of the fine or the probability of getting caught would affect the speed at which cars travel. Not surprisingly, this paradigm has been used extensively to design government interventions, with the classic work in economics being that of Gary Becker (1968). Legal scholars refer to this as the "imperative theory of law" (Raz 1980).[4] My aim here is to argue that the paradigm is flawed in an important way. I spelled out this critique in an earlier work (Basu 2000) and will briefly draw on that here. But my aim is to then pursue the argument further afield and derive its policy implications. Later in this chapter, I will contend that the more sophisticated view of law's role in the economy that I outline here is likely to enable us to construct more effective policy interventions. This altered view also helps explain why so much of our laws go unheeded. Before going into that, though, I want to describe in greater detail and the context of game theory the standard perspective that was sketched above, since that will provide the building blocks of what I want to discuss below.

Consider the Prisoner's Dilemma game. Let me outline this in the abstract, storyless form in which it is told in contemporary game theory papers.[5] This is a game between two players, 1 and 2. Each of them, independently, has to choose between two actions, A and B. After they have made their choices, they are rewarded as follows. If both choose A, then each of them gets eight dollars. If both choose B, then each receives one dollar. If one chooses A and the other chooses B, then the one choosing A receives no money and the one choosing B gets nine dollars. This game can be summarized in a 'payoff matrix' as described above in table 1.

Player 1 chooses between the rows and player 2 chooses between the columns; in each box, the first number is the payoff earned by player 1 and the second number is the payoff earned by player 2. This game has been analyzed repeatedly since its discovery in the early 1950s. It is easy to see what will happen in this game if both players are fully (selfishly) rational. Note that if

TABLE 2
Prisoner's Dilemma Game, with Fine

		Player 2	
		A	B
Player 1	A	8, 8	0, 9-pF
	B	9-pF, 0	1-pF, 1-pF

player 2 chooses A, player 1 is better off choosing B, and if player 2 chooses B, then again player 1 is better off choosing B. Hence, no matter what player 2 does, player 1 is better off playing B. So player 1 will choose B. Since this is a symmetrical game, the same logic applies to player 2, and so they both will choose B. This game's outcome will be (B, B) and each player earns one dollar each. In brief, the Prisoner's Dilemma ends in a tragedy—one similar to the tragedy of the commons, where each shepherd overgrazes the common grounds available to all shepherds, and in the final outcome they are all worse off since the resource (of land and grass) is depleted more rapidly than is good for any shepherd.

The Prisoner's Dilemma has come to acquire some notoriety since it demonstrates with audacious simplicity how individual rationality need not lead to the common good. This became the classic counterdemonstration to Smith's invisible hand, discussed in chapter 2. But that is not my interest here. I want to show how the standard view of law would work in this context. Suppose the state enacts a law saying that anybody found using action B will be fined F dollars. Let us assume that the probability of being discovered using action B is p. Then every time a player uses action B, the player expects a cost of pF dollars. Thus, the law alters people's payoffs. As Douglas Baird, Robert Gertner and Randal Picker (1995, 15) observe, describing the standard view of law and economics, "We can capture the change in legal rules by changing the payoffs." The new game—that is, with the altered payoffs—is depicted in table 2.

If the government sets F = 4 and puts in a level of police vigilance that ensures that p = ½, then it is easy to verify that for each individual the rational thing to do is to choose A. Hence, the law alters the outcome that occurs in this game to (A, A). Both individuals are better off. In the final outcome no one actually pays the fine; but it is the presence of the fine (unused though it may be) that causes the outcome to be different. As in the speeding example, the law alters the payoffs or returns that are associated with different actions, and through that, alters the way that individuals behave and thus the outcome that society achieves.

The Law as Focal Point

To see what is wrong with the standard view just described, consider first the speeding example. In that case, the motorist decided to drive slower after the law was enacted because of the concern that speeding might have led to the motorist being caught by a police officer. What we did not ask ourselves was: Why will the police officer suddenly catch a motorist driving at eighty-five mph when earlier the officer did nothing about such motorists? To respond by simply saying that "because that is the law now" is to treat police officers like robots who automatically do what the law requires them to do. In reality, a police officer is also a player, like the motorist, and there is no reason to deny such agents the scope of rational cogitation that the motorist is capable of. So we need to explain why the police officer will catch a speeding motorist when a new law is instituted against speeding, whereas the officer will not do so when there is no such law. In many developing countries, and also some developed ones, the police often do not alter their behavior because of the law. There are instances of police officers not stopping motorists when they are openly in violation of the law, and also of police officers stopping motorists even when they are not violating any law and charging them 'fines,' which they then rapidly insert into their pockets.

To understand such violations of the law as well as adherence to it, we need to ask why the police implement the law when they do. The answer must, in turn, lie in the police officer's rationality calculation. We could argue that to not do their 'job' too often is for officers to risk being caught and being fined or sacked by the magistrate, and that is the reason why they stop a motorist driving at eighty-five mph when there is speed limit law and do not stop a driver doing the same when there is no speed limit law.

This would have been a good explanation, except for the fact that this now opens up another question—that concerning the magistrate's behavior. Why would the magistrate fine or fire a police officer who does not stop motorists driving at eighty-five mph when there is a law prohibiting speeding above sixty-five mph, and not fine or fire a police officer who does not stop motorists driving at eighty-five mph when there is no speed limit law? Why should the mere existence of a law change the magistrate's behavior? One can try to explain this by referring to what someone else will do to the magistrate if the magistrate does not behave appropriately, and so on. A good explanation must cover everybody's behavior. The standard view of law, described above, looks fine as long as we are willing to assume the free availability of robots that enforce the law mechanically, simply because it is the law. But there is no basis for making such an assumption, and therein lies the weakness of the standard approach.

To better understand this critique, let us return to the Prisoner's Dilemma example. The standard view of law seems fine as long as we do not ask who catches a player playing B and imposes the fine. If there was a police officer available for doing so, the officer should have been represented in the original game. The original game was then never a two-player game, as described above, but a three-player one—the two players, as before, plus the police officer.

If we now go ahead and begin with an n-player game, with all the characters involved—ordinary citizens, the police, the magistrates, and so on—as players, then we will soon see that the law cannot be viewed as an instrument that changes the players' payoffs or the game, because there is no one left to alter the payoffs (that is, to enforce fines or dole out incentives). To look at it another way, the law cannot change the payoffs since for every player, all actions that were available before the law are available after it.[6] If everybody took a certain set of actions, the payoff to everybody would be the same. The fact that some law exists or does not exist cannot in itself alter anybody's payoff. Even before the law was passed, the police officer could have asked you to pay a fine for driving at eighty-five mph and the magistrate could have looked the other way in the face of the police officer's misdemeanor.

As I have argued in an earlier book (Basu 1993, 217), the law is, after all, nothing but some ink on paper. It is not surprising that it does not change the game people play. People, when everybody is counted, would be found to be playing the same game they would have played in the absence of the law.[7] Surely the mere noting of some words on paper cannot change the strategies available to a person or the payoff functions of citizens. The method of analysis in the standard view of law and economics is evidently flawed.

Let me illustrate this with the Prisoner's Dilemma example. If to start with we want to write down the full game with all the players involved, we may have to characterize not just what is played by the two players described above but also the game played by the police officer. What we would then need, minimally, is to think of the police officer as having two available actions: L and V, where L stands for lax and V for vindictive. If the police officer chooses L, the game played by the two citizens is portrayed in table 1; if the officer chooses V, the game they play is depicted in table 2. Of course, we would have to also write down the payoff that the police officer would receive with each possible outcome. If we want to go further and bring a magistrate into this, then we have to also specify what the magistrate can do and how that could affect the two citizens, the police officer, and the magistrate. This fully described game then tells you what everybody can do, and the actions available to each person and the payoffs received by everybody under every contingency. This game, it seems natural to assume, cannot be altered by announcing a new law, because there is no one beyond the game to change the payoffs.

Therefore, the traditional view of the law is valid as long as we are willing to assume that there are robotic agents in the wings waiting to come out and enforce whatever law happens to be in place. Clearly, the traditional view is not a compelling one, since laws are not enforced by robots but rather by individuals, who have their own aims and ambitions.

At first sight this critique seems to be paralyzing. If the law cannot alter the game or, to put it another way, the strategies available to the players and the payoffs that players receive under different configurations of actions chosen by all the players, then it appears that the law can do nothing—it cannot alter the behavior of individuals and the outcome. The law seems to be nothing but chimera. Surely that cannot be right. After all, we do see cars stopping at stop signs, traffic police fining speeding cars, motorists not speeding for fear of being fined, and citizens paying taxes.

Clearly, even if the law cannot alter the game, as argued above, it can alter the outcome of the game. The only way to reconcile these two features of the law is to recognize that the law has the power to change the beliefs of individuals concerning what others may do. This is where we are led to inexorably by reason and this is going to serve as the foundation of the view of law that I wish to espouse. After the speed limit law is passed, I *expect* or *believe* that if I drive at eighty-five mph, the police will stop me and ask me to pay the fine. After the law is passed, the police officers *believe* that if they do not stop a motorist driving at eighty-five mph, then they may be pulled up by their senior and be charged for dereliction of duty. One can continue in this manner. If these beliefs are consistent and, when taken together, self-fulfilling, then the law is obeyed. The law thus affects behavior even though it leaves the game unchanged.

What is interesting is that while the law appears to be concrete and binding on each individual, there is nothing to it but a set of beliefs. This is similar to Hume's notion ([1739] 1969, [1758] 1987) about the authority of the state.[8] Hume maintained that government works—to the extent that it does—because of nothing else but the opinions and beliefs of the citizens. If it appears that this grants too minor and vacuous a role to the law and the state, this is only because we are so habituated to underestimating the power of beliefs.

To go a step further and explain more precisely how the law works, it is necessary to introduce Thomas Schelling's concept (1960) of a 'focal point.' So here is a brief digression into game theory. Suppose two friends have decided to meet after coming out of the customs area in London's Heathrow airport at noon, but they forgot to decide where they will meet. Each person now has to choose a spot to wait for the other person. Let us, for simplicity's sake, assume that the two of them meet only if they choose the same spot. Effectively, what they face now is a 'game.' Each 'player' has to choose a spot. If they happen to choose the same one, each gets a reward (in this case, the reward of meeting a friend); if they choose different spots, neither gets the reward.

This is a good place to introduce the concept of 'Nash equilibrium,' named after the famous economist-mathematician John Nash. A choice of action (or strategy) by each player constitutes a Nash equilibrium, if these choices have the property that, given every other player's choice, each player feels that it is not possible to do better by altering his or her choice. If we consider the Prisoner's Dilemma described in table 1, note that both players choosing B—we may cryptically describe this as the outcome (B, B)—is a Nash equilibrium. If the other person chooses B, you cannot do better by deviating unilaterally to A. In the Prisoner's Dilemma, it so happens that you cannot do better by deviating to A, *no matter what the other player does*. But in other games, this is not necessarily true.

The central idea in game-theoretic analysis is that what is rational for one player may depend critically on what is rational for the other, and of course there is an infinite regress involved in this. To fail to anticipate the other's rationality could expose one's own deficiency in rational analysis. This is best illustrated by this tale that I first heard in India. A hat seller, on waking from a siesta under a tree, found that all his hats had been taken to the treetop by a group of monkeys. In dismay he took off his own hat and flung it to the ground. The monkeys, known for their imitative urge, threw down the hats, and the hat seller collected all the hats and continued on his way. Half a century later, his grandson, also a hat seller, set down his wares under the same tree for a nap. On waking, he was dismayed to discover that all the hats were taken to the treetop by some monkeys. Then he remembered his grandfather's story, took off his own hat, and tossed it to the ground. But mysteriously, only one monkey came down. It took the hat firmly in hand, walked up to the hat seller, gave him a tight slap, and said, "You think only you have a grandfather?"

Here are some little exercises to make sure that you are fully comfortable with the idea of the Nash equilibrium. Take the game in table 2 and assume that $p = \frac{1}{2}$ and $F = 4$. In that case, the game will have only one Nash equilibrium. This occurs at (A, A)—that is, when player 1 chooses A and player 2 chooses A.

Not every game has a unique Nash equilibrium. Consider the game shown in table 3, which is called by various names, such as the Coordination game

TABLE 3
The Assurance Game

		Player 2	
		A	C
Player 1	A	2, 2	9, 1
	C	1, 9	10, 10

and the Assurance game (Sen 1967). In this game there are two players, 1 and 2, who have to each choose between actions A and C. It is easy to see that the game has two Nash equilibria, (A, A) and (C, C). If the other player plays C, you will have no reason to deviate from C yourself; but if you are assured that the other player will play A, you have no reason to play anything but A. Recall that a Nash equilibrium is a pair of strategies (one for each player) or, equivalently, an outcome, starting from which no player can make a gain by deviating unilaterally to some other strategy.

Return now to the Heathrow game. There each player has not just two strategies or alternatives to choose from but instead a huge number of them, since each person can choose from among lots of available spots where to wait. In this game, it is not hard to see that there are lots of Nash equilibria. In fact, as long as both players choose the same spot, no matter which spot that happens to be, that pair of choices will describe a Nash equilibrium. If both players decide to wait in the bookstore W. H. Smith, that is a Nash equilibrium. If both decide to wait at the coffee store, then that is a Nash equilibrium. Of course, not every choice pair is Nash: if player 1 chooses W. H. Smith and player 2 chooses the coffee store, then that is not a Nash equilibrium.

Now, with so many Nash equilibria we have a problem—one that also arises in a smaller measure in the Assurance game. When deciding what action you should choose, which Nash equilibrium should you target? Clearly, you want to aim for the same Nash outcome as the other player. If that is not so, the outcome will be non-Nash, and at least one of you (or in the Heathrow and Assurance games, both of you) would be better off with another strategy. But how should you coordinate your actions since each of you chooses your action independently? (And in asking that question, it becomes clear why the Assurance game is also called the Coordination game.)

This is where the somewhat mysterious but extremely powerful idea of a focal point comes in. It has been seen that in games like Heathrow, the players, especially if they happen to know each other, often manage to guess right about where the other player will go. If both are book lovers, and each knows that the other is a book lover, they may be able to guess that W. H. Smith is the best bet. The Nash equilibrium, which stands out in their psychology and enables them to coordinate their actions, is called a focal point.

Suppose I tell you and another person to choose one number (an integer) from two to a hundred, and that if both of you choose the same number, I will give you one thousand dollars each; if you choose different numbers, I will give you nothing. Then again we have a game with lots of Nash equilibria—ninety-nine of them to be precise. Which number will you choose? It turns out, and I have tried this on several batches of my students, people choose one hundred, which means that they expect others to choose one hundred. Hence, both choosing one hundred is a focal point or a focal outcome of this game. I should stress again that the focal point has no hard definition. It is a psychological concept, and there are no guarantees that all will agree on which is the focal point.

In choosing which side of the road to drive on, we also face a game with multiple Nash equilibria. If others choose to drive on the left, it makes sense for me to drive on the left, and likewise for the right. Of course, in most countries the choice of side is enforced by law. In India, the law is to drive on the left. Now consider two bullock carts approaching each other on a village road, where there is no chance of there being a police officer to enforce the law. Moreover, I am not sure (and likely the villagers will not be sure either) if the law "drive on the left" applies to bullock carts. But almost invariably you will find that each cart will choose to stay on the left. Thanks to the fact that this is the law concerning cars and it is enforced in the cities, driving on the left is a norm even in other contexts in India. This also demonstrates the close connection between norms and focal points.

My claim (originally made in Basu 2000) is that a law influences behavior, to the extent that it does, by creating new focal points.[9] So a new law does not alter the game, but it can nevertheless alter the outcome of the game by creating a new focal point and so new expectations of how others will behave. A new law affects the behavior of ordinary citizens by altering their expectations about how the police will act if they behave in certain ways; the police will act in those ways only because given *their* expectations of other people's behavior (for instance, the behavior of the magistrate, the chief of homeland security, and also the citizens) it is in their interest; and so on for all agents.

In some real-life game-theoretic contexts there are examples of focal points deliberately being created. In the Heathrow case, for instance, the problem today is not so hard because the airport has posted a sign in the middle of a large concourse that reads "Meeting Point," thereby making that spot a focal point. If you have decided to meet a friend but forgot to fix a place, then it makes sense for you to wait under that sign.

Of course, games in reality, unlike in most of the above examples, are seldom symmetrical. Different people have different choices open to them. Thus in the speed limit problem, once a new law is announced setting a speed limit at sixty-five mph, the focal point is an outcome in which if drivers break the speed limit, the police officer catches them, and if they do not break the speed limit, the police officer does not catch them; if a driver breaks the speed limit and the police officer does not catch the driver, the senior office catches the police officer for dereliction of duty; and so on. This entire set of choices becomes focal once a law is announced setting a maximum speed limit at sixty-five mph. Each player expects others to behave according to the above description and this in turn reinforces the behavior. I am not claiming that this invariably happens—after all, we do know that speed limit laws and other laws are often violated.[10] But when they are enforced and obeyed, what makes that possible is the fact that the law creates a new focal point.

For ease of reference, I will call this new approach the 'focal view of law.'

I am aware that like the concept of a focal point, the focal view of law is not an idea that can be easily described formally and given mathematical shape. It is, I believe, nevertheless a valid idea, and one that clearly breaks from the traditional view of the role of law, as discussed above. This also has implications quite different from that of the traditional model, as I will explain in the remainder of this chapter.

Implications of the Focal View of Law

Laws differ greatly in terms of their efficacy. In some cases laws are rarely violated, and the rare violators are generally punished. Some laws, on the other hand, are observed in the breach. The view of law propounded here helps us understand at a fundamental level why some laws are more effective than others.

The focal view of law, developed above, suggests that there can be two broad classes of violation of a law. First, if a law is announced that is not a Nash equilibrium of the economy-wide game being played, then it is preordained to fail. To understand this, recall that a focal point is a Nash equilibrium that is psychologically salient. As we have just seen, for a law to be effective—that is, for it to be obeyed—it is necessary for it to recommend behavior that constitutes a focal point. Since a focal point is a Nash equilibrium, it is necessary for the law to recommend behavior that is a Nash equilibrium. I believe that lots of laws fail in developing countries purely on this count. They are simply not compatible with every player's interest in compliance even when everybody expects everyone else to comply with it.

A part of this understanding was already there in the standard view of law, but only a part. To see this, return to the speeding example. In the standard view, a lot of care is taken to make sure that the fines and the probability of getting caught while speeding (which depends on the level of monitoring that the government chooses to put in place) are such that it is worthwhile for drivers to comply with speeding laws. Suppose the benefit to drivers of driving fast is the equivalent of B dollars. Consider the case where $p = 1$—that is, whenever you drive fast, you are caught for sure. Now, if F happens to be less than B, clearly no driver will comply with the law. This was always known. What I am saying here, however, includes yet goes beyond this. To check that a law is individual-incentive compatible, in the sense of being a Nash equilibrium, it is important to check not only that it is in the driver's interest to comply with the law but also that it is in the police officer's interest to catch a driver who violates the speed limit law, in the senior officer's interest to charge a police officer who does not catch drivers who violate speeding laws with dereliction of duty, in the magistrate's interest to punish a senior officer who does not charge a police officer who does not catch speeding drivers, and so on.

According to the focal concept of law and economics being proposed here, just being compatible with the 'final' round of agents—agents who are the object of the law, or in this example, the drivers—is not good enough. I can think of many examples of laws where the punishment is so severe that if it were enforced, it would not be in the interest of citizens to violate the law. The reason they do not abide by the law is that the incentives on the police officer and bureaucrats for enforcing the law are not right. So they do not convict the offenders, and the offenders, knowing this, are willing to offend. Hence, the first condition for a law to be successfully implemented is that it must be such that adherence to it can be supported by a Nash equilibrium of a game that includes everybody—the citizens and the enforcers of the law—as players.[11] I construct an example later in this chapter to illustrate this point with actual numbers.

But that is not sufficient, and this brings me to the second class of violations of the law. If an economy has several Nash equilibria, then even if the law picks one Nash equilibrium (that is, it does not make the mistake of trying to realize a non-Nash outcome), it may not be realized because it may not be focal. This can happen for various reasons. If there is already some focal outcome, then the announcement of a law (and therefore a new outcome) may fail to replace the prior focal point. The important idea to comprehend is that a game cannot have multiple focal points. If someone tries to create multiple focal points then effectively there is no focal point.

Return to the Heathrow airport example and confine the attention to a single terminal before the "Meeting Point" sign was put up. Assume that there was a bookshop, WHS, that was so prominent that people treated it as focal. Friends trying to meet at the airport who had forgotten to specify where they would meet went to WHS. Suppose this was widely known and commonly used. Now to make meeting up even easier, someone from the airport authority thought up of the idea of installing the "Meeting Point" sign. Would this help and make people go to where the sign is? The answer is not evident. The WHS practice could be so deeply ingrained in the psyche of travelers that they would continue to use the bookshop as their meeting place. And in fact things could actually get worse because now some people may go to WHS and some to the "Meeting Point" sign, thereby defeating the very purpose of the sign.[12]

The same is true of the law. When a new law is announced, it is a bit like a new "Meeting Point" sign being put up. It may fail to create a new focal point. Much will depend on the government's reputation and the strength of the preexisting focal points. If the government has a reputation for announcing laws that are not followed, then the next law may not be followed simply because no one will expect it to be followed. Recall that a focal point must have the (admittedly somewhat indefinable) quality that each player expects every player to consider it focal. In fact, for a point or outcome to be focal, it must be common knowledge that it is focal.

Thus, in countries where laws are widely violated, when a new law is announced, it is likely to fail to be focal, because everybody expects it to be breached. This explains why failed laws come in clusters. In some countries most laws seem to be ineffective, and in other countries most laws tend to be effective. This is best understood in terms of the focal point conception of the law being proposed here.

These are ideas that will need to be further developed and formalized, but this view of law as focal point clearly opens up new avenues for understanding why some laws are followed whereas others are not, and also why some nations are prone to having laws that are wantonly violated whereas other nations are more law abiding.

This focal view of law influences the way we perceive the relation between law, growth, and efficiency. It is widely recognized that bad laws can lead to bad economic outcomes. If a country (especially a small one) imposes a legal ban on imports (out of fear, say, that all its foreign exchange will get drained) and this is fully implemented, then it is reasonable to expect that the country will do badly. Its growth will falter, and the country will operate below its full efficiency level. If a government places a ban on all forms of money lending (and this is properly implemented), it is probable that this will greatly hamper a nation's growth, since entrepreneurs will not be able to make investments by borrowing money.

But what the above analysis of law and economics tells us is that if a law banning imports can cripple an economy with trade grinding to a halt, then the same can happen even in the absence of such a law. Likewise, if a law prohibiting money lending can hurt growth by deterring investment, then growth can get hurt and investment deterred even without such a law. This is because as the focal view of law demonstrates, a law cannot create a new equilibrium; it can simply lead us to a preexisting equilibrium, or to put it differently, it can help us select one among the set of preexisting equilibria. But since an equilibrium is an outcome that by definition can occur on its own and persist, whatever outcome can occur because of a law can do so in the absence of that law. So if a law is oppressive, then so can nonlaw be. If a law can hurt some people, so can nonlaw. If a new law can take away people's freedom of speech, it can be taken away even in the absence of such a law. The suffocating control that the subalterns of the state establish over K's life in *The Trial* has all the trappings of being caught in a legal snare, but it happens with no law being used.

These claims are not easy to understand, certainly not in the deeper sense of the intuitive understanding discussed in chapter 1. Take the last claim in the previous paragraph. When we talk of guaranteeing freedom of speech, we typically mean that the state should provide legal guarantees for such freedom. The law should have provisions like no one can ban a book and no journalist can be silenced for saying something that someone powerful does not like to hear.

These are extremely important principles, and can contribute greatly to creating a civilized and democratic society. The big mistake that one can make, and we often do make, is to suppose that once a nation desists from using laws to silence people, people will not be silenced—they will have freedom of speech. But in reality the same curbs that arise in some nations because of the absence of legal guarantees of free speech can arise in nations where laws protecting the right of writers and speakers are in place.[13] One can see some evidence of this in the United States, where through a variety of nonlegal means, freedom of speech is often curtailed. In such times mainstream television channels and major newspapers express opinions that are monolithic, even though by law they need not do so. Corporate sponsorship, advertisers' interests, and government's permission to let journalists travel as embedded personnel with the military create constraints, which may have little to do with the law, yet are constraining on free speech, as are legal restrictions on the freedom of expression.

If an alien searched the mainstream media for the opinions of radical critics of the system, such as Noam Chomsky, Howard Zinn, and Michael Moore, or tuned into major radio channels to listen to the songs of the Dixie Chicks and Nathalie Mains, in particular, they would find so little that they would conclude that there is a gag order on their speech. The alien would be wrong, of course, and that is exactly what illustrates my point.[14]

To understand the power of nonlegal control, consider the case of caste rules in India. These rules have no standing in the eyes of the law. Yet thanks to the fear of ostracism, in traditional sections of Indian society and especially in rural India, people adhere to caste rules, and in many places these rules have a force equal to or even greater than a state-sanctioned law (Akerlof 1976).[15] The reason it is so strong is that it relies on a system of natural peer monitoring. If an individual violates an important caste norm—for instance, if an upper-caste person shares a meal with a low-caste person, then the individual expects to be ostracized by others in society. This anticipation makes them conform to the caste norms. This raises the question of why those who ostracize the breaker of caste norms do so. Interestingly, the answer is the same. If a person did not ostracize someone who broke caste norms, then that person in turn would be ostracized by others. This interlocking web of monitoring one another can be an immense disciplining force.

There are other domains of our social and political life where this argument can be used (Havel 1986; Basu 1986, 2000). Economists puzzle about why the dowry system persists in India, or why U.S. teenagers in ghettos indulge in practices that can be self-destructive. Once economists recognize the powerful role of peer approval and peer ostracism, the angst that they feel about the world not fitting into their demand-supply models may get lessened.

It is then not surprising that even when there are no legal restrictions on press freedom, press freedom can be curbed with as much force as occurs when legal bans are used. I have maintained before, and continue to do so, that even though the U.S. press has more legal freedom than the British press, it has less effective freedom than the latter.[16]

To recognize this is to realize that if we want certain freedoms and individual rights, it is not enough to simply have the laws in place and prevent government from curtailing these individual rights. We need awareness that these freedoms can get eroded with no change in the law, simply through subtle intercitizen dynamics, and so we need continuous social vigilance to keep these freedoms alive. What is so frightening about the McCarthy period curbs on civil liberties in the United States is that they were achieved with no changes in the law.[17] This should alert us to the fact that such erosions can happen again.

A Game-Theoretic Illustration of Law as Focal Point

It is possible to think of numerous real-life situations to show how this altered view of law would change our predictions of how particular laws would or would not influence economic outcomes.[18] I will demonstrate my argument with a simple example, fully aware that there is a trade-off between simplicity and realism. Nevertheless, some readers may wish to skip over this relatively technical section.

Consider a three-person society in a remote hill resort, consisting of an ordinary citizen, Sai, a police officer, and a judge. Sai can turn on music at different volumes: C (very loud), B (loud), and A (soft). The police officer can punish her (action p), depending on how loudly she plays her music. If the officer does punish her, her utility drops to zero, irrespective of whatever she may do and whatever the judge does, and irrespective of what volume her music was on. You can simply think of the punishment as taking all the joy out of her music. If the police officer does not punish her (call this action n), Sai gets a utility of 3 from playing music at level C, 2 from B, and 1 from A, with her youthfulness creating a preference for higher decibels.

The standard approach to law and economics would already be in a position to predict the outcomes. If there are no laws on sound pollution, Sai will play her music at level C; if C and above were declared illegal, she would choose B; and, if B and above were illegal, she would choose A. To see this, consider the last case. B and above are illegal. So she expects to be punished if, and only if, she plays at B and above. If punished, she gets a utility of zero. Hence, she would prefer to play at level A and get a utility of 1. This approach takes for granted that the enforcers of the law do indeed enforce the law. What I am maintaining is that despite the rhythm of the sentence, it is false. In a more correct model, the enforcers of the law ought to be treated as human. We need a description of what moves them. So to continue with the portrait of this society, assume that the judge and the police officer have a complicated relationship, the details of which will be suppressed here in the interests of keeping the central narrative uninterrupted. How well each person does depends on what the other does and also on the noise level in this remote hill resort where they live.

In this example, the police officer has to choose whether to punish Sai (action p) or not (action n), and the judge has to choose between two actions, which I will denote with the nondescript L and R. The judge's action has no effect on Sai (as already explained), but it has an impact on the police officer. And it so happens that the police officer's action also affects the judge, who is overly sensitive to what is happening because they also live in this neighborhood.

TABLE 4

Game G_{AB} (for Sound Level A and B)

		Judge	
		L	R
Police officer	p	1, 1	0, 2
	n	0, 0	2, 2

If the noise level on the hill is less than C, then the payoffs earned by the police officer and the judge are summed up by the payoff matrix depicted in table 4. The police officer chooses between p and n, the judge chooses between L and R, and for each pair of numbers shown in a box, the left is the payoff of the police officer and the right is the payoff of the judge.

If the sound level on the hill is C, though, the payoffs earned by the police officer and the judge are shown by the payoff matrix shown in table 5.

It is now easy to see that if the police officer and the judge are in an environment where the sound level is A or B—that is, they are engaged in playing game G_{AB}—then no matter what the police officer does, the judge is better off playing R. That, in turn, will imply that the police officer will choose n. Thus, if Sai chooses to play music at level A or B, it is never rational for the police to punish Sai, and the judge will for sure choose R.

Note next that if Sai turns the music up to level C, the game between the police officer and the judge has two (Nash) equilibria: the police officer chooses p, and the judge chooses L—which we can describe in brief as (p, L)—and the police officer chooses n and the judge chooses R—which we can describe as (n, R). The reader should verify that in neither of these equilibria (this is, in fact, the meaning of a Nash equilibrium) can the police officer or the judge do better by *unilaterally* changing his action.

If there is no law restricting sound levels, one entirely possible outcome is that Sai will play music at level C, the police officer will not punish her, and the judge will choose action R. Notice that no one can do better by unilaterally changing his or her behavior. In other words, the outcome is a Nash equilibrium.[19]

Now suppose that a law is announced that requires that sound levels be kept below C in this hill resort. Like all laws, this comes with the presumed injunction on the police officer—what I call the 'anterior law' (Basu 2000)—that should anybody play music at levels that violate the law, the police officer should punish her.

As I have contended above, the law cannot alter the game. Why should something written on paper alter what people can do and what they earn by

TABLE 5
Game G_c (for Sound Level C)

		Judge	
		L	R
Police officer	p	1, 1	0, 0
	n	0, 0	2, 2

doing so? But interestingly, it can still alter the outcome that occurs. The law can make the police officer expect that if Sai plays music at level C, the judge will expect the police officer to punish her and so play L, and if the judge plays L, it is in fact better for the police officer to punish her. And Sai, knowing this, will choose to play music at volume B.

Next consider a law that says that music at level B or above is not allowed. This law cannot be focal—that is, it cannot give rise to self-fulfilling beliefs. This is because if Sai plays music at level B, the police officer will not punish her, because the police officer knows that in this case the judge will choose R. Hence, Sai cannot be deterred from playing music at level B. This law will not be effective, even though, had the police officer been completely diligent in enforcing the law, Sai would have complied with it.

A Research Agenda

The example above, while contrived, illustrates how the focal view of law can lead to a distinctly different understanding of the role of law in economic life. It also highlights how this perspective can enable us to understand why some laws are effective and some not, and why in some nations laws are generally effective and in other nations they rarely are. This is a crucial ingredient in our understanding of economic development and stagnation.

In general, the focal view of law opens up a large research agenda. Consider the idea briefly mentioned earlier of anterior law, which is the implicit injunction that requires the enforcers of the law to enforce the law, whatever that happens to be. For instance, when a nation lowers its speed limit to fifty mph, we can say that it is the law that no one should drive above fifty mph. This law, however, comes with the implicit injunction that the police, the sheriff, and the magistrate should punish anybody who drives above fifty mph. A police officer who does not do so violates the law even if they diligently drive below fifty mph themselves. What the officer violates is not the speed limit law but rather the anterior law, which is a concomitant of the speed limit.

If the anterior law in a nation is well understood and already focal for a whole set of laws, that helps a lot in enforcing the law. In the above section, if the judge and the police officer each know that the other will obey the anterior law, given a violation of the law, then it is in each person's interest to obey the anterior law for any law that prohibits music above level B. This will mean that as soon as a law, from within a set of a priori possible laws, is announced, the enforcers of the law know that they are supposed to enforce the law and other enforcers of the law will punish them should they not do their job. This line of inquiry, whereby we separately study the incentives and beliefs of the official enforcers as well as the ordinary citizens, provides a better understanding of the efficacy of law.

While the focal view of law significantly expands our understanding of the effect of law on an economy beyond what is possible under the standard paradigm, there is room to take our analysis even further. Some of the germs of such extensions have already been discussed. As we bring those to bear on the subject of law and economics the terrain gets intellectually demanding, and all I can do at this point is to indicate some worthwhile research directions.

We have seen in the discussion of the public good urge, social norms, and incentive compatibility in chapter 3 that there are important ways in which we human beings self-impose restrictions on our own choices. There are actions and behaviors that we do not even consider. There are actions that are not chosen by an individual but at the same time cannot be described as rejected by the agent, for rejection suggests agency on the part of the individual. As pointed out earlier, most of us do not steal wallets from other people's pockets in buses not because the expected pickings are meager (since we know that on average, people do not carry wads of money when traveling by public transport) and fail to offset the expected cost of getting caught but instead because we do not even consider stealing wallets to be a choice. These social norms do vary across time and space. In fact, different civilizations are defined in part by the kinds of self-imposed restrictions that people place on themselves.

In the spirit of the earlier look at anterior law, people probably have two kinds of persona within themselves: one that dictates their behavior in the marketplace, in making investment decisions, and so on, and another that gets activated when they are called on to provide a social service, or to be a judge, a minister, or a police officer. In this second role, a person is more than just a citizen; they are a metacitizen. This can help us understand why anterior laws function as well as they do. Yet this recognition does not take us back to the traditional view of law; it urges us to build further on the focal view.

Hence, a person's set of feasible actions is defined not simply by what is physically possible or what is possible by "nature's rules" but also by "society's rules" and the person's self-imposed restrictions, some of which may be so deeply embedded in the person that they could be unaware of them.[20] We do not properly understand where these restrictions come from, and why and when they change over time. The new behavioral economics takes a stab at it, but there is still a great distance to go. Once we become aware of this, we ought to recognize that the announcement of a new law could alter some of our self-imposed restrictions. The idea of the expressive function of law, whereby the mere announcement of a law alters the preferences of citizens, entails this kind of reasoning.[21] We know from experimental economics that the wording or a framing of a decision problem can alter behavior. There are studies (for instance, Ross and Ward 1996) showing that if players are made to play the Prisoner's Dilemma by calling it the "community game," they play the game more cooperatively than when the same game is given to them but called the "Wall Street game."

Particularly relevant here is the paper by Iris Bohnet and Robert Cooter (2001), in which they report on both the framing effect and the role of law in creating a focal point that makes it possible for the players to anticipate one another's behavior, and thereby coordinate their action. There are also real-world examples of a society collectively moving from one equilibrium into another. An engaging discussion of the ability of such social engineering to shed the age-old practice of foot binding in China in a dramatically short time is discussed by Gerry Mackie (1996). The trick is to persuade all citizens to make a coordinated move to some new behavior, which is self-sustaining in the sense of Nash. This falls nicely within the ambit of the focal view of law. But when law alters human preferences, maybe because in some societies people are preprogrammed to love the law they have, we are forced to modify our view of law and economics even further than is suggested by the focal view. If laws can change the preferences of players, then this means that the law can change the game. At first it may seem that we are back to the traditional paradigm in which it is assumed that the law *does* change the game. On reflection, it becomes evident that the alteration in the game occurs in ways different from what is assumed in the traditional law and economics literature. In the presence of expressive effects, the mere framing of some act as illegal alters behavior in novel and as yet ill-understood ways. Recognizing these behavioral features of human decision making not only takes us into newer territories of law and economics but also calls into question the very interpretation of a game.

Another way in which a law can affect citizen behavior is if the very announcement of a new law is treated by ordinary people as a signal of some new information on the part of government. All this merely points to the fact that the critique of the standard paradigm and the alternative approach suggested here are best viewed as a prelude to further research. The focal view of law opens the door to a deeper and richer understanding of how laws impact on economic outcomes, how we can make our laws more effective, and how we can use the law to achieve greater economic growth and prosperity.

CHAPTER 5

Markets and Discrimination

Do Free Markets Reduce Discrimination?

There is a view, propagated by conservative intellectuals, that free markets and unfettered capitalism reduce discrimination. Permit capitalism to flourish unhindered, and not all at once but gradually we will see racism and discrimination wither away, somewhat like the way white vinegar diluted with water, left standing without further interference, makes some of the worst residues and crusts on glass vanish. Milton Friedman (1962) advocated this viewpoint vociferously in his *Capitalism and Freedom*. Talking about "minority groups" that, according to Friedman, benefited most from this property of capitalism but failed to understand it, he argued, "They have tended to attribute to capitalism the residual restrictions they experience rather than to recognize that the free market has been the major factor enabling these restrictions to be as small as they are" (109).

Friedman made it clear that he personally believed that no one should be discriminated against for their race or religion, and he disapproved of the "taste" for discrimination that some people had. But he asserted that "the appropriate recourse is for me to seek to persuade them that their tastes are bad and that they should change their behavior, not to use coercive power to enforce my tastes and my attitudes on others" (111).

I will contend in this chapter that when it comes to some people's taste for prejudice and discrimination against persons of a specific color, religion, or gender, we should be prepared to interfere in the market and thwart the exercise of such prejudicial preference. It may not be enough to leave it to the art of suasion.

The argument for market intervention is not an easy or obvious one, and is rooted in some of the foundational issues raised in this book. Friedman reached the conclusion of nonintervention precisely because of his view that the worst cases of prejudice will vanish under capitalism. Hence, his somewhat touching faith that telling people with bad taste not to have such taste is enough. And even if this were not effective, unfettered capitalism would take care of its worst excesses.

This conservative claim deserves to be banished, but it cannot be dismissed out of hand. Free market capitalism does indeed have a natural corrosive effect on discrimination. We need to understand this in order to see why this may not be effective enough, however, and how there may also be situations where the free market actually exacerbates the problem of prejudice.

There are two basic claims about why capitalism may have a tendency to lessen discrimination against some groups of people. The first is more a by-product of capitalism than capitalism itself. As has often been pointed out, and not without merit, as capitalism flourishes, people become more materialistic and money minded, and are driven by the urge to maximize profit and accumulate wealth. We may well take a pejorative view of this transformation of human preference, but there can be no denying that this same preference tends to squeeze out the preference in favor of or against different groups. If women who are as productive as men are available in the market at a lower going wage than men, an entrepreneur who is solely driven by the urge to maximize profit will prefer to employ women, unlike the alleged feudal landlord who may be willing to incur a cost in order to have a female-free labor force. I believe there is some merit to this argument. One reason why caste prejudices are eroding in India is because entrepreneurs and shareholders are now much more single-minded about money than they were earlier. This is a simple enough contention that it need not be labored further.

The second argument is complex. It is frequently associated with the 'Chicago school' view of labor market discrimination. Consider an industry where there is perfect competition. New firms enter the market freely when there is profit to be made, and old firms exit with little pain when they begin to experience persistent losses. Now suppose there are some entrepreneurs who have a taste for racial or gender-based discrimination. They want their labor force to be, for instance, male and white. This will typically tend to depress the wage rate for nonwhites and women. But that, in turn, will enable entrepreneurs who do not have any racial or gender bias to earn more profit since they will take advantage of this wage disparity to employ more nonwhites and women.

Note that if there is free entry of new firms into this industry, as we just assumed, more prejudice-free entrepreneurs will enter the industry, lured by the profits. This will then cause the price of the product that this industry produces to go down, eventually driving down the profit earned by all entrepreneurs. In the ultimate equilibrium, the profit earned by prejudice-free entrepreneurs will be driven down to zero (which in the jargon of economics means that firms earn nothing above what we call 'normal profits'—that is, the minimal profit for a firm to continue in the industry). But if a prejudice-free firm earns zero profits, then discriminatory firms, which we have already seen earn a lower profit than prejudice-free firms, must earn a negative or subnormal profit. Since normal profit is by definition what it takes to keep a firm in the industry, discriminatory firms will exit from the industry in the perfectly competitive equilibrium. End of proof.

But not end of analysis. Of course this argument has implicit assumptions. Some of those are reasonable. It is, for instance, assumed that when we say some entrepreneurs are willing to pay a price for their discriminatory preference, we are nevertheless maintaining that they will not be willing to stay on in an industry and make losses in order to discriminate. What is being assumed is that people are willing to make a smaller profit, as long as they are not actually incurring a loss, to indulge in their preference for prejudice.

The force that the 'Chicago argument' refers to is certainly present in capitalistic markets, and one cannot dismiss it out of hand. At the same time, there is reason to believe that free markets even when they are fully competitive often do not work that way, and discrimination can flourish despite markets being free and there being no government intervention. Fortunately, to demonstrate this one does not have to start from scratch. There is a large literature in economics that may once have been viewed as heterodox, but is today a part of the mainstream that shows how free markets and wanton discrimination can persist, giving rise to the need for intelligent intervention. The contributors to this discourse are a bit like a who's who of economics: Arrow (1972), Michael Spence (1974), Akerlof (1976), Edmund Phelps (1972), Stiglitz (1974). Before moving on, it is useful to briefly recapitulate the ground covered by some of these people.

The Literature

To see how the market may lose its property of naturally eliminating discrimination, let me begin by assuming that people are solely interested in profits. They have no innate discriminatory preference. This makes my argument harder. If discrimination persists under this assumption, it will in all likelihood persist when some people have racial or gender-based preferences.

Unlike in the above model, but as is often so in reality, assume that entrepreneurs cannot always judge the productivity of each laborer and use average group characteristics to form a judgment. These are called 'statistical discrimination' theories. In the simplest version, suppose all entrepreneurs believe that members of group X are less productive. Even though they have no innate group-based preference, the entrepreneurs then will be willing to pay less to members of group X. This simplest model is not persuasive because it relies on entrepreneurs having a false belief about the average characteristics of groups. The analysis becomes more compelling if it can be shown that having such a belief about a group makes members of the group behave in such a way that the belief turns out to be true.

There are elegant models in economics that demonstrate just this. Spence's (1974) classic work on job market signaling is a case in point. It is frequently remarked that what we learn in college—abstract mathematics, classical poetry, theories of business organization, and even the theory of job market signaling—really does not equip us any better to handle reality; such education does not enhance our productivity. This claim may be a bit extreme but it is not outrageous. So let us go along with it. What is undeniable, however, is that the more productive people (those who are smarter, innately harder working, and better organized) find it easier to do better in college and acquire their degrees. Of course, productive people are the ones that firms are after. So if it were the case that college degrees are more likely to be earned by the more productive persons, then even though productivity may be innate in human beings and not altered by earning a degree, statistically an average person with a degree will be more productive than an average person without a degree.

What is not hard to see is that this model may exhibit multiple equilibria. Education can certainly be of different amounts, measured in terms of the number of years of education or the number and level of degrees earned. It is entirely possible that if employers believe that all those with a high school education are highly productive, then this will be borne out in reality, and if they believe instead that those with a college education are highly productive, then this will be borne out in reality. Since these are self-fulfilling prophecies—the more productive people want to signal to their employers that they are indeed more productive—there can be several employer beliefs that are fulfilled in reality. Since the more productive people find education less costly, they and only they find it worthwhile to get the level of education that the employers believe indicate high productivity. Once they acquire such education, the employers' belief turns out to be valid, or in the parlance of economics, their expectations happen to be rational.

Now comes the problem. Suppose employers believe that blacks are less productive and thus need more years of education to reach the same level of productivity as whites. It may be entirely reasonable for productive blacks and productive whites to get different levels of education. That, in turn, means that the conjecture of the employers is borne out by the data that the market throws up. In reality, there are people with racist preference. But the above theoretical model shows that even without such people, the market could lead to an equilibrium in which blacks have to go the extra mile to demonstrate that they are as productive as whites. The free market is not as unfriendly a terrain for nurturing racism and other forms of discrimination as it may have appeared at first sight.

Though I have stated much of this analysis in terms of race, it is possible to carry this over to gender-based discrimination. In recent years there have been new theories that apply specifically to gender discrimination. Patrick Francois (1998) offers an ingenious model, where there is no difference ex ante anywhere but simply an ex post facto difference in *outcome*. His is also a model of market equilibrium, but one in which within-household arrangements depend on the wages that prevail for males and females in the labor market; the wages that prevail in the labor market are, in turn, a response to the arrangements within the household. Basically, there are two kinds of jobs available on the market, and within the household there is scope for specialization and 'gains from trade' between the partners. These gains are possible only if one of the partners has the better job. Firms in this case have an interest in ensuring that the better jobs go to only those who live in households where only one person has this kind of a job.

There are other models of discrimination that make critical use of the organization of the household. It is a fact that people within a household share their incomes, with children, the elderly, and the unemployed. In addition, in poor countries, from a firm's point of view it is better to employ those who consume most of their income themselves so as to ensure that they have better nutrition and are therefore better able to work. There is some evidence that women share their income more generously with other members of the household than do men. This has been noted not just in developing countries such as India (Desai and Jain 1994) but also in developed countries such as Britain (Lundberg, Pollak, and Wales 1997). In Britain, for instance, in the late 1970s when child benefits were shifted from being handed over to the mother instead of the father, expenditures on children's clothing went up. This implies that firms will prefer to employ men.

One can make a similar argument even if all human beings are ex ante identical—that is, if there is no innate difference between individuals in terms of their propensity to share. It seems reasonable to expect that in communities in which unemployment is high, sharing will be greater, since each employed person will have more unemployed friends and relatives. If firms find laborers whose income is dissipated by sharing to be less attractive, then in fact communities that have more sharing will have more unemployment. The two assertions reinforce each other. More unemployment leads to more sharing, and more sharing leads to more unemployment (see Basu and Felkey 2008).

In South Africa, the interracial differences in the rates of unemployment are quite shocking. The nation's *Labour Force Survey* of 2003 reveals that unemployment among whites is 10 percent, whereas among blacks it is 50 percent. The argument just presented can explain this, even when there may be no innate differences between blacks and whites.

A set of new empirical studies has generated new interest in the subject of discrimination in the labor market. I want to comment on some of them here, because they provide the setting for some novel ways of thinking about the problem that I explore below. Marianne Bertrand and Sendhil Mullainathan (2004) sent out fictitious résumés in response to actual job advertisements in Boston and Chicago newspapers. Some of the résumés used first names that are conventionally given to whites—Allison, Anne, Carrie, Brad, Brendon, and Geoffrey—and some used first names associated with blacks, such as Aisha, Ebony, Keisha, Darnell, Hakim, and Jamal. The aim was to find out how callbacks for job interviews vary by race even when other applicant characteristics are the same or similar. Since the résumés were created by the authors, they could control for other characteristics, such as education and experience. The authors found that applicants with black names needed to send out fifteen applications to get one callback; white-named candidates needed ten applications. A black needed eight years of additional experience to get the same number of callbacks as a white.

Thanks to the excellent control of the experiment, it firmly establishes the discrimination that blacks face on the U.S. labor market. The authors point out that since the employers use race as a factor when choosing employees, this fits the legal definition of discrimination. Similar results have been found recently by Zahra Siddique (2008), who conducted a comparable study in India by sending out job applications with caste-specific names. She discovered that high-caste candidates needed to send out 6.2 résumés to get one callback, whereas low-caste candidates needed to send out 7.4 résumés to get the same result. What I will argue later, however, is that this kind of callback difference can occur even when employers do not care about race or caste per se.

The other empirical finding that captured a lot of public attention is that of Richard Sander (2006), who demonstrated that in getting entry-level jobs in prestigious law firms, blacks do not face any disadvantage, but when it comes to being partners, blacks seldom make it. The proverbial glass ceiling seems to thwart blacks' trajectory. Sander's own explanation of this striking empirical phenomenon is that firms use affirmative action when hiring blacks, so that the average grades of blacks getting these jobs is lower, and their weaker long-run career and failure to rise to sufficient seniority reflects this.

Sander's analysis has received strong criticism. In a closely reasoned paper, James Coleman and Mitu Gulati (2006) note that while Sander's data on the rarity of black partners in top law firms is compelling, Sanders does not have enough information to reach the *explanation* that he gives. They make an important technical point. Black associates are hired mostly from elite law schools, and it is possible that even the whites hired from elite schools may have weaker grades. Hence, minimally, one needs to put in controls for this by, for instance, comparing the performance of blacks and whites from similar schools. While this will need statistical testing and so remains to be resolved, from my point of view the more significant criticism leveled by Coleman and Gulati is that black associates receive little mentorship, lower-quality assignments, less client contact, and less interaction with their senior partners than white associates do. It is not surprising that at the end of a period of such treatment, blacks appear to be less productive, and often leave a firm or usually fail to rise to more senior positions.

This interactive part of work will be a key ingredient in the analysis later in this chapter. That analysis will entail distinguishing between the concepts of "collective discrimination" and "individualistic discrimination." I contend that a lot of discrimination in social life takes the form of collective discrimination, and this could lead to different policy prescriptions from the ones that arise in response to the more familiar individualistic discrimination.

The Self-Reinforcement of Productivity

Another kind of evidence that provides foundations for the theoretical analysis that is developed below pertains to the indeterminate nature of human productivity. The conservative view that in markets, left to themselves, individuals earn according to their marginal productivity, takes a beating when it is recognized that people's productivity depends not just on their respective education, motivation, innate skills, and ability for hard work; there is an essential *social* component to productivity. From some striking recent experiments this seems to be beyond question. A person's productivity is highly sensitive to factors connected to the social setting in which the person works, the person's social status, and other collective features.

Through a set of experiments in India's Uttar Pradesh, Karla Hoff and Priyanka Pandey (2005, 2006) demonstrated a remarkable result. Low-caste children solve mazes (an indicator of intelligence and analytic skill) with as much dexterity as upper-caste children. But if, before administering the same kind of test, each child's caste is publicly announced, then the lower-caste children perform worse. The public proclamation of a person's caste has a withering effect on the psyche of those belonging to historically disadvantaged groups.[1]

These results—following in the tradition of earlier work in psychology, such as by Claude Steele and Joshua Aronson (1995) and Nalini Ambady, Margaret Shih, Amy Kim, and Todd Pittinsky (2001)—highlight the connection between social context and performance, and makes the general point that people's productivity depends not just on the obvious variables, such as how much they have studied or their innate ability, but on their social situation and identities that are salient to them at that time. This opens up a whole new set of policy options for enhancing human capital and productivity.

This general point receives reinforcement in some data that I acquired from an NGO-run teaching institute for slum children in Calcutta called Anandan (see Basu 2007c). Anandan is a teaching institute that is meant to supplement the education of slum children. Children are taught basic numeracy, logic, and English; they are made aware of world affairs. The idea is to take the poorest children and spark their curiosity as well as intellectual interests. I have an insider's view of Anandan since three of my sisters are among the founding members.

The institute collects basic information about the children's background—their household income; whether their households have radios, bicycles, and watches; and their number of siblings—and of course basic information about each child—age, sex, mother tongue, and so on. In addition, it has answers to questions directly administered to the children about the social conditions in their households, such as if their parents beat each other, if their parents talk to each other (and if so, how much), and if these parents talk to their children.

Furthermore, in 2006 the school administered some basic IQ, arithmetic, and general knowledge tests, which I helped Anandan design, to sixty children, from ages nine to sixteen years. The questions they were asked are reproduced in an appendix at the end of this chapter. The data were not collected with special statistical care and were not intended to be used for formal social science inquiry. They were meant for the school's internal use. The data can nevertheless be used to get a sense of what is most important as a determinant of a child's aptitude. One can glean some useful correlations and run some minimal regressions to get a sense of which variables go together, and then speculate about causes. These caveats are meant to warn the reader not to overinterpret the results. As discussed earlier, causality at a fundamental level can never be established. It is a construct of the observer's mind rather than a fact of the world. I mention this in order to clarify that not being able to establish causality is not as great a flaw as it appears to those who are deluded into believing that causality can be established.

What turns out to be most important for a child's aptitude is not income, wealth (as measured by the possession of radios, watches, and bicycles), or, within some limits, age, but instead whether the parents talk to each other and whether the child lives with his or her family.

The reason I report this result, though it will need more investigation, is the suggestion that a child's *social* conditions matter significantly in how the child performs in school, and in this case, they seem to matter more than the economic conditions of the child's household. One possibility is that a person's 'citizenship' status matters. If a person feels a proper 'citizen of the household,' this bolsters his or her self-confidence, and again results in intelligence and human capital. If your parents talk to you, it bolsters your status in the household, which in turn aids your intellectual performance.[2] This is further reinforced by the fact that children who live with their parents do better, on average, in aptitude tests. In fact, on average they get 6.76 marks more—that is, one standard deviation higher marks. Clearly, children have a more secure status at home when they reside with their parents. These results are basically similar to those found by Hoff and Pandey (2008) and Field and Nolen (2005) on children's performance when they are reminded of their marginalized status in society.

The Entrepreneur

As a precursor to theory, it is important to revisit the idea of an entrepreneur. The 'entrepreneur' is, at the same time, a critical and an elusive character. They are critical because an economy's growth and development relies so heavily on the entrepreneur. They are elusive because it is so hard to define who is an entrepreneur. It is this elusive character of the concept that has made it a source of intellectual curiosity and investigation. Attempts to understand the entrepreneur predate Smith's *Wealth of Nations* to the writings of Richard Cantillon in the mid-eighteenth century, particularly his *Essai sur la Nature du Commerce en General* ([1755] 1964), which was published after Cantillon's death and after circulating for a quarter century in the form of notes.

Cantillon's life is as obscure as some of the ideas he pursued. He was of Irish extraction (it is not clear why he had a Spanish name), lived most of his life in France, and died in London in 1734. What we do know about him is that he had a flair for entrepreneurship, and made a fortune for himself from a variety of risky and speculative ventures, especially those pertaining to currency fluctuations.

Among the many pioneering ideas in *Essai* is the concept of an entrepreneur. Cantillion's entrepreneur was essentially an absorber of risk, a person who, for instance, bought goods at a fixed price in order to later sell them at an uncertain one, or bought inputs at the going price and converted them to some final goods, without quite being sure what the price of those goods would be. The entrepreneur made money out of this speculation.

The subject of entrepreneurship continued to intrigue political economists over the next two hundred years. There were the contributions of the French school, most notably Jean-Baptiste Say, but also others like Jeremy Bentham and Johann Heinrich von Thunen, who drew a clear distinction between the manager and the entrepreneur; ultimately, Schumpeter made the most important contribution to this subject. For Schumpeter, the key feature of an entrepreneur is the ability to innovate, whether by creating a new product, discovering a new way of producing, or finding a new market. Unlike Cantillon, Schumpeter did not view the entrepreneur as a risk taker, since without any capital, the burden of failure did not fall on the entrepreneur's shoulders.

One reason for the many definitions of the entrepreneur may be that fundamentally, it is an 'indefinable' concept or one that is "essentially contested," as Walter Gallie put it (1955). So our understanding of the idea of entrepreneurship may have to rely on not one definition but rather an evolving appreciation of its many facets. In this spirit, I want to emphasis one critical feature of an entrepreneur that seems to me to be central and yet has received little attention. This is the view of an entrepreneur as a person who solves other people's "coordination problems," of the kind discussed in the previous chapter.

Consider the following scenario. There is a cobbler, with poor marketing skills, who produces shoes (efficiently) and then markets them to customers (in his own inefficient way). Then there is the natural marketer, who spends half her day clumsily making poor-quality shoes and then sells them rapidly to gullible customers.

It should be obvious that if the cobbler and the gifted marketer could be told to concentrate on what they are good at, so that the cobbler produces shoes all day and keeps handing over the wares to the marketer who spends all his time selling shoes, the two of them could earn more. An entrepreneur is a person who takes a bird's-eye view of this situation, telling the cobbler to produce shoes and do nothing else, and the marketer to just sell the wares that are made available to them. The entrepreneur suggests a salary to each person that is a little more than what each person was getting and pockets the margin between the total revenue earned and what is paid out in salaries.

What is being suggested here is nothing novel. The literature on entrepreneurship is so voluminous that it is not possible to say anything that has not already been said. For one, I am picking up on Smith's ([1776] 1937) and Allyn Young's (1928) idea of how wealth is created by specialization, and combining it with the thought that wherever a new firm is formed, there is an underlying game with two equilibria—one in which there is no firm and each person works in isolation, and another in which they coordinate their work and create greater value. I am also picking up on ideas pursued by contemporary sociologists. Ironically, this game-theoretic, coordination-solving facet of entrepreneurship has been emphasized more often by sociologists than by economists. Ronald Burt (1993), for instance, talks about how an entrepreneur is the 'third party' who brings others unable to unite on their own together. He refers to the mildly derogatory Dutch phrase *de lachende derde*—the third person who has a laugh at the expense of the other two. AnnaLee Saxenian (2000, 312), in her study of systems firms in Silicon Valley, points to the critical role of coordination: "The guiding principle for Sun, like most new Silicon Valley systems firms, is to concentrate its expertise and resources on coordinating the design and assembly of a final system."

It is interesting how some of the most innovative ideas of contemporary social science have their roots in Georg Simmel's writings. This critical role of the entrepreneur who helps coordinate people's action and thereby generate value was developed by Simmel (1950) via the expression *tertius gaudens*, which means "the rejoicing third."

There are two alternative game-theoretic stories in pursuit of this idea. It is possible that a group of people (who may or may not know one another), such as the cobbler and the marketer discussed earlier, is engaged in a game that has two equilibrium outcomes: the one they are currently locked into, and another in which they would all be better off but is currently unrealized. The entrepreneur is a person who enables them to secure the better outcome and then syphons off some of the benefits that these people achieve.

A second interpretation is that these people are currently locked into a low-level equilibrium, but there is another choice of strategies that does not constitute an equilibrium yet would lead each of these people to be better off. The Prisoner's Dilemma game is an example of this. The entrepreneur, then, is a person who can alter the incentives and payoffs so that the other superior choice of strategies now becomes an equilibrium. So the entrepreneur creates an equilibrium that is better than the existing one and takes away a part of the benefits.

As a digression, it should be remarked that if we begin with a description where all agents, including the entrepreneur, are part of the game, then this basic game must have at least two equilibria for us to be able to explain the role of an entrepreneur. The entrepreneur is a person who knows the art of steering everybody to the new equilibrium. The argument here is similar to the one developed in chapter 4, where it was the law that helped people select one from among the multiple possible outcomes.

As economists have noted, we owe a lot of our societies' progress, organizational innovation, and growth to entrepreneurs. But it should be recognized that the impact of an entrepreneur does not have to be beneficial for others. Entrepreneurs are resourceful people, and there can clearly be contexts where they steer agents in directions and destinations that, once reached, constitute an equilibrium in which others are worse off and the entrepreneur is better off. The new outcome being an equilibrium means that once individuals are in it, no one can unilaterally deviate and do better.

Cases where, contrary to textbook economics, entrepreneurs and industry chiefs actually leave the population impoverished are not difficult to conceptualize. To understand this, let us first understand the textbook claim. An entrepreneur offers workers the lowest wage that the market will bear. This is often called the worker's reservation wage or market wage. As more and more entrepreneurs start up operations, this market wage rises because of competition. No individual may be big enough to influence the market wage, but the rise in aggregate demand for labor pushes it up and all workers are better off.

There are reasonable scenarios where life does not work this way, however. First of all, many entrepreneurs are big enough to be able to influence the worker's reservation wage. We have already seen how shrewd entrepreneurs can alter the game that people otherwise play. It is possible to create scenarios where the games are altered in a manner where the players (all but the entrepreneur) are worse off in the end. Further, if a large new corporation starts up a big factory that causes the groundwater level to drop, all the laborers in the region can become worse off, causing their reservation wages to drop, and they would then agree to work for the entrepreneur for a lower wage. Large corporations often deliberately use such strategies to hold workers to a low wage.

This can also happen with small entrepreneurs who cannot single-handedly affect the reservation wage, but the entry of numerous entrepreneurs can have the same net effect. In chapter 7, such arguments are formalized under the title of 'large numbers argument,' which shows how the totality of a large number of innocuous or even mildly beneficial moves can in the end leave people worse off. This is close to the Marxian view of what capitalist enterprise does, even though my *method* of analysis is different.

For the purposes of the theoretical model constructed later in the chapter, note that entrepreneurship is not a trait that has to be equated solely with the founders and chiefs of firms and corporations. Since in all but a few totally unskilled or autistic jobs, people need to interact with one another and a person's efficacy depends on how that person can mediate between others, there is scope for entrepreneurship in many different walks of life. In this sense, even workers in a firm may have scope for being entrepreneurial. A lawyer who works in a corporation or even a law firm may have to deal with laborers, customers, judges, and government officials. A more entrepreneurial lawyer is someone who can mediate effectively between these multiple players and so would be more productive from the firm's point of view. This will play an important role in the outlines of theory that I develop below.

Toward a New Theoretical Model

The next chapter studies group performance and group conflicts, which are founded on assumptions that go beyond methodological individualism. Here I want to show that some important forms of group discrimination and disparities can be understood even within the foundational assumptions of mainstream economics, as long as we are careful about reality and choose some of the other more proximate assumptions with care. So for now I will continue to assume that individuals have no innate identity-based preference.

We do observe all around us correlations between a person's performance and community identity—the group with which this person is associated—including identity markers that seem to be unconnected to the person's 'fundamentals' or innate qualities, like IQ or productivity. Men are higher income earners than women, Native Americans do worse than non–Native Americans in terms of economic well-being, members of the supposedly backward Indian castes get lower wages than Brahmins, and so on.

In traditional economics, there is a tendency to explain people's earnings differentials and other performance differentials in terms of fundamentals rooted in the person. Thus, in mainstream neoclassical economics we encounter statements like "i earns more than j because i has greater innate productivity or because j has a stronger preference for leisure than i has." Such economics is uncomfortable with a theory that concludes "i earns more than j *because* i is white and j is black."

For one, if markets led to the latter kind of income disparities, then markets would lose some of their neoconservative luster. A free market would no longer be viewed as a fair and neutral mechanism that delivers greater income to those who work harder, or are more innately productive or are willing to take intelligent risks.

Some of those who believe in this description of the free market outcome may nevertheless find a mechanism that gives greater reward to the innately more productive *instead of the more needy* to be unattractive, but they reconcile themselves to the fact that it is more fair than a system that arbitrarily rewards individuals, or benefits someone just for belonging to a particular race or religion.

What I am claiming here, and will shortly develop a theory to demonstrate, is that the market mechanism may not have even this minimal quality of rewarding the more productive. Its system of rewards may be much more spurious and vindictive. A free market can reward a person of race X or religion Y simply for being of race X or religion Y. In short, identities, which may have nothing to do with qualities that have a bearing on production, may matter.

The view that once markets are properly freed from government intervention, racist practices and caste-based rewards will wilt under competitive pressure and ultimately wither away, is plain wrong. In the case of caste practices, we know that these rose to prominence in India at a time when there was little by way of government, and the aim of the theory that follows is to show that such phenomena can flourish with no propping up by the state.

As mentioned earlier, there are important works by Akerlof, Spence, and others that construct models of discrimination that survive without the hand of the state or community. The argument developed here is related to but distinct from this literature. Here one community can get higher wages even when its profile of productivity (natural or acquired through education) happens to be the same. In fact, this can happen even when all human beings are identical.

There is a small empirical literature in economics that highlights what at an intuitive level we all know: that in different markets, people from certain communities do well and tend to corner a disproportionate amount of the market. Marcel Fafchamps (2000; see also 1992) has described how, in East Africa, Europeans and Indians manage to get loans and credit to start and expand businesses, whereas Africans are left devoid of funding. More recently, Abhijit Banerjee and Kaivan Munshi (2004) in their study of the garment industry in Tirupur, Tamil Nadu, India, find that one particular community, the Gounders—an elite cultivator caste that has had a record of being prominent in business and finance—controls a disproportionate amount of capital.[3] The Gounders are a close-knit community, and when they go into business they do so with a greater abundance of capital than do the non-Gounders, who comprise 42 percent of the exporters in Tirupur in the sample that Banerjee and Munshi study.

What these authors manage to demonstrate is that capital in the hands of the non-Gounders is as productive or even slightly more productive than capital in the hands of the Gounders. The output is smaller in a new non-Gounder firm compared with a new Gounder firm, but the former typically overtakes the Gounder firm within five years.

Why, then, are the Gounder firms flush with capital? Banerjee and Munshi conclude, rightly, that this suggests the presence of 'community effects.' Clearly community identity matters per se. They go on to suggest, however, that *this contrasts* with a model "where the allocation of capital is guided entirely by its marginal product in alternative uses" (41). I maintain that community identity effects are entirely consistent with capital being guided by the market principle of seeking higher productivity. Except in a tautological sense, a community can corner more capital even without having any innate capital cost advantage. In brief, not only are markets no guarantee against racism; they can actually nurture it.[4]

The basic idea is simple. Barring those involved in completely unskilled work, human beings go through life signing contracts, exchanging assurances, and making promises. As explained earlier, most jobs entail some amount of 'entrepreneurial skills.' A person (called E) starting a business raises start-up capital by implicitly promising to the investor that E will use the money prductively, and pay it back with interest or a profit share at a later date. The same person, E, may then go to someone to raise working capital. E may get raw material from some supplier and promise the supplier that E will sell E's final product to the supplier at a cut-rate price. E will, in the course of time, also try to get into contracts with customers. If this were a lawn maintenance company, homeowners may offer E contracts that take the form of a fixed monthly charge with the promise that E will maintain the lawn to the best of E's ability.

Now suppose you are one of the persons offering E a contract (for instance, providing E with working capital). Before doing so, you will try to find out how productive and efficient E is (to make sure that your money is safe and will yield a return). So you may look at E's educational attainment, size up E's penchant for hard work and promptness at returning calls, and so on. But E's productivity depends not just on his or her own characteristics. A large part of what E does depends on what others who offer contracts to E do (the moneylenders, consumers, and so forth, or what I refer to here as 'investors').

If consumers do not sign contracts with E, then E will not be able to pay you back. If the provider of raw material refuses to sign a raw material supply contract, E will not be able to pay you back.

Of course, the same is true of the consumer and the raw material supplier. Before signing a contract, each of them will wonder about E's productivity and efficiency. In each case, this will depend in part on E's own characteristics but also on how others view E, since whether E will be able to serve consumers well or pay back E's raw material supplier within the stipulated time will depend on whether E has enough working capital, enough start-up capital, a steady source of supply of the inputs, and so on.

And herein lies the rub. Assume that a person's religious, racial, or community identity has no bearing on the person's productivity. So whether a person is a Christian, Brahmin, black, white, Jew, or Gounder makes no difference to his or her business or work acumen, or preference for leisure and work. But if a belief forms that a person from community C is more productive, then this may turn out to be true in retrospect. A person's community identity could begin to matter in determining how effective a life the person can lead, even though it has no innate significance, and it may also involve no special behavior or choice on the part of the person involved. Everybody believing that persons of community C are more productive makes everybody want to interact with such persons and sign contracts with them, and that *makes* them more productive.

This explanation paves the way for important government interventions, like affirmative action. Hence, it is useful to try to understand the argument more closely by formalizing it a little more. Suppose the amount of value that a person E—the entrepreneur planning to start a lawn maintenance company—can generate depends on whether or not E gets a contract with a customer to provide the service, and manages to get working capital. If E gets neither of these, there is no company and the value generated is zero. If E gets both a customer and a supplier of capital, E generates a substantial amount of value—so much so that E is able to pay the market interest to the supplier of capital, charge the customer the going rate for lawn maintenance, and still keep some profit. There is nothing exceptional about these assumptions.

Let me now assume what seems quite realistic: that if E finds a customer but not a supplier of capital, then E has to use more-expensive funds from personal sources and so the profit (the lawn maintenance charge minus the costs) is negative; and if the supplier of capital agrees to work with E but E does not get a customer, E again incurs a loss, because the entrepreneur does not have good ideas for the use of capital beyond lawn maintenance. What I have just assumed has a name in industrial organization theory, borrowed from mathematics. It is called 'supermodularity' between the two activities: the value that entrepreneurs can deliver to their customer is greater if they have capital, and the return they can get on the capital is higher if they find a customer. What supermodularity implies is that E will be able to pay back the investor enough for that person to find it worth investing if, and only if, E finds a customer; and E will be able to provide the customer satisfactory service if, and only if, E finds an investor.

This immediately places the customer and the investor in a quandary. When E tries to get into a contract with each of them, each of them has to form a conjecture about E's productivity. If, for instance, the investor is sophisticated enough to understand the way the world works, the investor will wonder if E will be able to find a customer, since E's ability to repay the investor depends on E's finding a customer. If the investor is unsophisticated, E will simply believe that E can be of two types—high or low productivity (without understanding what makes E either)—and will try to guess which type E is. The practical upshot is the same. The investor has to form a conjecture about E's ability to deliver; likewise, the customer also has to form a conjecture about E's productivity, which depends, in turn, on whether or not the investor invests in E.

Now suppose people form race-based conjectures. They believe that whites are more productive than blacks. Or what amounts to the same thing, they believe that others believe that whites are more productive than blacks. This belief, if acted on by several people, will turn out to be true because of the supermodularity assumption. If lots of people demand your service and interact with you, that actually makes you more productive. This can work for other kinds of identity as well. If it is believed that men are more productive, graduates of Ivy League colleges are more productive, or that someone who speaks proper English can better deliver on the job, then these all will be self-fulfilling for the kind of reason discussed above.

This model has one similarity with Spence's model of job market signaling as well as Stephen Coate and Glenn Loury's model (1993) of affirmative action. Racial prejudices, even when they have no actual basis, get borne out in equilibrium. But the similarity ends there. In those models, innate productivity varies across people, and people use schooling or other indicators to signal their productivity. In my model, the entrepreneurs across races are not only same ex ante but they may not even choose different actions. It is other people's attitude to them that makes them more or less productive. This is an implication of the supermodularity assumption, which, despite its abstract sound, is a worldly and realistic assumption when it comes to entrepreneurship.

It is therefore possible to have an equilibrium where community identity matters, and people of one race or graduates of an elite college get all the contracts and earn more. In other words, the market exhibits racism (or other forms of group discrimination), and the racism or discriminatory practice can be entirely a product of the free market. Note that no person individually is discriminatory, but collectively they all are. So what we have is a phenomenon of 'collective discrimination,' even though there is no individual-level discrimination.

The model carries over easily to the labor market. As observed above, barring some completely mechanical work (tightening screws into cars) or closed-door work (a design artist), most work entails some amount of entrepreneurship. An associate of a law firm would typically have to deal with clients, clerks, judges, and bureaucrats. The value they generate for the company depends on how well they interact with these various agents, and each of these agents will find it worthwhile to interact with the associate if each believes that the associate will be able to interact with the others. If a black associate in a law firm is believed to be less productive, agents that the associate needs to interact with will be reluctant to reciprocate since they will expect to get less from the black associate, and this in turn will make the black associate less productive and less valuable to the firm. No one in this analysis wants to deliberately discriminate, but the market perpetuates collective discrimination.

I am not saying that there is no discrimination in society prompted by innate individual racism but rather showing something even more disturbing: to wit, that even if there were no innate individual racism, we could end up with an outcome that exhibits racism. The invisible hand does not always have to be benevolent. The context that I have just described is different from the one in which the Invisible Hand Theorem works, yet it is no less realistic.

The way to correct the unfairness of the market is by a determined government or other forms of collective action. Different kinds of affirmative action can correct this. For example, subsidizing the education of disadvantaged groups or providing subsidized capital to such groups can help. Of course, in reality failure can be habit forming. Persistent discrimination can lead to habits of tardiness and sloth, and it can take time to break out of these habits. Hence, unlike in the theoretical model, where a subsidy can cause an instantaneous switch in equilibrium, in reality the change can take a long time, and may need sustained effort and some financing for some length of time.

In India, some of the worst discriminatory practices of caste seem to be on the wane. This is not because of the rise of the market. Caste has survived for millennia, through periods when there were virtually no governments, and also through the last years of British rule and the early years of

India's independence when the government was a larger presence. It began to weaken as a consequence of government action that banned caste practices and the repeated appeals of national leaders immediately after the nation's independence.

Models can be put to good and bad uses. Clearly there are lessons in the above analysis for groups that want to engineer discrimination in their favor. A group of people doing some positive discrimination in favor of people of their own type can end up rendering their own types actually more productive and therefore attractive to others. In the final analysis they do not have to deliberately promote their own kind, since once the collective discrimination is in place, their own type will actually be more productive. I do not need to develop this theme any further. There are enough bad ideas floating around without me promoting more by working out a blueprint.

Appendix: Aptitude Test Administered to Slum Children at Anandan in Calcutta

Type I

1. Name India's capital.
2. Is Pakistan part of India?[5]
3. Who is the prime minister of India?
4. Who is the chief minister in West Bengal?
5. What is the name of the highest peak in the world?

Type II

6. There are ten students in a classroom. One student leaves, and two students enter the room. How many students are in the classroom now?
7. There are ten students in a classroom. Each student was asked to bring two biscuits. One student forgot and brought three biscuits. One student did not bring any. How many biscuits are there in the class?
8. The teacher gives fifteen biscuits to six students and asks them to share equally. How many does each student get?

Type III

9. What number should go in the blank space below?
   1, 3, 5, ( )

10. What number should go in the blank space below?

0, 3, 6, 9, ( )

11. What number should go in the blank space below?[6]

1, 0, 12, 0, 123, 0, ( )

12. There are ten girls in a class. Two boys leave. How many girls are left?

13. Red, Blue, Sandesh, and Green go for a stroll.[7] Which one should not have been part of the group?

14. In a strange village, two plus two equals five. There are two biscuits plus two biscuits. Also, there are two other biscuits and two more. How many biscuits are there in this village altogether?

15. From a, b, and c below, choose the one that best fits in the blank space following the three words: hand, head, ear, ( )

a. cat

b. foot

c books

CHAPTER 6

The Chemistry of Groups

Identity and Methodological Individualism

Our sense of self or identity can influence our social, economic, and political behavior. There are people willing to lay down their lives for their flag, boycott products that they believe are produced by an enemy people, and take actions that hurt themselves but hurt people of another religion or ethnicity even more. While there may be ways to contort the traditional models of economics and society to explain such behavior, the more reasonable method is to make explicit room for the individual's sense of group identity in our models. This requires us to step beyond the bounds of methodological individualism or define methodological individualism so tautologically that everything fits into its mold.

As discussed in chapter 3, ever since Carl Menger's classic book in 1883, methodological individualism has been such a deeply entrenched cornerstone of economics that we refuse to admit that persons can act in their national interest, class interest, caste interest, or the interest of humanity at large.[1] The assumption in most of economics is that an individual will act in his or her collective interest—for instance, by providing a public good efficiently—only when the collective interest *happens to* coincide with the individual's self-interest.

Ordinary human beings, unschooled in the social sciences, routinely believe that a group's ability to do well depends on the ability of the group members to hold in abeyance some of their self-interest in order to contribute to the cause of the group. Sociologists, political scientists, and recently some economists have written about the importance of trust and altruism among people, and how these are critical for more complex relationships to thrive as well as for a group or nation to progress economically.[2] Revolutionary writers of colonial times have observed how the imperial masters colluded among themselves and 'divided and ruled' the native inhabitants. The subject of *in-group* trust and altruism is a crucial special case of trust and altruism in general, and it belongs to the larger theme of group identity. The significance of identity and group formation, and the effort to formalize and measure these, are only now beginning to be appreciated in economics.[3] In the social sciences outside of economics, though, this has had currency for quite some time and continues to be a topic of interest.[4]

My analysis here belongs predominantly to positive social science. While I do comment on some normative matters, I deliberately do not take a normative stand on the cooperative spirit, or the ability of individuals to withhold their self-interest in the interests of the group, community, or nation. This may seem quizzical since the cooperative spirit is usually singled out for praise and commendation. But once we ponder on the matter for a while, it becomes evident that the same spirit of cooperation that can promote economic progress and lead to greater wealth can be—and in the long history of humankind there are many instances where it has been—turned *against* other groups, usually minorities, but also majorities that are disorganized and unable to promote their own cooperative spirit of resistance. It is not difficult to see that cooperation promoted by a group, such as a nation, racially homogeneous community, or collectivity of coreligionists, against others can be more ruthless than oppression promoted by individuals. One reason for this is that it allows for the free-riding of guilt. It allows each person to think, "It is not my action that oppresses them because I am a small fry." Hence, the heart of my analysis here is the study of the implications of the cooperative spirit in the mode of positive social science, with the awareness that there may be a case for commending or castigating the cooperative spirit depending on the context.

Models of identity can also be used to study conflict. It is interesting to see how a particular identity can play a major role in our behavior even when it is ex ante of little significance. To me, the intriguing feature of identity for understanding conflict is its malignancy—the fact that it can start innocuously and become large through normal, everyday interaction and exchange. This is not to suggest that all identities take this form. Identity can often be a significant part of our preference (as in Akerlof and Kranton 2000) and the glue that cements society. Yet it remains puzzling as to which of our identifying marks become salient and of consequence in the market, politics, and society.

The malignancy of identity is interesting for three reasons. First, given the rise in conflict in many parts of the world (the Middle East, Kashmir, Sri Lanka, and Northern Ireland), the basis of which is patently that of group identity, the topic deserves attention. Second, there seems to be casual evidence that human differences that remain innocuous over long stretches of history can, over a short time, become markers of passion and conflict. Finally, the possibility of identity emerging out of virtually nowhere seems analytically intriguing.

Each human being has thousands of identifying marks ranging from skin color, ethnicity, and civilizational history, to height, weight, and the contours of the thumb impression. Some of these identifying marks become symbols of identity, and reasons for conflict or cooperation, while others are treated as personal idiosyncrasies.[5] We hear about religious wars, ethnic tensions, and the coming clash of civilizations, but we do not hear about friction between short and tall people, the bald and the hirsute, or those who can do mathematics and those who cannot (though there is an economist friend of mine who believes that this is the next big clash). Using the sociology of human life, one can narrow down the list of identifying marks that can potentially be the source of major conflict and those that cannot. For instance, it is unlikely that there will ever be a pitched battle between men and women, since they have to share living space. There is little scope for any lasting conflict between the old as a group and the collectivity of young because each of us will feel empathy for the other side, knowing that we will be (or have been) in the same boat at some point in time.

Even after we have isolated the list that survives this paring down, there seems to be some indeterminacy about the markers that become sources of conflict. Samuel Huntington (1993) was right in his suggestion that the basis of conflict can undergo major shifts. What seems an unimportant distinction today may become a matter of pride and war tomorrow, and vice versa. Nationalism and its concomitant, patriotism, seem like natural emotions today, and to stand up for these is often seen as noble. But I remain persuaded that if wars do not bring the world to a premature end, there will come a time when we will find it baffling and shameful to contemplate that we once went to war for reasons of patriotism or national identity.[6] Today it appears normal to have newspapers or television channels in the United States count the tragedy of war by reporting the number of Americans who die each day, but we would find it abhorrent if a newspaper reported the number of white or Christian Americans dying each day. But morally, there is not much difference between these different kinds of group identities and presentations of mortality statistics. Hopefully, someday, there will be easy agreement on this.

There is an apocryphal tale about an American Jew who goes to China and meets with a colony of Chinese Jews. On being introduced, the Chinese are pleased but cannot help asking, "Funny, but you don't look Jewish." In telling this joke in a *New York Times* review of Frederic Brenner's book of photographs of Jews from around the world, Grace Glueck (2003a, 2003b) makes the point that much of our identities are constructed rather than innate. The empirical validity of this extreme position can be questioned. But that this *can* be so is a theoretically interesting observation and well worth investigating, since identities can play a major role in conflicts even when they are socially constructed.

One frequently hears people of race X say that they have nothing against people of race Y, yet the latter behave so aggressively toward them that they have no option but to fight back with aggression. There may be truth to these claims. Racial conflict may emerge from no innate racial preference. The basis of such conflicts could be founded on the use of race to form conditional judgments about people's behavior. Moreover, there are contexts where racial conflict is inevitable even though *if* individuals had common knowledge of their preferences, there would be none. Understanding the process that gives rise to such conflict is the key to crafting policy to restrain such conflict. Though I will only briefly comment on policy, the theory that is developed here is motivated by the need to inform ourselves about what causes identity flare-ups and how they can be doused.

One of the most critical results of this model is how the injection of a few people with special preferences can transform a society in harmony into one in which racial groups are balkanized. In particular, the arrival of one new person, aggressively inclined, can transform a peaceful society into one in which people of two races are pitted against one another (and that is then the only equilibrium). Thus, in curing the problem it is important to recognize that a randomly selected person who is aggressive against another group may have no *innate* aggressive preference. This model resists the view of conflict where the 'other' side is innately wicked. There is a tendency among us—one that has been with us from primitive times—to view those on the other side of the bush as evil.

This simplistic propensity has been a major hindrance to understanding conflicts and stopping them. As Hume ([1739] 1969, 397) wrote, "When our nation is at war with any other, we detest them under the character of cruel, perfidious, unjust and violent: But always esteem ourselves and allies equitable, moderate and merciful." To the extent that both sides in a war hold this view, at least one of them must be wrong. Typically, I would argue, both are wrong.

Below I will analyze cases where people have idiosyncratic powers of recognition when it comes to people of their own race and those of another. Much has been written on this topic.[7] To a white colonial master all Rwandans may appear indistinguishable, but the blacks of that region will probably have no problem figuring out who is a Hutu and who a Tutsi.[8] This general idea finds reinforcement in the experiments of James Li, David Dunning, and Roy Malpass (1998), which found that whites who are basketball fans, and therefore familiar with black features (since a disproportionately large number of basketball players are blacks), are better at recognizing black faces than whites who do not watch basketball. The subjects were shown a number of unknown black faces on a video monitor and later tested for their ability to recognize them. Blacks and white basketball fans did equally well, and significantly better than whites who were not basketball fans.

Recognition can give dignity to a group, as Charles Taylor (1994) has argued effectively. But it can do more. It can act as a brake in the escalation of identity wars. When a person from a race or religious group X acts aggressively toward another, if the latter can identify the aggressor as belonging to a smaller group—for example, a sect of X or a member of X with a specific history—then this act of aggression will not taint the person's view of everybody of race X, and this can be a crucial step in the prevention of escalating aggression. That one should get to know one's enemy is therefore not just highfalutin moralistic advice but rather a recommendation for peace that has a foundation in formal theory.

The Ingredients of Theory

It is not within my ability to break away from methodological individualism to the extent that we will eventually need to in order to have a more powerful social science and at the same time retain rigor. What I hope to do in this and the next two sections is take some small, first steps in that direction. To do this successfully, I need to introduce some ingredients of analysis that are not common in mainstream economics. These may be summed up as the need to recognize that (1) the cooperative instinct or the public good urge is innate to human beings, and that (2) this instinct flourishes when it is reciprocated.

By constructing some (admittedly simplistic) models, the next two sections of this chapter will try to show how (1) and (2) can vastly enrich our understanding of social phenomena, such as why some economies succeed and others fail, why some groups advance and others stagnate, and what explains the success of imperial powers and, reciprocally, the succumbing of the colonies.

But let me first elaborate on (1) and (2), for these are not axioms in the formal sense of the term but instead suggestive foundational assumptions. In these assumptions, the term "cooperative instinct" is used in a general sense to cover prosocial characteristics like altruism, a sense of fairness, the urge to trust and be trustworthy, and so on. These assumptions have now found plenty of corroboration in the behavioral economics and experimental game theory literature.[9] In fact, were it not for the huge brainwashing effect of economics, assumptions like these would never have had any novelty value. My main interest here, though, is not in upholding these assumptions but in tracing the analytic consequences of using them in economic theory.

Related to (1) is another key ingredient of my analysis: the need to distinguish between an individual's choice and an individual's welfare or utility. In traditional economics, it is presumed that if a person chooses an alternative x over y, then the person must receive at least as much utility from x as from y. Let me call this the 'choice equals utility' or 'choice equals preference' axiom. This is called 'selfish behavior,' by definition, in microeconomic theory and game theory. This is so fundamental to economics that most economists try to hold on to this assumption even when they concede to (1). Their response is that a person may behave 'altruistically,' but that is only because they get utility from other people's happiness. Hence, the effort is to absorb altruism and other-regarding behavior into a larger concept of selfishness, and to retain the assumption that choice is always equivalent to utility maximization. From a purely behavioral point of view it does not matter if we assume one's other-regardingness as part of one's selfish utility evaluation or something beyond it, which affects a person's choice.[10] The difference occurs in our welfare evaluation of outcomes.

I am here contesting the assumption that choice equals utility. It can be argued that when most economists say that they believe that actions reveal a person's preference (the choice equals utility axiom), they do not really believe in this. If they did, they would be led to some pretty absurd policy positions. Consider the following problem. In the Salt Lake area, which is a large part of the city of Calcutta, homeowners are not allowed to sell their houses. The government sold these homes at subsidized rates to the not-so-rich, and the politicians in charge did not want the rich to deprive these people of their property by buying them up. Thus the law.

To most economists this law seems misconceived, and I agree (Basu 2003a). The reason is the 'Pareto principle,' which as explained in chapter 2, says that any change that makes one or more persons better off and no one worse off should be considered desirable, and therefore should be permitted. Now, when someone wants to sell his or her property and someone else wants to buy it, then by the revealed preference of their choices both of them will be better off by this trade. Permitting this transaction seems to be a 'Pareto improvement.' So this transaction should not be stopped.[11]

But now, if we take the choice equals preference axiom seriously, we will have to admit that since a politician objects to this transaction (this is revealed by the fact of the ban on such transactions), it means that at least one person exists who is worse off by this transaction—to wit, the politician. The deal is thus not a Pareto improvement. In fact, allowing the deal and not allowing it are both Pareto optimal. If it is allowed, the buyer and the seller are better off, but the politician is worse off. If it is not allowed, the buyer and the seller are worse off, but the politician is better off.

By this argument, any time a bureaucrat or politician chooses to stop any transaction, that transaction ceases to be a Pareto improvement, and the orthodox economist should then support such an intervention. In other words, any transaction can be stopped at will by a politician on the grounds that it is not Pareto improving, since the politician's very act of stopping it makes it so. The orthodox economist has clearly got himself (or herself, in case any female economist wishes to be included in this category) trapped into a corner.

The fallacy lies in the choice equals utility axiom. What we need to recognize is that there are different kinds of choices with different kinds of utility implications. A bureaucrat choosing to disallow a transaction is not the same as a person choosing to buy an apple or accept a certain job. It is likely that the bureaucrat's policy choice does not have any direct utility implication for the bureaucrat. This immediately compels us to make distinctions in the notion of preference. Are the utility implications the same for a person who hates jute carpet and therefore does not buy it, and a person who does not buy a jute carpet as a form of boycott against products that use child labor?[12] The latter choice probably does not have a direct utility effect on the buyer; it is akin to a bureaucrat's objection to a certain transaction.

Relatedly, when a politician expresses a preference against an unknown young person's clothing (or the absence of it) and when a mother expresses a preference for her teenaged son's clothing, in the former case there may be no direct utility implications for the person making the choice (hence we will be right to ignore it), whereas the mother may feel actual pain or joy depending on what her son wears. To grant minimal recognition of this problem, in this chapter, I will allow an individual's preference to be represented by two numbers: one that represents the individual's welfare, and one that guides choice. The two numbers will have interconnections, of course; this will be explained later.

Assumption (2) above refers to the fact that our moral preferences have an inherent tendency to reciprocate. Each of us has an intrinsic altruistic urge, but tend to bottle up that urge vis-à-vis individuals who do not evince a similar spirit toward us. I will capture this through the structure of the game that will be described and analyzed later in this chapter.

It should be immediately obvious that once we admit (2), we can understand why, despite our instinctive altruism or social spirit, some societies collapse into selfish disorder, with all individuals serving only their self-interest. Traditional economics has been obsessed with how individual selfishness can lead to cooperative outcomes and social order. By chipping away just a little from the standard methodological individualism assumption, we can understand the reverse, equally important phenomenon of how, despite our natural cooperative spirit, societies can be reduced to utter selfishness and disorder.

In what follows, I employ some simple canonical games to illustrate how the use of these new ingredients can enrich our understanding of social and economic processes.

Altruism, Trust, and Development

The aim here is to understand and formalize what the cooperative instinct does for human society and the economy. People are self-seeking, but they also have other 'social' characteristics like altruism, a sense of fairness, and the public good urge that temper their selfishness. Just as self-interest creates drive and ambition, so can these other, social concerns. More important, it is these other social characteristics—mainly the cooperative instinct—that glue society together and prepare the ground for markets to function effectively. Minimally, a proper understanding of economics requires recognizing that our economic relations are a part of a larger sphere of social and cultural interactions and institutions.[13]

There are many different kinds of games that can be used to understand the connection between trust, altruism, and identity—most notably the Trust game, but also the Ultimatum and the Traveler's Dilemma games.[14] But let me use what is likely the most familiar game in the social sciences, and was discussed earlier: the Prisoner's Dilemma. This is illustrated below in table 6. Though the payoffs are different from those used in chapter 4, the essential story is the same. What is shown above are the dollar payoffs, and I will assume (purely for expositional ease) that each number represents an index of each person's overall well-being measured in utils—units of utility. That is, it is being assumed that utils are a one-on-one match with dollars. So in this game, player 1 can choose between C and D, and likewise for player 2. It is a useful mnemonic to think of C as 'cooperative behavior' and D as 'defection behavior.' If player 1 chooses C and 2 chooses D—something that can equivalently be described as "if players 1 and 2 choose (C,D)"—then player 1 earns zero dollars and player 2 earns eight dollars. If they choose (D,C), they earn eight and zero dollars, respectively, or $(8,0)$, in brief. If they choose (C,C), they earn $(6,6)$, and if they choose (D,D), they earn $(3,3)$. This entire information is summarized in the adjoining table.

TABLE 6
The Prisoner's Dilemma

		Player 2	
		C	D
Player 1	C	6, 6	0, 8
	D	8, 0	3, 3

The standard analysis of the game, it is worth repeating, goes as follows. Place yourself in the shoes of player 1 and observe that if player 2 chooses C, you are better off choosing D instead of C, since that way you get eight dollars instead of six. And if player 2 chooses D, you are better off choosing D instead of C, since D gives you three dollars and C gives you zero. Hence, no matter what the other player does, it is better for you to choose D.[15] Because the game is symmetrical for the two players, each player will reason the same way. The outcome will be (D,D)—both players will choose defection—and so they will earn three dollars each. It is an unfortunate outcome, since they could have earned six dollars each if both chose C, the cooperative strategy.[16]

In reality, people do not just maximize their own dollar incomes or even their own utilities (in the present analysis these are the same). People have feelings for their fellow human beings, altruism, a sense of fairness, and the urge not to hurt others (or in some cases, to hurt others). To keep the analysis as simple as possible, I will simply allow for one kind of social feeling in this formal analysis: altruism.[17] This is captured by assuming that one dollar (or what is assumed to be the same here, 1 util) earned by the other player is valued by this player as equal to α dollars of his or her own, where α is some number between zero and one. Later I shall allow for the possibility of α varying depending on who the other player is. Thus, my index of altruism, α, may be 1 for kin, ½ for kith, and 0 for an alien, and so on. For now, however, let us treat this as fixed. So if player 1 plays C and player 2 plays C, player 1's behavior is predicted by treating the player's *effective payoff* as 6 + 6 α.

Two important clarifications are worth placing on record here. First, one question that may arise in the reader's mind is about the meaning of selfishness. It appears at first sight that once the α is treated as a part of a person's preference, the person can, from then on, be thought of being perfectly selfish, since it is *the person's preference* to give a weight of α to others' income. So it seems probable that given the preference as just described, the person is just as selfish as a person who values only his or her own dollars.[18] The problem with this critique, as discussed above, is that it reduces selfishness to a tautology; selfishness then becomes impervious to criticism. To counter this, what has to be kept in mind is that contrary to what many economists claim, it is not a tautological definition of selfishness that economics uses. Economists would not have been able to derive any testable proposition if they did so, because all behavior would then be compatible with selfishness, and so the selfishness assumption would not be able to predict any particular behavior.

Therefore, the way I view α here is not as an innate part of a person's utility but instead simply as a guide to a person's *behavior*. This is where the separation between choice and utility occurs; α is something that we typically acquire through socialization. Indeed, it may not be a part of our preference; it could be that we merely behave *as if* we valued other people's dollars by that amount. A player's welfare or level of utility is measured throughout by the payoffs shown in table 6. It is simply that people do not play to maximize their utility but rather a hybrid of their utility along with their social and moral values captured by α. Consider a person who gives a thousand dollars to a charity in Africa. It would be reasonable to say that this person chose to give this money (that would be a pretty normal use of English). But would we say that he or she is better off by giving the thousand dollars to the charity? Many mainstream economists would say yes. I would contest this, and argue that the person *is* worse off (in terms of most reasonable interpretations of well-being and personal happiness), but that the person nevertheless chose to make that little sacrifice for a good cause.[19] Otherwise, "making a sacrifice" would have to be removed from our lexicon. This divergence between the index of individual well-being and what guides individual behavior needs some getting used to since it is alien to traditional choice theory. Fortunately, there is a small literature in game theory that inclines toward this.[20]

To sum up, there are three indicators associated with each person: the dollars earned, the utility enjoyed, and what I call the 'effective payoff.'[21] Here I treat the first two as the same. This is an innocuous assumption, made purely for expositional convenience. I treat the third as distinct from the other two, in the spirit of the discussion above. This is a significant assumption—one that is crucial to my analysis. What is being assumed, then, is that the effective payoff numbers are guides to human behavior. People behave as if they are maximizers of those numbers. Their well-being is related to but distinct from those numbers, though. The well-being numbers are given in table 6, and the effective payoffs are the numbers we get by making the α-based corrections to them, as explained above.

Second, while formally what I am modeling is altruism rather than trust, it is reasonable to think of the model as an idiom for trust or other indicators of a person's sense of society. As will be evident soon, a person's likelihood of cooperation depends on the expectation that the other person will cooperate. Hence, we could think of the player's decision as follows. If the player trusts that the other person will cooperate, then the player will be more inclined to cooperate.[22] While explicitly that of altruism, the analysis that follows from this could also be thought of as a mutual trust model.

We could similarly introduce stigma into the model by assuming that there is some stigma attached to being selfish and playing D. Of course, the person who chooses D need not be selfish but instead could be playing this in anticipation of the other player choosing D. But one of the functions of stigmatization, as pointed out by Herbert Gans (1972), is to scapegoat individuals in order to maintain certain norms of behavior. Further, in a more sophisticated and realistic model, we may wish to allow for the fact that the α I attach to the other player's utility would generally depend on how this was achieved. I may attach a higher α to the other player's utility if he or she achieved it through (C,C) than through (C,D). I will stay away from such complications here.

Suppose we have a society with lots of individuals, and players are randomly matched with each other and made to play the Prisoner's Dilemma. Note that a society in which players cooperate a lot will become richer over time. This is because they will have a higher income that way. And if we append to this simple model a larger economy so that people can save a part of their income (over and above what they need to consume) and earn interest on that, then a society that manages to reach the outcome (C,C) often could become many times more prosperous than a society that always reaches the outcome (D,D). If, for instance, 3 is subsistence consumption, then the latter society will presumably have no savings, whereas the former will not only earn more but also save and become even richer in the long run.

Keeping in mind that the cooperative spirit, captured here by the altruism parameter, is natural to human beings, I want to first show how the same group of people may behave differently. As such, by looking at differences in behavior we should not jump to conclusions about fundamental differences in people's orientation or preferences. Aggressive behavior and cooperation can both emerge from the same group of people.

Consider a case where everybody's altruism parameter, α, is given by half. Then, if the other player cooperates and I cooperate, I will get an effective payoff of nine dollars (or utils), or six from what I directly get myself and three that is my valuation of the other person's gain of six dollars. This is easy to see from table 6. Likewise, if the other player plays C and I play D, my effective payoff is eight dollars. Next suppose the other player is going to choose D. If I choose C, I get an effective payoff of four dollars, and if I choose D I get an effective payoff of four dollars and fifty cents.

Observe now that the strategic nature of the interaction has changed. If I am assured that the other person will play C, I will play C. If, on the other hand, I expect the other person to play D, I will prefer to play D. Once we allow for a modicum of altruism, the Prisoner's Dilemma effectively becomes an Assurance or Coordination game, both of which we encountered in an earlier chapter. As always with the Assurance game, we now have multiple equilibria. The same society can behave totally cooperatively or noncooperatively. By seeing one society behaving cooperatively and getting prosperous, and another remaining disorderly, selfish, and poor, we cannot conclude that there are innate differences between the people of these societies. It could simply be the case of both behaviors being self-sustaining in equilibrium, and so two ex ante identical societies could exhibit different kinds of outcomes.

To complete the taxonomy, it can be checked that α being one-half is not the only case where we get multiple equilibria. If people's altruism, α, lies anywhere between one-third and three-fifths, the society will have multiple equilibria. On the other hand, if altruism is low—in particular, if α is less than one-third—then this society will never have cooperation, since all persons will prefer action D, *no matter what they expect others to do*. The other polar case occurs if altruism is high—in particular, if α exceeds three-fifths. Then cooperation is the only equilibrium. Each person prefers to cooperate no matter how others behave.

Models of this kind can also lead to threshold effects, as in Granovetter and Soong (1983), whereby behavior can swing over from one extreme to another—say, from peace to strife—in response to a small exogenous shock. One kind of change that can do this in a somewhat unusual manner, which I will discuss later, is the arrival of a few people with a determinedly aggressive attitude.

There is some important policy wisdom that emerges from the above model. What I have modeled here as altruism is part of a generalized idea of trust, other-regardingness, and the social spirit. There are situations in life— for instance, in starting a business—where we have to take the risk of vulnerability for the business to work. This is akin to playing C in the Prisoner's Dilemma. If your business partner (player 2) is cooperative (chooses C), you both do well, but if the partner betrays your trust, you will do badly (get zero). As already suggested, the altruism parameter α could also be thought of as a propensity to trust. So what this model shows is that altruism and trust are critical ingredients for a society to do well and prosper. In the present model I have treated α as exogenous. But we know at an intuitive level that people (especially children) can be taught or inspired to be more or less altruistic, more or less trustworthy, and more or less trusting.[23] One person being more altruistic (having a high α) would not help that person economically. In fact, such a person would be vulnerable to being cheated. But if *at a societal level* all individuals were more trusting—for example, with α going from less than one-third to over one-third, then there would be the possibility of greater cooperation, and if α went above three-fifths, cooperation would occur for sure, with all the attendant economic benefits of higher income.

Greater altruism and trust among a people is therefore like a public good. We do not fully understand how exactly a government or an educational institute can create as well as nurture a more altruistic society.[24] But at the same time, we do know that these traits change and can be changed. People can be taught not to litter in the streets. Societies can cultivate habits of charity. Corporations can become environmentally conscious or develop other forms of codes of ethics (Sacconi 2000). Even if we do not as yet understand how these things happen, it is important to recognize that unselfishness and altruism, or more minimally, the capacity for these traits, are innately present in human beings and so can potentially be nurtured and modified; and that such traits are valuable for development. So much of standard economics was a celebration of selfishness that we did not even make room for the fact that greater altruism is a useful trait and can contribute to economic efficiency. At one level, we have known this since the arrival of game theory. Yet the awareness has not spread widely enough to reach popular discourse, and as I also try to argue in this book, these observations have roots that go beyond standard game theory.

The analysis developed here can be extended to heterogeneous societies— in particular, where the cooperative spirit varies across individuals. This allows us to illustrate how the introduction of a few noncooperative individuals can cause cooperation to unravel totally. The basic idea is easy to convey in words. Recall, as we assumed above, that people like to cooperate typically when the recipient of their generosity or altruism reciprocates the generosity. If the intensity of the cooperative spirit varies across individuals, once societies harbor a few die-hard noncooperators, individuals who have the weakest cooperative urge—that is, they need the strongest assurance that the other players in the game will cooperate—will now cease to cooperate (since with the introduction of the die-hard noncooperators in society, the probability that you will be pitched against a diehard becomes positive). Once these weak cooperators start behaving noncooperatively, the probability of being pitched against a player who plays noncooperatively goes up even more, thereby making even more people opt to play noncooperatively, which in turn further raises the probability of meeting a noncooperative player. Cooperation can unravel altogether by this process. A simple example illustrates this idea.

Suppose society consists of two kinds of people: those with an altruism level of one-third (that is, their α equals one-third), and those with an altruism level five-elevenths. Let us call them, respectively, people of types A and B. Note that type Bs are more altruistic. Assume that the population of this society is large, say, one billion, and half of them are type A and half are type B. As assumed before, a person's type is not outwardly visible. So when an individual in this society is matched to play another individual, all each person knows is that there is half probability that the other person is type A and half probability that the other person is type B.[25] Suppose to start with that all players decide to play cooperatively. It is easy to check using table 6 that people of type A will be indifferent between playing C and D, and people of type B will prefer to play C. Hence, no one has a reason to deviate and behave differently. In other words, everybody being cooperative is a Nash equilibrium.

Now suppose one completely nonaltruistic person arrives in this land. This person's α is zero. So this person will always play D. Unlike earlier, when a person is matched randomly with some player to play the Prisoner's Dilemma, the person will now know that there is a tiny possibility that the other person will play D. It is easy to see that this is enough to make people of ethnicity A abandon cooperative behavior and switch to playing D. So now when you meet a person at random, the chance of that person playing C is certainly less than a half, even if you do not know by how much. Recall that all type As and the one new person all play D. It can be checked that for type Bs, that is reason enough to switch to D. In other words, the introduction of one congenitally noncooperative person can have a domino effect, resulting in a total breakdown in cooperation.[26]

Since I derive this result using simple arithmetic, one may have the impression that what I just described is just a special case. In reality, one can extend the same logic to consider more general cases where people have differing levels of altruism, but to start with, they all cooperate. The entry of one innately noncooperative person in this society can have a huge domino effect, making the least altruistic person switch to aggressive behavior, thereby vitiating the atmosphere a bit and prompting the next least altruistic person to abandon cooperative behavior. This will worsen the atmosphere further, prompting altered behavior on the part of the next in line, and so on, until cooperation breaks down altogether. The logic is exactly the kind described in the simple example above.

The Janus Face of In-group Altruism

We usually treat altruism as a desirable trait, and most often it is. There are, however, important contexts where that is not so. This happens most frequently (though not always) when there is in-group altruism—that is, when a person's altruism is restricted to people with whom they identify. I will argue here that in-group altruism can be a bit Janus-faced. It can result in the creation of wealth, prosperity, and goodwill, but it can also be a powerful instrument of oppression and exploitation of other groups.[27]

This recognition of the human ability, and indeed propensity, to differentiate between in-groups and the rest is a critical ingredient for a deeper understanding of the history of development, why some nations have grown and others have failed, and why some groups have prospered and others have stagnated. To try to understand these without the chemistry of groups is a handicap, and one that conventional economics has had to contend with. The reason why traditional economics made so little room for this is an unwitting consequence of the kind of methodological individualism utilized by the discipline.[28]

The assumption that we can fully describe the individual without reference to society, that individuals are powered by utility maximization, and that each person's utility is a function of the person's consumption, savings, and wealth creation is a useful assumption for a lot of analysis, and has contributed to the elegance of economic theory. But this same convenient methodology has also blinded us to some facets of reality.

To make room for this, we have to first allow for the kind of norms-based behavior discussed in chapter 3—namely, that human beings can and do hold back on many a personal gain in order to live by certain customs, and in order to be part of society. From this it is just another step to allow for the fact that these little gestures could well be dependent on the person and, in particular, the group that one is interacting with. I may respect the property boundaries of individuals (even when they are not walled or policed) when I am in my own nation, but not respect that when I have landed somewhere else. This group specificity of norms-based behavior and altruism opens the door to a much richer analysis of economic development along with the prosperity or poverty of nations and groups. The terrain is large; all I want to do here is to take some first, tentative steps.

I will not deal here with general social norms but rather, for reasons of simplicity, only with altruism and other-regarding behavior. In the sections above, it was assumed that the altruism that person i feels is directed toward everybody. Of course, that need not be so. People do have different ethics and altruism for in-groups and out-groups. There are many societies fractured along lines of race, gender, religion, country of origin, languages, and caste, and people often show extra trust and have an altruism premium for those with whom they share some a common identity.[29] Furthermore, there are some groups that are known to have the quality of being more trustworthy. Others are then willing and more eager to do trade and business with such groups, and these groups, as a consequence, tend to do well in the relevant markets.

In the early 1980s, soon after settling down in Delhi, I tried to buy a used car and went through a copious amount of newspaper advertisements. I was impressed that many of these advertisements would mention that the car was owned by a "South Indian lady." It soon became clear to me what was happening. Many in India believe that South Indians are the more dependable people, and that women are more trustworthy than men. Since political correctness never gets in the way of free speech in poor countries, advertising that a car was owned by a South Indian woman was a way of telling potential buyers in the treacherous world of used cars that they were buying the car from a trustworthy source. So strong was the urge among North Indian males to signal that they were South Indian females that, frequently, the information in the advertisement was doubly false. On several occasions, when after having talked to the North Indian man showing me the car, I asked to see the owner, I was told that "she was away on government duty," thereby giving another cue of the owner's goodness, since duty to one's government is widely viewed as more noble than devotion to one's own business. It is not difficult to see that if a real South Indian lady who frequently was away on government assignments wanted to sell her car, she would have a natural advantage.

Hardened economists are generally troubled by this. How can this situation persist? Surely *individual* South Indians will take advantage of this good reputation of their *group* to cheat customers and do better individually. As more and more of them do so, the good reputation of their group will get eroded. I do not deny that this possibility exists, but to believe that this will necessarily happen is to make the mistake of methodological individualism, and fail to recognize that people do have an innate cooperative spirit or the public good urge. And when this is sufficiently hardwired into one's psyche, one may not think twice about letting go of the possibility of small individual gains in order to be true to one's values.[30]

To return from this digression, the general point seems valid that there can be group-specific differences in trust and trustworthiness. With this recognition comes the possibility of many complexities. The simplest case is where in-group trust partitions the society into different alcoves, within each of which there is trust and altruism, and across which there may be little of those social feelings. But situations can also arise where i treats j as belonging to i's in-group, unaware that this feeling is not reciprocated. Cooperation in a nation or group can break down when there are these crosscutting allegiances. If a nation tries to create solidarity among its citizens, but a subset of citizens have allegiance to an identity different from that of mere citizenship, then cooperation can break down.

Moreover, in the previous section altruism always led to good outcomes. But in a society that is fractured, with altruism and trust confined to in-groups, these traits can become instruments of group oppression—where one group oppresses another, building up greater power in the oppressing group than it would have managed if the members of the group tried to atomistically carry out the oppression.

These directions of inquiry would take a lot of time and effort to pursue. What I can do here is take some tentative steps to illustrate the scope of research that opens up once we allow altruism to be limited to those with whom a person shares a common identity. Where this sense of identity comes from, whether it is malleable or permanent, and whether it can be contained from malignancy are large topics, and while there has been some exploration into them, much remains to be written.[31] Here I will treat these altruism characteristics as primitives by simply assuming that when playing such games, people make use of some preexisting sense of identity to decide how they will classify their opponents and how they evaluate their dollar payoffs.

Let me return to the assumption where α is a constant and equal to $\frac{1}{2}$. It is not as if I am assuming that everybody feels altruism toward everybody else but rather that when i feels altruism toward j, it is always at a constant altruism parameter of α. We could in principle allow the αs to differ across people, but that would complicate the analysis unnecessarily, and more important, complicate it beyond the capability of the author.

Suppose society consists of two groups. Let a fraction p belong to group A, which can represent race, caste, or the fact of having belonged to the same college fraternity, and the rest belong to group B. If we suppose that people feel (instinctively or through cultivation) altruism only for their own group members, then we could do the same analysis as in the section above, but think of each group as a society. The analysis then is trivial. When people play across groups, they are selfish—they choose D. But within each group there could be cooperation or defection, as in the above section. So we could, for instance, have an equilibrium, where group A cooperates and progresses economically, whereas group B is a fractious community living in poverty and disarray.

A more interesting case arises where the group B people think of A *and B* as a common identity—that is, their identity is a general national identity—whereas those in group A share an in-group identity. One special case is where members of group A recognize each other, because, say, they belong to a secret society and have a secret handshake, whereas to members in B everybody (individuals of types A and B) looks the same.

Assume that members of B feel altruism for all individuals in this society. In any case, since they cannot tell who belongs to A and who belongs to B, they cannot harbor different feelings toward different people of different groups. But members of A can tell a member of A from a nonmember, and they have cultivated altruism α only toward their own group members.

Now, when a type B meets another player, the probability that the other player will not cooperate is not less than p. This is because type As do not cooperate with type Bs. If p is sufficiently small it could be worthwhile for each type B to cooperate. Every now and then they will get jilted by their opponent who will not cooperate, but if the population of As is small and all the Bs cooperate, then it is worthwhile for all the Bs to cooperate. Given the numbers in table 6, it can be shown that the technical condition under which this happens is when the population of type As is less than two-thirds of the entire society's population. Let us suppose this is true, and that all type Bs cooperate. Type As, on the other hand, cooperate only with their own types.

In this equilibrium, type As earn an expected *dollar* income of $6p + 8(1-p)$ every time they play the Prisoner's Dilemma. This is because whenever they meet a type A (probability p), they earn six dollars, and when they meet a type B (the trusting type whom they let down), they earn eight dollars.

On the other hand, the expected income of each type B is $6(1-p)$. Hence, type As earn more than Bs. But not just that: by forming an in-group collusive block, type As earn even more than what they would have if they cooperated with the entire population. The latter would give them a per game income of six dollars. It is the ability to exploit the out-group members that gives them the extra edge.

There is a Machiavellian lesson tucked away in this algebra. Consider the case in which the population of type As is sufficiently large that the above equilibrium does not work. If all the As play action D against the Bs, the type Bs will get cheated too often to trust strangers and so they will also begin to play noncooperatively.

It is in the interest of type As, however, to get them to play cooperatively, because that way they can be better 'exploited.' One way of restoring the 'exploitative equilibrium' is for the type As to decide, collusively, not to play D against the type Bs always and to occasionally play C. This will enable them to delude the type B masses into believing that they all share one common identity, and then play collusively at all times and end up getting exploited. This is a rather repugnant strategy for group A to use; what this model does is to alert us that there can be subgroups of people who use such a strategy.[32]

It is in fact likely that some of the most successful colonial exploitations relied, deliberately or unwittingly, on strategies of this kind. For a ruling oligarchy or race keen on exploiting the masses, a useful strategy is to disrupt the formation of identity among the masses by picking out some from among them, and enriching them and giving them a modicum of power. This will create the feeling among the masses that they can make it if they try. The ruling race can facilitate this feeling by frequently pointing to the few who have made it. Whenever a group becomes restive, the technique is to disrupt group identity by weaning away some key figures into the folds of the elite. This was routinely done by the apartheid regime in South Africa. One also sees this among some conservative intellectuals in the United States today, who are wary that blacks will get restless about their widespread poverty and demand more. They draw attention to how blacks have done well by pointing to the few who have, or by pointing to not how they have done vis-à-vis whites (since they have done badly by comparison) but instead using the dubious benchmark of other failed societies, which has the subtext that they have done well and so should be content. Here is Pat Buchanan on the subject: "America has been the best country on earth for black folks. It was here that 600,000 black people, brought from Africa in slave ships, grew into a community of 40 million, were introduced to Christian salvation, and reached the greatest levels of freedom and prosperity blacks have ever known."[33]

I should clarify that it would be wrong to presume intentionality every time we observed this kind of behavior, which enabled the exploitation of one group by another. As, in reality, with those who are oppressed, oppressors are also a mixed bag. A study of the colonial history of India should leave one in no doubt that there were many among the British rulers in India who were genuinely interested in helping the lot of their colonial subjects, some of whom believed that this was indeed their mission there. This was true not just for some minions in the colonial administration but also for some of the rulers appointed by the Crown to administer India. But intentions are one thing and consequences are another. What I am claiming is that when one group rules over another while cohabiting the same space, the behavior patterns of the rulers take the form that I have just described so as to lull the oppressed into believing that they all have common interests and a common identity. In fact, the presence of some good people among the oppressors may in effect turn out to be the facilitating factor for the oppression to persist, for it has the effect of raising the level of cooperation with the ones being controlled up to the mark that makes their belief of common identity credible. Modern India's founding father, Gandhi, it is worth recalling, believed for many years that the Indians and British were equal partners in the subcontinent, and resisted the call for independence from early radicals. It took many incidents and actions on the part of the Crown before he changed his mind.

One question that may arise is about the general applicability of these results, since all the derivations here are using the Prisoner's Dilemma example and a certain class of payoffs. This would indeed be cause for concern if I were trying to establish general results—what will always be true in society. Instead, the aim of this chapter is to illustrate how society *can* exhibit certain kinds of behavior that have been treated as impossible in our textbook models of the economy and society. I have just shown how some groups can use their innate traits of (in-group) altruism and trust to control or even exploit other groups. I am not claiming that this will always happen but rather that it can happen under plausible conditions. Hence, the depiction of this argument with a game that is accepted as a good model for some social situations suffices in the present context. Testing the frontiers of its generalization would be an interesting exercise for the future.

The discussion of in-group trust draws attention to another difficulty that could arise with identity-based collusive behavior. As we have already seen, even if people want to trust others and cooperate, one problem could arise from there being no 'focal identity' in the society. In the section above, I assumed that an entire nation shares a common identity and is bound by a common altruism toward all.

One variant of this problem can lead to a total failure of cooperation in society. It is well recognized that we have multiple identities, and that this can often (in fact, I believe, more often than not) help societies stay united (Sen 2006; Dahrendorf 1959). But this can also lead to a failure of cooperation. To see this, suppose people in a country resolve to be cooperative among those with whom they share their primary identity. If this society lacks a focal identity or has overlapping identities instead of partitioned identities, cooperation may fail to occur in equilibrium.

Suppose in a nation there are two races, 1 and 2, two religions, 1 and 2, and two language groups, 1 and 2. Using notation in an obvious way, we can describe a person as $(1,2,1)$ or $(2,2,1)$, and so on, where $(1,2,1)$ means a person of race 1, religion 2, and language group 1. Let me use A to denote the set of all people of type $(1,2,1)$, B to denote all those of type $(1,1,2)$, and C to denote $(2,1,1)$. Assume that one-third of the population is of type A, one-third is of type B, and one-third of type C. As explained earlier, I also assume that the population is large, so that when an individual knows his or her own type, it does not affect the player's calculation of the probability of another random player's type.

Let us now assume that all As think that race is the primary identity (that is, they try to be cooperative with all those who share their race), all Bs think that religion is the primary identity, and all Cs think that one's mother tongue is the primary identity. In this society, each person will find that at least half of the time when they expect the other player to be their type and so cooperate, the other player chooses to defect. Under reasonable conditions, this does not make it worthwhile for anybody to cooperate.

This has the policy implication that if a government or some collectivity wants to encourage cooperative behavior in the country or among its members, it must try to create a focal identity among its citizens. Various repressed groups that fail to rise collectively against their oppressor probably do so for reasons of an absence of a focal identity among themselves. This is an equally useful result for a tyrant or powerful government trying to prevent some group or nation from acting cooperatively within itself. The aim must be to destroy the group's ability to form a focal identity. Through a deliberate policy of splintering the group's identity into various overlapping and conflicting identities, it can keep the group under control and keep the possibility of group rebellion at bay. At times this happens naturally. During the rise of colonialism, small imperial countries established control over large swathes of people. This is impossible to understand until one brings identity and trust into the picture. The handful of British officers who established control over India had a shared identity and in-group altruism, which enabled them to make personal sacrifices to enhance the cause of the group. The Indians, on the other hand, had no focal identity. In many ways, the idea of India itself was born through the experience of colonial subjugation, and so was not available to counter the subjugation.

The model above is best treated as an allegory of the real world. Nevertheless, it points to policy, and like all science, it does so whether our aim is noble or mean. It indicates how to prosper economically, and offers hints and suggestions for people trying to cooperate among themselves and escape oppression, and also for people wanting to cooperate in order to oppress others. It shows, for example, that one way to exploit a large mass of people is to form a collusive subgroup, the members of which identify primarily with the subgroup, but deludes the large mass into believing that it identifies totally with the large mass. Of course, and mercifully, the subgroup's effort can be foiled by other subgroups trying to do the same.[34] If too many opportunistic groups come into existence, society could crumble into the low-output equilibrium of selfish disorder. Such kinds of behavior are not morally commendable, but being positive theory, the analysis simply interprets how the world works. This knowledge can be put to good or bad use.

A central lesson that emerges from this allegory, and one that contrasts sharply with popular wisdom, concerns the ubiquitous invisible hand. The Invisible Hand Theorem, which has come down to us from Smith, and was discussed at length in chapters 2 and 3, has had enormous influence in shaping economic policy.[35] It also has been prominent in the advice that various think tanks and organizations, not to mention legions of economists, have given to the governments of developing countries. One inadvertent implication of the theorem that many have taken away from it, and that has had considerable influence on the organization of our economic and social life as well as on the way we conduct ourselves, is that it is fine to be selfish, since in the end, thanks to the coordinating power of the invisible hand of the market, this leads to a good outcome for society at large. This selfishness axiom has in recent times spilled over into other disciplines, such as parts of sociology and the new political science.

We are taught that not only are consumers and producers self-seeking but so are politicians, bureaucrats, and judges, and more significantly, that this situation is fine. This has some alarming consequences. It means, as discussed in chapter 3, that all we can expect of judges is for them to pass verdicts that best serve their own interests. So the only way to make judges and magistrates issue a just verdict is to design the institutional and incentive structure of the courts in such a way that it is in each judge's self-interest to be just.

This ubiquitous philosophy has been damaging not only socially and morally but also in terms of economic growth and development, because the truth about development is that it needs human beings to be other-regarding, fair, and trustworthy.[36] Since these traits are innately available to most of us, what we need is not to have them muted through training and socialization. Take the problem of bureaucratic corruption, which has been eating into the fabric of so many societies and blighting the possibility of development. The standard policy response to this, inspired by the popularity of the Invisible Hand Theorem and the visible global economists, is to argue that government ought to redesign the system of incentives and punishments for bureaucrats. What we do not say is that the ubiquity of corruption has a lot to do with the lack (or more appropriately, suppression) of personal integrity and individual moral commitments (Minkler and Miceli 2004). The design of incentives plays a role, but our own sense of values and morals plays a bigger one. Governments that are noncorrupt are largely so not because of third-party monitoring of such corruption but instead because of the self-monitoring of bureaucrats and politicians. There is no scope for this in standard economics and economic sociology because these disciplines provide little space for *self*-monitoring.[37]

There is no reason to believe that countries with rampant corruption are populated by citizens who are innately less moral; rather, they *act* less morally in equilibrium. This is related to the findings from the celebrated experiments by Robert Frank, Tom Gilovich, and Dennis Regan (1993). They showed that in games where one can be selfish to different degrees, economists play the most selfishly. There are different ways of interpreting the result, but I take the view that since economists learn from their textbooks that every-body is selfish and it is fine to be selfish, they try to conform to what they take to be standard behavior.[38] In corrupt environments, people begin to treat corruption as the norm (moreover, deviating from that norm also has larger costs than in more honest environments), and like economists in the above-mentioned experiments, they try to replicate what they take to be normal behavior.[39]

In the early 1990s, I used to take a team of research students to a cluster of villages in one of the most lawless and poor regions of India—now in the state of Jharkhand. Seeing the utter chaos in the region, the hollowness of the pop-ular advice that what India needs is less government was evident. There was no trace of any government there for 'less government' to be a feasible option. Also, there was no dearth of individually selfish behavior. What was lacking was the fauna and flora of social values that make economic development pos-sible. What these villages had perfectly re-created was what some economists recommend: a complete resignation to unfettered self-interest. This observa-tion holds true beyond the villages that we were studying. Contrary to what many textbooks teach us, the regions of the world that are economically the biggest disasters are the ones that are in many ways models of the free market, with amoral individuals seeking nothing but their own self-aggrandizement, no trace of law, and a suppression of individual respect for fairness and justice.

The starkest examples of this appear in the streets of third world coun-tries. Drivers are willing to break every rule in the book and show a relent-less commitment to serving their own interests, swerving through traffic with abandon. With little evidence of any intervention from traffic police, the streets of the third world should be textbook cases of neoclassical efficiency. The fact that they are not should alert us to the possibility that the central message of so many of our textbooks may be wrong.

Human beings are not innately selfish, though they can learn to be so if it is drilled into them that that is normal or they grow up in societies caught in an ethos of totally selfish behavior. If we want society to progress and eco-nomic development to occur, we need to nurture our innate sense of social values—such as altruism, trustworthiness, integrity, and a sense of fair play. And if we do not want the world to be fractured and broken up into oppressors and the oppressed, we should try to inculcate these values across all human beings and not just narrow in-groups, defined by race, religion, or nationality.

The Malignancy of Identity

The framework developed thus far can help us better understand one of the most urgent problems of our times: the clash of identities and civilizations. Why do identities that may have been no more than dormant markers for long periods of history sometimes flare up into symbols of conflict and aggression? When people say that they have no latent animus toward the other group but behave as though they do, can they be speaking the truth? The tools of analysis developed in this chapter enable us to supply at least some answers to these kinds of questions.[40]

As I did before, I will allow for the fact that the actual payoffs that an individual earns may be different from the numbers that guide the individual's choice. The basic game that I will use here, introduced early in chapter 4, is variously called the Assurance game (Sen 1967) and the Coordination game (see, for instance, Weibull 1995). This was described in table 3, in chapter 4, and will be referred to here as the 'basic game.'

Consider a nation with lots of individuals. Each person has certain visible characteristics—that is, visible to all—and some invisible characteristics that the person knows about but others do not. For reasons of simplicity I will assume that the visible characteristic is race, and again to keep the analysis simple assume that a person's race can be either black, B, or white, W. And I will assume that the invisible characteristic captures a person's affinity for their own type (that is, who is visibly like them). The workings of the invisible characteristic will be explained later.

Individuals in this economy get paired off randomly and play the basic game against each other. The payoffs in the basic game should be thought of as direct, visible payoffs that players receive. For simplicity, we can think of the numbers as dollar payments, and these payoffs are presumed to be common knowledge. The strategies A and C denote "aggressive" and "cooperative" behavior, respectively. As always with games, the left-hand number in each box denotes the payoff earned by the player choosing between rows, and the right-hand number denotes the payoff of the player choosing between columns. So if player i chooses C and j chooses A—that is, i opts to be cooperative, while j opts for aggression—then we can see from the payoff matrix of the basic game described in chapter 4 that i will get one dollar and j will get nine dollars.

The game captures the idea that cooperative behavior leads to desirable outcomes, but one does not like to be cooperative when one's opponent is being aggressive. There are many different interpretations possible for this game. Action A could be an act of violence against the other player, and the game could represent people's penchant for hitting back at someone who hits you. Die-hard pacifists do not figure in this game.

Another interpretation, the more widely applicable one, is where C stands for cooperative behavior, such as in business, and A stands for cutthroat behavior in business. To be cooperative against a cutthroat is to do badly. If both can be cooperative, they both do well. It would have been possible to use a more elaborate game (as, for instance, in Basu 2000, sec. 4.6) where being cutthroat in business is always in one's individual interest, but for the purposes of this chapter the additional complication would not be worth it. In other words, the idea being captured here is in the spirit of Francis Fukuyama's discussion (1996) of how trust among a people can aid their progress and prosperity. In this game, if a group of people can trust one another and play cooperatively, they will earn more and prosper.

There are two Nash equilibria in this game, (A, A) and (C, C), that is, choices of strategy such that, given the other player's strategy, no one would prefer to unilaterally change the strategy. If (A, A) were to occur, each player would earn two dollars, and if (C, C) were to occur, each player would earn ten dollars. Hence, game theorists who believe that when several equilibria are available people manage to coordinate on a Pareto superior outcome, would predict the outcome in the basic game to be (C, C). For the most part, I will go along with this presumption.

When the two players are of different races, the game that they play is not the basic game, however, because there may be psychic costs and benefits involved in being aggressive and cooperative (that is, each player's invisible characteristic now comes into play), over and above the commonly visible payoffs described in table 3.[41] The actual game that two players, i and j, of different races and matched against each other at random, play is a little different from the basic game because now we have to factor in the psychic costs and benefits.

Let us allow that people have a small psychic cost in being cooperative with a person of a different race. In particular, an individual i feels a cost of c_i when the individual plays cooperatively with a player of a different race. This psychic cost can vary from individual to individual, and unlike the payoffs of the basic game, are not visible to others. This will introduce some uncertainty into the minds of each player when there is an interracial game. Each player will have to play without knowing how large the other person's psychic cost is. This is akin to what we have already seen in the previous sections: each person's altruism parameter is not visible to others.

I will assume throughout that the psychic cost has a value of anywhere from 0 to 2. There can be different interpretations of this cost. For the most part, c_i is to be interpreted as follows: it captures the innate unfriendliness that person i feels toward an alien—that is, someone different. It could be thought of as a person's index of chauvinism. The psychic costs may also be referred to as a player's latent characteristic, since it is not visible to others.

If $c_i = 0$, then person i makes no distinction between an own type and an alien. In the present context, people are race blind. As long as c_i is less than 1, a player prefers to respond to cooperative behavior with cooperation. This should be obvious from table 3. The outcome (C,C) now gives player i a payoff of 10-c_i. If c_i is less than 1, this is greater than 9. Since (A,C) gives player i a return of 9, the player is better off responding to the other player's C with a C. Hence, from now on I will refer to all individuals whose c_i happens to be less than 1 as cooperators.

If c_i exceeds 1, player i prefers to be aggressive vis-à-vis anybody who is visibly different *from* i, irrespective of what action the person chooses.[42] This is easily verified using the payoffs of the basic game.

What I first want to demonstrate is that in this setting, even if people have $c_i < 1$—that is, they are cooperators—playing aggressively against the other race may be the only rational strategy for them. Expecting aggression from the other side, we respond with aggression, and moreover, given some weak conditions, this is the only expectation (that is, the expectation of aggression) that can occur in equilibrium. In other words, huge amounts of racial animus can be founded on the most flimsy basis.

If i and j both belong to the same race, as already explained, they play the basic game (there are no psychic cost corrections to be made) and there are two Nash equilibria in this game. In keeping with my assumption, they should reach the Pareto superior outcome—namely, (C,C).

Now suppose that one player is white and the other is black. While the race is visible to both, in deciding what to choose, A or C, a player now has the handicap of not knowing the other player's latent characteristic and not knowing the other player's belief about his or her own latent characteristic.[43] As usual under such circumstances, the natural equilibrium notion to use is what game theorists refer to as a Bayes-Nash equilibrium. In the present context the idea of this equilibrium is straightforward, and I will spell it out with an example.[44]

Consider a society with six persons, three of each race. The profile of latent characteristics within each race is identical. So within each race, I will refer to the three individuals as being of types 1, 2, and 3. Let $c^1 = 0$, $c^2 = \frac{1}{2}$, and $c^3 = 7/6$. In other words, on average, two persons in each race are cooperators—one of them is, in fact, race blind—and only one person in each race prefers aggression unilaterally. Actually, what I will assume (though this can be generalized) is that each of the three persons has an equal probability of being of types 1, 2, and 3. Though each player knows of his or her own type, when a player sees another person, the player thinks that the person could be of type 1 (that is, have $c^i = 0$) with a probability of one-third, type 2 (that is, have $c^i = \frac{1}{2}$) with a probability one-third, and type 3 (that is, with $c^i = 7/6$) with a probability of one-third. What type I am, in short, does not influence my expectation of what type the other person is. It is easy to do without this assumption, but I will go along with it. In the present model this is a harmless assumption, since the question of the other player's type assumes significance only when the other player is of a different race; so my being of type t has no bearing on what type the other player is. Further, this assumption becomes much more natural if we are dealing with large populations, as would be the case in a host of real-life situations.

The game proceeds as specified in the previous section. People are picked at random in pairs and asked to play. If a player finds themselves pitted against a person of the same race, then the payoffs in the basic game are the payoffs they get (and this is common knowledge). If, on the other hand, a person i is pitted against a person j of another race, then the payoffs will have to be corrected using c_i and c_j. In particular, the psychic cost c_i will have to be deducted from person i's basic payoff to get the actual payoff that guides their behavior, and likewise for person j. Each person i knows c_i, but can only guess at the other person's psychic cost, c_j.

It follows that whenever two players are picked at random to play, as long as neither of these players happens to be the third type of the groups of blacks and whites, the game has two equilibria, (A,A) and (C,C). Hence, it would be plausible to expect they will reach the high-returns equilibrium, (C,C). It follows (and it is easy to demonstrate this formally) that if person 3 in both racial groups did not exist and everything else remained as described, then a natural equilibrium is one where everybody plays C, against people of their own race and others. In other words, there is cooperation all around.

If the two omitted persons are brought into this society, then playing C ceases to be an equilibrium.[45] The probability of encountering this extreme racist, person 3, makes aggression the only rational strategy for each person to use against everybody of the other race. Society, to put it another way, will now be divided along racial lines, with people cooperating among their own group and being aggressive with the other.

To prove this, first note that person 3—that is, a person who is of type 3—in each race will play the aggressive strategy, A, because he or she prefers to do so no matter who the player is pitted against, as long as the other player is of a different race. Now consider person 2. When this person meets the opponent, he or she cannot see the latent characteristic of the other person but instead knows by deduction (the same deduction that I just made) that there is at least a one-third probability that the opponent will play A, since there is one-third probability that the opponent is of type 3. It is easy to verify that if the probability of the opponent playing A is greater than or equal to one-third, then it is best for person 2 to play A.[46]

Person 1, or more precisely, a person of type 1, knows by deduction that the opponent will play A with a probability of at least two-thirds, since the probability that the opponent is of types 2 or 3 is two-thirds, and it is known by deduction that both these types will play A. But if the opponent is expected to play A with a probability of two-thirds or more, a person of type 1 will clearly play A. Therefore, all players will play A for sure. There is unconditional aggression between the two races, even though two-thirds of the players are cooperators.

To appreciate the frustrating nature of this result, let us compute the average value of c. This is equal to five-ninths. When you confront another person to play the game, then, the other player's expected value of c is way below 1. And the other player's expectation about you is identical. These expectations are in fact common knowledge. Hence, at a casual glance, it seems reasonable to expect both players to play C and earn a payoff of close to 10. But from the above analysis we know that despite both players knowing this, an outcome of (C,C) can never occur. They will both play A and earn a payoff of 2 each. Conflict is the unique equilibrium.

Since this result is derived for a special case, it is worth asking what the special features of the example are that drive the result. The answer is: this will be true for any any distribution of Cs such that at least one person has a dominant preference for aggression toward the other race and the Cs are closely packed for everybody in the sense that for every person, k, $c_k - c_{k-1}$ is less than or equal to $2/n$, where n is the population of each race. The result does not seem unrealistic. Moreover, I am not claiming that every society will have these characteristics but rather that these characteristics are possible and this kind of a configuration can occur in any country, and when it does, the malignancy of identity will spread rapidly. The entry of one person who is innately aggressive toward the other race can cause an escalation of aggression through society.[47] Understanding this cause of racial aggression could help governments, NGOs, or other groups wanting to diffuse a crisis to think of new forms of interventions.

There is a different way to interpret the above game. We could think of a society with exactly two persons, one black and one white, playing the above game. Both have c equal to 0. But this is not common knowledge. Each player has a prior belief about the other's 'type,' and this prior probability distribution is the same as the one described above. In that case, the formal analysis of the game remains identical to what we just did. The Bayes-Nash equilibrium of this game is unique, and both players will be aggressive to each other, though cooperation is a Nash equilibrium (for a game with common knowledge of payoffs when c is low enough) and the cooperative outcome is Pareto dominant.

Although this is contrary to the standard wisdom in economics, understanding and appreciating the positive or negative externalities of our individual actions often encourages us to undertake the actions with greater or diminished zest, even if this is contrary to one's self-interest. Moreover, awareness that some action undertaken by a large number of people can be detrimental to society frequently deters us from taking that action, even when one person choosing it is inconsequential for society. People are usually persuaded to switch off lights when leaving a room by being told that if everybody was careless about this, the whole country could suffer an electricity shortage. Good citizens tend not to throw garbage out of their car windows, even if that in itself makes no difference, simply because of the awareness that if everybody threw garbage out onto the streets, it would make the city dirty. I am ignoring exceptions such as the one noted by Wade Davis (1997, 19) in his lyrical account of exploration in the Amazon basin. Traveling by train in Colombia, he observed a sign posted by the rail authorities on the back of the seat in front of him: "It politely asked all passengers to be civilized enough to throw their garbage out of the windows of the train."

A better understanding of a phenomenon can itself have a policy impact. If we realize that the other side is not innately evil and that our own tendency to form race-conditional expectations of other people contributes to conflict, we are likely to resist this tendency. Moreover, the above example shows how a tiny change in our preferences (or everybody's preferences, or even that of one or two persons) can make a big difference. Hence, this gives government and civil society some hints on how to 'educate' people.

One important way in which the above model can be generalized is to take away race consciousness from everybody except the person(s) whose latent characteristic exceeds 1. What I mean is this. Suppose (again assuming that there are n people of each race) for every person $k < n$, the psychic cost of cooperation, c_k, occurs *no matter whom* they are playing against, and for person n this cost, c_n, occurs only across racial lines. That is, if person n is playing against a person of the same race, he or she feels no psychic cost, whereas c_n becomes effective whenever the person is matched against a person of another race. Everybody except person n in each race is, in other words, totally race blind. It is easy to see that the Bayes-Nash equilibrium remains exactly as described above. People are always nasty across racial lines. Racial identity in this model emerges from virtually no race-identity variable in people's utility function. This result demonstrates how this model is distinct from that of George Akerlof and Rachel Kranton (2000). It argues that identity can emerge from virtually no innate sense of identity. The word 'virtually' is important because some innate identity preference is needed (in this example, I assume that this is true for person n) for the balkanization of society to occur.

There is another possible modification that will illustrate how a quasi-balkanization of society can happen with *no* identity variable in anybody's preference. Consider a society in which there are $n-1$ whites and n blacks, and they have preferences as described in the above example, with the additional feature that the psychic cost c_i occurs no matter who one is playing against. In their preferences people have no sense of race. Note now that only one person, the nth person in the group B, has an unconditional preference for A (*against whites and blacks*). Since race is a visible characteristic, it is easy to see that every Bayes-Nash equilibrium will have the following feature: blacks choose action A against whites and blacks, and whites choose action A against blacks. We can have a Bayes-Nash equilibrium that has this property and also has whites playing cooperatively against whites. This mimics the kind of control that one in-group can exercise over a large mass of people in society. In this case, the race-based behavior occurs even though people have completely race-neutral preferences.

There are other interesting patterns of aggression and cooperation that one can explain by modifying the informational assumptions of the above model, and that is what I do below.

The assumption that human beings have some characteristics that are invisible and some that are visible (with the implicit assumption that these are visible to all) overlooks the other realistic case where people have characteristics that are idiosyncratically visible—that is, visible to some and not to others. The common refrain that "all natives look alike," coupled with the fact that to the natives, the natives do not look alike, suggests the presence of idiosyncratically visible characteristics.

Consider a case where people know one another within their own racial groups, but cannot distinguish between individuals in the other racial group. In other words, if person i, who is white, is aggressive to a white person, the information that registers in the latter's head is not simply that "one white person was aggressive to me" but rather that "a specific person i from the set of whites was aggressive to me." On the other hand, if person i, who is black, were aggressive to the same white person, the information that registers in the head is that "a black person was aggressive to me." This can drastically change the nature of equilibria that arise, since it changes the nature of the conditional variables used in the formation of probabilities and expectations of behavior.

To see this, consider the case discussed above, with $n-1$ whites and n blacks with characteristics exactly as described there: no one has race-based preferences and only one person (the nth black) has a dominant preference for being aggressive (toward one and all). Since whites cannot tell the difference between blacks, they will begin with the belief that a randomly chosen black has a probability $1/n$ of playing A. And if the c_ks are sufficiently closely packed, this leads to a cascade as before with all whites being aggressive toward all blacks and vice versa.

When a black player (not n) meets another black person i, however, the former's behavior depends on whether i is n or not. If i is n, the player will necessarily be aggressive, but if i is not n, the black player need not be aggressive. As such, the cascade does not occur in this case. The following is a Bayes-Nash equilibrium outcome of this game. Whenever players are pitted across racial lines, they are aggressive to one another, every black i that is not n is aggressive when playing black n, and of course black n is always aggressive. Apart from this, blacks play cooperatively against blacks and whites play cooperatively against whites.

This model provides a formal basis to an oft-heard recommendation on how to control ethnic or racial conflict (Varshney 2002): the importance of getting to know the other side. The reason why this works may not be quite the same as what prompts this advice, which generally has to do with how knowing someone fosters warmth and affection. The contention here is that if we know the other side, we are able to think of one act of aggression as an act by one particular person instead of an aggression by a race or an ethnic group.

Much has been written about cultural traps, or why people fall into certain stereotypical behavior patterns even though that may not seem to yield any benefit (Swidler 1986; Wilson 1987; Basu and Weibull 2003; Gray 2009). As Ann Swidler (1986, 275) quizzes, "Why doesn't a member of the 'culture of poverty' ... take advantage of opportunities to assimilate to the dominant culture in conduct and dress, acquire the appropriate educational credentials, and settle down to a steady job?" One way to answer this is to argue how human preferences can vary, and interestingly, there can be a self-fulfilling element in this. Once one recognizes oneself as belonging to a certain group, one develops a preference for the symbols of that group.

But by using the structure of analysis developed in this chapter, one can also assert that even when people's preferences remain unchanged and they would prefer to be in the shoes of the other race, they may not wish to exercise the option of changing their culture. The argument I am suggesting here has much to do with 'recognition' (Taylor 1994). Suppose now that an individual has three traits: an innate, publicly observable trait (like race or nationality); a chosen cultural characteristic, such as dress style, coiffure, or college degree; and a latent characteristic, as before. What is new here is the chosen cultural characteristic. Suppose that this can be of two types: green and blue. That is, each person can choose to be green or blue. If the chosen characteristic is one that is idiosyncratically visible—in particular, it is visible only to your racial type—then it is easy to see why no one may want to switch. Consider a model just like the above one, but with fewer blacks than whites, and with all blacks choosing green and whites choosing blue. The latent characteristic, let us suppose, depicts one's animus toward anybody who looks different from oneself.

By now it is easy to see how we can have an equilibrium in which i and j are aggressive to one another if, and only if, they belong to different races. Since one earns a larger payoff the more one cooperates and there are fewer blacks, blacks are worse off in this equilibrium. Now consider one black who wants to wave a conciliatory signal to the whites to say that he or she is willing to cooperate with them (for instance, in business ventures). If this person tries to do this by altering the chosen cultural signal, such as by choosing blue instead of green, the person will be worse off. Since to whites all blacks are the same (that is, they do not observe the chosen variable), their behavior will not change toward this person. And since other blacks will notice this person's altered cultural trait, some of them (those with sufficiently high c) will now be aggressive. Overall the outcome will be worse. Hence, blacks choosing green and whites choosing blue will persist.

The anthropologist M. N. Srinivas (1955), who coined the term 'sanskritization' to denote the conscious change in culture that some lower-caste groups in India affected in order to get some of the advantages of the upper castes, also noted why this phenomenon was not more widespread. This had much to do with the opprobrium one faces for attempting to be different (see also Basu 1989). Not surprisingly, the successful cases of sanskritization were usually associated with groups that migrated to and started life afresh in a new locale.

This model can be used to address other interesting phenomena. The world has seen, mercifully not too often, the emergence and flourishing of 'secret societies.' By a secret society, I mean a group of people who know that they belong to a special group—let me call this group S—but the larger society to which they belong is unaware that they share a separate (and among them known) group identity (Robson 1990). Freemasons in some stages of history may have functioned as such a group. Underground revolutionary movements frequently have the character of a secret society. CIA agents, trying to infiltrate a society, may recognize one another as CIA agents even though no one else is supposed to.[48] Such secret societies are a *social* counterpart of the military strategy of the Trojan horse. They form a special, coherent group within a larger society that is unaware of their secret association.

To understand how this could play out in the model, let us consider a society of 2n people, with two subsocieties, B and W, with a population of n each. As in the case discussed earlier in the chapter, a person of type B cannot tell the difference between a B and W, whereas a W (maybe through a secret handshake, meaningful only to those who know the handshake) can tell if a person is a W or B. In other words, we are assuming that all people (B and W) have the same skin color and looks, but when people shake hands a W person wiggles the middle finger and only a W person realizes that this is a signal that the wiggler is a W. Clearly in this case a W person will be able to condition the behavior on whether the gaming partner is a W or B, but a B person will not be able to use such a conditional strategy. This opens up a host of analytic possibilities that are worth studying in the future.

Despite the abstract character of this analysis, its main motivation is to help us craft policy to diffuse racial and other identity-based tensions and turmoil in the world. The first step in this is to understand the politics of identity, and how identity, through the simple mechanism of individuals using statistical information and group characteristics to form expectations about the behavior of individuals, can come to acquire certain malignancies. Innocuous differences turn into significant markers for which people are willing to die. To prevent this from happening, we need to desist from certain individually rational behaviors, just as one way to control pollution is for us to behave in socially responsible ways, and desist from smoking in a crowded waiting room and discarding plastic bags carelessly. Such behavior is not individually rational, but society functions on human beings having acquired these behavior traits simply on the knowledge that such minor individual sacrifices can lead to large social gains. To keep identity-based strife at bay we need to cultivate such little irrationalities, like ignoring the information that comes with a person's group characteristics or social identity. Equally important is to get to know the 'other side' better, and as a consequence to treat individuals as individuals rather than an anonymous member of a large group.

CHAPTER 7

Contract, Coercion, and Intervention

Principle of Free Contract

In 1995, soon after I moved to the United States, I got a letter from a lawyer in California requesting me to write a letter to a California Supreme Court judge in support of his client. Not being sure of the ethics of such matters, I will not reveal any names. His client, Mr. X, had been approached by an entrepreneur, Mr. R, for a loan of five hundred thousand dollars in order to open a restaurant. They agreed to an annual interest rate of 12 percent and a schedule of repayment in installments. For quite some time R paid X in accordance with the repayment schedule; then he began to default. After waiting for a while, X decided to take R to court for breach of contract. The case was proceeding well and seemingly in favor of X, when R's lawyers discovered that a 12 percent interest rate was a violation of the statutory limit on interest rates prevalent in California at that time, which set an upper limit at 11 percent for interest rates on loans. This was used by R's lawyers to argue that the entire contract was null and void, and therefore R should pay no interest; moreover, by this argument, he had overpaid X and so in fact ought to get money back from X.

It was at this stage that X's lawyer decided to seek the support of some economists (being aware, I suppose, of our profession's proclivity in such matters) and the letter arrived on my desk. Since I had never before had occasion to write to a Supreme Court judge, the novelty of this was lure enough; I acquiesced.

What I wrote, in a nutshell, was this: I am aware that what the law says has to be followed, but how severely a violation of the law has to be redressed often depends on our view of how reasonable the law happens to be. I went on to contend that in this case, the statutory interest law in California was quite unreasonable. When an adult, especially someone who is business savvy, agrees to accept a loan with a 12 percent interest rate and another person agrees to lend the money at a 12 percent interest rate, presumably both expect to be better off through this exchange. If there is no good reason to expect this to have any negative fallout on others, then no one should stop such a contract. Indeed, the ability among adults to freely sign contracts and rely on them is the bedrock of a vibrant, modern economy. Business, enterprise, and progress are made possible by such contracts, and equally, progress gets stymied if such contracts are disallowed.

Some months later, I met an economist who had received the same request from the lawyer and had also written to the judge. We discovered on comparing notes that we had taken almost exactly the same line. On consideration, this is not so surprising. It is a widely accepted principle of economics that if two or more sentient adults voluntarily agree to a contract or an exchange, which has no negative fallout on those uninvolved in the contract, then the government should not stop such a contract. This is often called the 'principle of free contract' (for a discussion of this, see Basu 2003a), or PFC, in brief. This has a close connection to the idea of the Pareto principle, which was mentioned on several occasions earlier, and through this it is also related to the idea that free markets achieve Pareto optimality, which was explored in the guise of the Invisible Hand Theorem in chapter 2. I will return shortly to the connection between the PFC and the Pareto principle.

Although I will argue in this chapter that this rule must not be treated as sacrosanct, I want to stress its importance in enabling an economy to function effectively. My critique of this principle must not be treated as an alibi for reckless intervention by governments, or any well-meaning or ill-meaning outsiders, in other people's contracts. I believe that a lot of harm has been done by ill-conceived interventions. Most people underestimate the significance of the ease with which we can rely on contracts for economic development. Many government policies would be unnecessary if only there was an effective institution for contract enforcement. Ordinary people would be able to strike innovative contracts and improve their lot. This relates closely to some of the topics discussed in chapter 3. Economists typically think of contract enforcement as a job meant for governments. While governments do play a large role in this, it is much more critical to have a 'culture of trust,' whereby we can rely on one another's word simply because that is the social norm and people instinctively adhere to it.[1] The reason this is important is that we need to rely on one another's word on so many occasions that it is just not feasible to sign a contract each time and then call on the government or the courts to enforce it. Also, enforcement by natural means—social norms or instinctive adherence to the culture of trust—makes it much cheaper than third-party enforcement. It is not adequately recognized that one of the preconditions for development are these kinds of norms of trust.

Government is key in all this because it often ends up playing a negative role. Consider the law concerning property in the Salt Lake area of the city of Calcutta that I mentioned in the previous chapter. The Salt Lake area was once a marshland on the eastern flank of the city. It was developed by the regional government, which decided that plots of land and apartments in this newly developed area would be sold at a subsidized price to not-so-rich people, thereby enabling the middle and lower middle class to own property. It was essentially a scheme for subsidizing the relatively worse off, and as such, was a good idea. It struck the politicians dealing with this that left to the forces of the market, these subsidized plots and apartments would change hands over time and likely end up with the rich. To prevent this, they enacted a law that said that property in the Salt Lake area could not be sold.

To me this seems like a mindless violation of the PFC. If someone wishes to buy a property and the owner wishes to sell it, presumably both expect to be better off by this transaction, and there is no reason to expect uninvolved others to be worse off. This is a good example of a situation in which the state should stay out of the transaction. In fact, the relatively poor person to whom the property was sold by the government could only be better off by having the additional freedom to sell the property. When that person gets an attractive job in Bangalore or Dubai, he or she will be able to easily move by selling off the Salt Lake property. Not being allowed to do so can only hurt the person. Indeed, I believe that the mobility and ultimately the well-being of the people of Calcutta have been hurt by laws like this.

In the United States, the principle of free contract is usually viewed as protected by the Fourteenth Amendment (passed in 1868) to the Constitution. The freedom of contract is often alluded to as a "property right," and there are celebrated cases, such as *Lochner v. the New York State* (1905), in which any effort to curtail work hours or legislatively raise wages has been struck down by the courts as being in violation of the freedom of individuals to sign contracts as they wished. It is likely that one critical ingredient in the outstanding performance of the U.S. economy since the late nineteenth century is the faith that the U.S. courts evinced in the principle of free contract and the natural culture of trust that flourished among the citizenry, even though, as we will presently see, this is a principle that can be overdone. There is a body of writing in economics that upholds the PFC (see, for example, Friedman 1962), and more significantly, there is a widespread, unwritten acceptance of this principle.[2]

Despite the value of this principle, what is worrying is that its terms are, on reflection, ill defined and it has its share of ambiguities. For instance, since it refers to voluntary choice, its proper use presumes an understanding of what is 'voluntary' and thus also coercive. And these concepts are ill understood in economics. It is ironic that while philosophers and legal scholars have debated and analyzed these concepts along with the validity of the principle of free contract, there is little discussion of these in economics, even though so much of economics is founded on this principle.

This has caused a lot of policy confusion. On the one hand, we find wanton violation of this principle by governments and bureaucrats. On a variety of matters governments specify terms of contracts exogenously. In India, any firm that employs over fifty laborers must follow the prespecified terms spelled out in the Industrial Disputes Act of 1947 in order to lay workers off, and any firm employing more than a hundred laborers has to have prior permission from the government before it can lay off workers. A contract voluntarily entered into by an entrepreneur and a worker that specifies terms of disengagement that are different from what the law requires (for example, that the worker's salary will be high, but the firm can ask the worker to quit with no prior notice and no severance pay) will be dismissed by the courts as invalid in the same way that the loan contract in California was considered null and void. So, if after having signed the contract, the worker or employer later reneges on it, the other side will not have any recourse to the law. Knowing this, people in India typically do not sign such contracts. Many economists have argued, and I find myself in agreement with them on this (see Basu, Fields, and Debgupta 2008), that the pervasive failure to respect the principle of free contract has harmed the Indian economy, including the workers, since entrepreneurs hesitate to start businesses in which demand is volatile (for instance, fashion garments), and that require the periodic hiring and laying off of workers.

There are mainstream economists and some legal scholars who take this line to an extreme, and do not recognize that the principle of free contracts can have any exceptions. But it is not difficult to find examples where a majority of thinking individuals would feel uncomfortable adhering to the principle of free contract.

First, consider a firm that puts a sign up outside the personnel office making it clear that the firm pays its workers excellent salaries, offers generous health benefits, and provides time off for vacations, but reserves the right to sexually harass its workers. It then leaves it to potential job applicants to decide if they wish to work for this firm. It would seem that if some workers choose to work for this firm, then under the PFC the state has no business stopping them. So should government allow firms to offer contracts of the above kind to workers?[3] Presumably, many firms will then have 'standard forms' for workers to sign, whereby they relinquish the right not to be sexually harassed.[4] Under the PFC we should not object to this.

Some people's first reaction to this is that sexual harassment cannot come under the ambit of the PFC because harassment is a form of coercion, and so when a worker is subjected to sexual harassment it cannot be thought of as a voluntary decision. On closer scrutiny, this objection turns out to be invalid. Harassment is of course an act of coercion, but the worker who opts for a package, one component of which includes harassment, need not be thought of as being coerced into choosing the package. It is a bit like a worker who chooses a job that entails six days of work every week. The worker may hate working on Saturdays, but *that* does not mean that they have been coerced into taking this job. I believe, however, that *contractual* workplace sexual harassment, even though it is part of a voluntarily chosen package, should not be allowed and that this is compatible with one's belief in the PFC. But the claim is a good deal more complex than it appears at first sight.

Second, in 1903 there was the celebrated case of *The Port Caledonia and the Anna*, in which a vessel experiencing a dangerous crisis at sea sought help from a tug (Wertheimer 1996). The master of the tug asked for one thousand pounds (an astronomical sum at that time), stipulating that it was a 'take it or leave it' offer. The master of the vessel, unsurprisingly, accepted the offer, but later went to court. The court declared the 'contract' or agreement void, and ruled that the vessel master needed to pay two hundred pounds. Evidently, the court's ruling violated the PFC.

Third, suppose a poor worker wants to be a slave to a rich landlord in order to have a regular supply of food, and the landlord sees this as an opportunity to add another slave to his retinue. Should such voluntary slavery be permitted? Prominent thinkers, including those otherwise committed to the PFC, have felt uncomfortable saying yes to this. John Stuart Mill ([1848] 1970) was troubled by this and took cover by using the rather arbitrary line that long-run contracts should be prohibited, because people are not able to judge their own well-being over long stretches of time.[5]

There are many other examples. Should we look the other way if a firm exposes workers to enormous health hazards as long as this is made clear to the workers in advance and they are not coerced into accepting the job? Is it all right for corporations in export-processing zones, or maquiladoras, to demand that any worker who wishes to work there has to give up the right to join trade unions? This is a practice that is becoming increasingly common in countries eager to woo multinational corporations to their shores. Should we not contend that, by the PFC, this is fine since no one is forced to work in an export-processing zone?

Interestingly, it was common practice in the United States until the 1930s for firms to make workers sign a standard form relinquishing their right to join trade unions before giving them employment. This was called a 'yellow dog contract.' But it was 'felt' that this was wrong, and yellow dog contracts were declared illegal in the United States by the Norris-La Guardia Act and the Anti-Injunction Bill in 1932.[6]

The trouble is that most of the time we react in an ad hoc fashion to these troubling questions. We outlaw some practices and allow others, but do not have clear rules of why and under what circumstances is it all right to violate the PFC. Without some such general rules, we are handicapped when we try to advise others. When a third world country declares that no one has the right to sell land, we rush to say that this is foolish because if someone wants to sell and someone wishes to buy, and there is no negative externality on an uninvolved third party (in other words, the conditions of the PFC hold), then we should not ban such exchanges. To do so is to harm the economy's growth and efficiency. But if the third world bureaucrat then turns around and asks how we can in that case justify the Norris-La Guardia Act or the blanket ban on sexual harassment in the workplace, we do not have a good answer, and often cite arbitrary nonwelfarist objectives.[7]

One widely used justification for disallowing free contracts is when this occurs between parties of asymmetrical power. Thus, for instance, in the *Henningsen v. Bloomfield Motors* (1960) case, the court disallowed the standard form contract by arguing that "freedom of contract is most at home when a contract is the result of free bargaining of parties ... who meet each other on a footing of *approximate economic equality*" (Wertheimer 1996, 45; emphasis added). This widely used assertion is invalid, however. If contracts signed between the rich and poor are not treated as valid by virtue of power asymmetry, the rich will refuse to sign contracts with the poor (knowing that the courts are likely to overturn the agreements). The poor will therefore tend to get excluded from the market. They will not be able to get loans easily or sign so many other kinds of contracts that one needs in order to get ahead in life. Hence, the asymmetry of power cannot in itself be construed as a reason for disregarding the PFC.

The aim of this chapter is to see how we can construct general and appealing rules for where we may violate the PFC, *while adhering to the basic axiom of the Pareto principle*. The route of using some deontological principle or nonwelfarist criterion to put aside Pareto is not a line that is permitted here. This is not an easy task since the principle of free contract is often viewed as a rule that is in fact a derivative of the Pareto principle. This discussion, in turn, will enrich our understanding of the nature and role of government interventions in general. It also helps us understand how through a series of seemingly insidious steps, huge moral wrongs can be committed, thereby alerting us to the need to be vigilant for such seemingly Pareto-improving steps. This provides a normative critique of the same kinds of risks explored in the previous two chapters from the purely positive perspective that traditional analysts run when they try to model the 'collective' as a mere aggregation of independently describable individuals.

It is worthwhile recalling the meaning of the Pareto principle, examined in chapter 2. For this it is useful to first define a Pareto improvement. A Pareto improvement is a change that leaves at least one person better off and no one worse off. The Pareto principle can then be described as a normative rule that says that a Pareto improvement is socially desirable, and so should not be thwarted by the state or anybody for that matter (except when it is self-contradictory in the sense that its repeated use leads to a Pareto inferior state). The qualifier within parenthesis can be ignored for now; its significance will become evident later.

The Pareto principle is not without its critics, but I am inclined to treat it as valid.[8] The general strategy here will be to uphold the Pareto principle, argue that this is not synonymous with the PFC, and look for justifiable violations of the PFC within the class of cases where the Pareto principle applies. In other words, I am seeking principles that allow us to disregard the PFC in situations where to uphold the Pareto principle does not mean upholding the PFC. If this sounds abstract, I seek the reader's patience only briefly, since the meaning of this will be made clearer soon.

One confusion that happens occasionally in the literature and is best cleared up at the outset is caused by confounding the Pareto principle with another related principle, the 'Pareto optimality principle,' which says that if an outcome is Pareto optimal, then it is desirable (and so should not be stopped by the state).[9]

Not only are the Pareto principle and Pareto optimality principle distinct but I also find the former an attractive normative axiom and the latter unacceptable. For one, if we wish to pass any judgment on distributional matters, such as wanting to shun extreme inequality, then we have to reject the Pareto optimality principle (Sen 1997). Another example that illustrates the moral separateness of the Pareto principle and the Pareto optimality principle can be seen in the case of torture. If a torturer feels pleasure by torturing, then by the optimality principle torture could be desirable. The state should not stop it. To see this, suppose in a society only two states are available: x, where there is no torture, and y, where person 1 tortures person 2. Since person 1 is better off in y than in x, it must be that y is Pareto optimal and so it is a desirable outcome by the Pareto optimality principle.[10] Notice that the rejection of y is permitted under the Pareto principle, since between x and y neither is a Pareto improvement on the other (since person 2 is better off under x).

Finally, we saw in chapter 6 how if we treat choice as fully reflecting the chooser's welfare, then every outcome can be made Pareto optimal by virtue of a politician or bureaucrat being against any deviation from the outcome. As we also saw earlier, if two grown-up and free individuals wish to conduct trade among themselves, when some bureaucrats suddenly appears on the scene and says that they do not want to allow this, then, by virtue of the bureaucrats' objection, the trade seizes to be a Pareto improvement, and the ban on trade becomes Pareto optimal. As explained in the previous chapter, I counter this problem by rejecting the assumption that choice always reflects welfare.

My main argument is developed later in this chapter, when I show that in a variety of situations, the Pareto principle and the PFC do not give us the same prescription, and this paves the way for rejecting the PFC while adhering to the Pareto principle. The other argument—to do with multiple equilibria— is more obvious, and for that reason is discussed only briefly, later in the chapter. In addition, this chapter explores some actual problems of government intervention, and looks at contexts where the rules developed below apply in practice. These practical applications are not an easy matter, and, as of now, there are many questions for which no convincing answer is available. There are situations, for instance, in which child labor can be banned even where no coercion is involved (Basu and Van 1998). This uses the multiple equilibria argument. Likewise, contractual sexual harassment in the workplace should be banned based on the claims below. As for hazardous work and giving up trade union rights in export-processing zones, these matters need to be further studied. Here, I outline the normative rules that can be used to analyze them.

In brief, the position taken in this book is that the principle of free contract is a good default rule; it is violated more often than it should be by governments. At the same time, it is not sacrosanct, and there are good moral reasons within the Paretian framework that allow us to suspend the use of the PFC in some contexts. This is not too far from the line taken by the so-called left libertarian school (see Steiner 1994; Vallentyne 2000). To have self-ownership and the freedom to contract, and then to expect the contract to be enforced, does not mean that all resources need to be carved out among individuals, nor does this mean that we have to abandon egalitarianism (Cohen 1986; Otsuka 1998).[11]

The section that follows deals with a prior matter. Recall that the PFC only talks about contracts, exchange, and trade that are entered into voluntarily. But what is a voluntary contract, and equivalently, what is coercion? I will argue that the PFC is often invoked spuriously by mistakenly taking certain actions to be voluntary when they are not. Though I do not succeed in giving a full definition of what coercion is (or what constitutes voluntary choice), the next section moves *toward* a definition that contradicts the position taken by much of economics.[12] It demonstrates that coercion is essentially a normative concept. Two observers can agree about the facts of a case, but can also legitimately disagree about whether coercion has occurred. Thereafter, in the sections that follow, I will proceed by putting aside the definitional problems—that is, by simply assuming that we all know what is voluntary and what is coercive.

Coercion and Voluntariness

In trying to understand coercion and voluntariness, the risk that many an analyst has succumbed to is that of falling into the tautological or near-tautological trap: seeing virtually all human behavior as examples of free choice or all behavior as an illustration of coercive action. The conservative neoclassical economist often bends over backward to show that virtually all choice is noncoercive. This is because, as David Zimmerman (1981, 122) pithily puts it, "Socialists and laissez-faire liberals alike ... have embraced the conviction that coercion is prima facie morally wrong." Given this, to admit coercion is to concede the need for government intervention. As Zimmerman notes on the same page, "If capitalist wage bargains did involve coercion, that would be one moral strike against them." Yet it is equally possible to err on the other side by jumping to conclude that coercion has occurred.

Suppose some workers choose to work in a low-paid hazardous industry. Did they choose this voluntarily? The correct answer is: We cannot say; we need more information about the circumstances before we can pronounce a judgment. So let me add to the above description the fact that these persons' only other option was unemployment, which would leave them abysmally poor. To some social scientists, this is enough information to be able to say that they did not make a voluntary choice because, effectively, they *had* no choice, since being unemployed is not really something one *chooses* (Macpherson 1973). On the other hand, there is a liberal position, best exemplified by Robert Nozick (1974), that argues that if other agents acted voluntarily and *within* their rights, then the worker can be described as having chosen voluntarily and without coercion. This is also wrong but for more complex reasons.

I am asserting here that both these positions are flawed (which shows that while my position will be Nozickian in some ways, it is not that of Nozick). With the information we have thus far, strictly, we cannot say whether the workers were coerced or not. The qualifier 'strictly' is important here. If we did indeed have this much information and no more, and we *had to* take a position on this, I would be inclined to treat this as a case of voluntary choice, since the accompanying conditions that we need for this to be construed as coercion (as we will presently see) seem empirically unlikely.

Those who race to conclude that this is a case of coercion, usually take the view that the 'choice' of being unemployed is not a serious one. They feel that no one should have to take a miserable job. But the mistake with this is its implicit tendency to assume that if "no one should have to take such a miserable job," then "someone taking such a job" must imply coercion. This and the opposite error of quickly concluding that this is voluntary can curiously stem from the same basic mistake: the tendency to equate "having choice" with "not being coerced."

Since I am not relying on an undisputed definition of these terms, let me proceed from an example in which we will presumably all agree that coercion has occurred to other more complex cases by analogy.

In 1971, when I was a student in Delhi, I was mugged at knifepoint one winter evening on the Delhi University campus. Three men in shawls came up to me on an ill-lit road, and one of them whipped out a knife and asked me for my watch. It took me a few seconds to decide what I should do. I took off my watch and handed it over to the man with the knife (somehow I seem to recall I thanked him), and then walked back to my dorm. The question is: Did I part with my watch voluntarily or under coercion?

Clearly, everybody will agree that this is coercion. If *this* is not coercion, then pretty much nothing is. But notice that this was not a situation of no choice. When the man pointed the knife at me and asked for my watch, he was giving me a choice: I could give him my watch or my life. I *chose* to keep my life. In fact, it was a bargain since mine was a cheap, unreliable watch. So having a choice cannot be equated with noncoercion.

It is depriving me of my right—namely, the right to *both* my watch *and* life—that made it a case of coercion. Given that one's rights are a matter of morals, I would, unlike Zimmerman (1981) and like Nozick (1969) in his paper on coercion, treat coercion as a moral concept. That is, what we think of as coercion depends on our notion of a moral baseline. This is quite distinct from the concept of coercion that one encounters (admittedly only suggestively) in mainstream neoclassical economics. And all this is closely related to the Pareto principle, since the Pareto principle is all about Pareto improvements being approved. As soon as we speak of an 'improvement,' though, the question of "from where or from which moral baseline" arises. What I have just claimed is that there may be ambiguities in relation to this. It should be clear that the moral baseline is indeed a normative matter, and not simply a matter of one's average, expected, or current utility level.[13]

Let us suppose that I knowingly choose to go for an evening walk to a dangerous neighborhood. Assume that there is a half probability that I will come back safe, in which case (let us assume) I will have a hundred utils of satisfaction, and a half probability that I will lose everything—the wallet, watch, and clothes on me—in which case I will have zero utils. Hence, when I choose to go out for a stroll to that area I am choosing to have an expected utility of fifty utils. Of course, if I am robbed of everything, we would all agree that I have been coerced, since I am worse off than any reasonable benchmark—for instance, the expected utility that evening (of fifty utils). But suppose now that the mugger instead takes only my cheap watch, which has merely forty utils of worth to me. So I return home with sixty utils. Note that this is a little more than the expectation I had at the start of my voluntary stroll. Would we now say that I parted with my watch voluntarily? Most of us would disagree with this. The reason is that most of us treat the baseline of utils not to be my expected utility level of fifty but rather one hundred—that is, with everything intact. Even though my choice to go for that risky stroll was voluntary, the fact of losing my watch is not.

This point of view can be bolstered further and made more complicated by bringing in a triadic interaction, which shows that everyone staying within their rights (which is not the case in the above example, since the mugger had no right to my watch or life) is not enough to guarantee voluntariness and noncoercion. This is a more controversial point, and a by-product of models of triadic interaction that have been used to study agrarian interaction and international relations.[14]

These models recognize that there are many contexts in reality where the interaction between individuals or agents is nondyadic; what happens between persons i and j can depend on what happens between i and some other person k. Using the Helms-Burton Act of 1996, for instance, the United States seeks to dominate Cuba by threatening to take action against other countries for trading with and investing in Cuba.

Let me here consider the case of a village in which there is a landlord (1), a laborer (2), and a merchant (3). I have argued elsewhere (Basu 2000) that what the landlord can extract from the laborer according to textbook models in economics, may be less than what he can extract in reality by using 'triadic threats'—that is, by announcing that he will boycott trade with the merchant if the laborer turns down the landlord's offer and, despite that, the merchant trades with the laborer. Without going into the formalism, the essential argument is easy to see. If the threat were credible, the worker would realize that to turn down the landlord's offer would mean losing out on not only what the landlord offers but also on what the worker was getting from the merchant.[15]

Knowing this, the landlord is able to make an offer such that by accepting it, the worker gets the same level of utility as (or maybe a little more than) what the worker would get if he or she got nothing from the landlord and nothing from the merchant. And so the worker will accept this offer, since it is as good as (or better than) the alternative. In other words, by accepting the landlord's offer the worker gets negative utility—they lose whatever net value was earned from the interaction with the merchant.

If we take the normative stance that the worker has the right to the level of utility to be had by interacting with the merchant, then we can see that the landlord's offer is akin to the mugger's offer, which makes the worker worse off than the moral benchmark. The greater complication here is that the landlord (unlike the mugger) is not veering outside of what is within his right—namely, to trade with whomever he chooses—since the landlord simply announces circumstances in which he will interact with the merchant. By doing this he manages to coerce the worker.[16] The worker, who gets a choice and exercises it, and may therefore seem to have made the voluntary choice, ends up worse off than the significant moral benchmark and so could reasonably be described as having been coerced.

This complicates the simplicity of our neoclassical analysis. Coercion can occur in subtle ways. And what we often take to be voluntary may turn out not to be so on closer inspection. Some cases of the PFC thus can be dismissed on the grounds that the preconditions for using that principle—that all choices should be voluntary—are not satisfied.

Having told this cautionary tale, let me now move to a domain where we set aside reasons that may be there to contest the voluntariness claim. Can we, even after that, reasonably reject the PFC in some situations?

The Large Numbers Argument

Suppose that individuals make decisions freely and sign contracts voluntarily. If these contracts have no negative fallout on others, must the state always allow them? As I have already indicated in the opening section, the answer is no; but at the same time, the negative answer must not be ubiquitous, nor based on whimsy. I will develop some principles here that can allow us to be Paretians, but still, on occasion, eschew the PFC. The importance of this analysis goes beyond the few examples that are discussed here and can help guide the development of general principles of government intervention.

The principle that I will develop here is what I have elsewhere called the 'large numbers argument' (Basu 2003a), which is the claim that there are situations where each of a class of actions (for instance, an act of exchange, trade, or contract signing) could be morally justified, whereas the whole class of actions may be morally unacceptable. This possibility of morally distinguishing between *single* acts and a *collectivity* of a large number of such single acts was first put forward by Parfit (1984).[17] But this raises the question: Is this logically possible? In this section I construct a formal game-theoretic example to show that the answer is yes. This creates a policy conundrum: Should such acts be permitted or not? Given that the state often has to go by rules and cannot afford the complication of a case-by-case consideration, the example in this section could be construed as an argument for a rule-based violation of the PFC. I have discussed this in practical, real-life contexts elsewhere.[18] What follows may be viewed as the construction of a formal analytic foundation for such arguments. I shall return to some practical policy discussions in the context of specific topics later later.

Suppose there is a society in which for every integer there exists a person by the name of that integer. In other words, in this society there is a person named 1, a person named 2, a person named 3, and so on. The population of this society is clearly larger than that of China. Every person in this society has the choice of either 'accepting' or 'rejecting' some action. The action in question could be the decision to participate in an exchange, sign a contract, trade commodities, or join a firm that pays a high salary but harasses its workers. From now on, let us suppose that the action in question is that of signing a contract (for a job, for instance). Of course, signing a contract typically involves another person. We can get around this by assuming that there is another person, called 0, who is always prepared to accept the contract with everybody in this society. In order not to let this person complicate our analysis, I shall suppose that the person's utility never changes. So we really do not have to bring the person into the analysis explicitly.

Hence, an *outcome* of this 'game' could be thought of as an infinite stream of decisions, with the first decision representing person 1's choice, the second decision person 2's choice, the third decision person 3's choice, and so on. An outcome could therefore look like this: (accept, reject, reject, accept, . . .). What this represents is a case where person 1 chooses the accept outcome, 2 and 3 choose reject, 4 chooses accept, and so on.

Alternatively, suppose the outcome of the game looks like this: (accept, reject, accept, reject, accept, reject, . . .). This represents the case where every odd-numbered person signs the contract and every even-numbered person rejects it.

Next, define player i's 'payoff function' to be a rule that associates with every outcome a number denoting the utility that person i gets. So I am allowing for the possibility that each person's utility can depend on other people's actions.

What I am looking for is a game that has the following properties. First, for every person j, whether or not person j decides to sign the contract has no externality on other players. More formally, if the only difference between two outcomes is that in one of them person j chooses accept (to sign the contract) and in the other one of them person j chooses reject (not to sign the contract), then a person i, who is distinct from j, is indifferent between these two outcomes—j's choice has no impact on i's utility. I will call this property 1.

This immediately means that if an individual is better off by signing the contract, this will come under the purview of the PFC (since that person is better off and no one else is hurt by it). By the Pareto principle we have no reason to stop this contract, since one person is better off and no one is worse off.

Next we want the game to illustrate the large numbers argument. That is, it has to have the property that if a large number of people sign the contract, then others (the nonsigners) will be worse off. Formally, there exists a set of individuals such that, if, starting from the case where nobody signs the contract, all members of this set switch to signing the contract, then every other person (those not in the set) is worse off than in the case where no one signs the contract. I will call this property 2.

At first sight properties 1 and 2 seem irreconcilable. What follows, however, is a description of a game that satisfies both these properties and thereby shows that Parfit's moral conundrum—whereby each of a class of actions may be morally justified even though the *class* of actions is not morally justified—is at least a *logical* possibility.[19]

For every individual i, define the person's payoff function as follows. (A) First suppose that by choosing the action, person i gets a satisfaction of 1 util and by rejecting it gets 0. (B) Further, if an infinite number of people choose the action, assume that this gives person i a utility of 1, and if a finite number of people choose the action then this gives person i a utility of 3. Each person's total utility is found by aggregating the utilities from (A) and (B) described above—that is, what is got from the person's own decision and from that of all others.

To make sure we understand what is happening, consider the case where all persons from 2 onward accept the contract and person 1 rejects it. Clearly, in this case person 1 gets an aggregate utility of 1. Since an infinite number of people choose the action, this gives 1 to person 1, and since person 1 did not choose the action, he or she gets 0 from that.

If all others reject the action and person 1 accepts it, person 1 gets $3 + 1 = 4$. The 3 comes from the fact of a finite number of people having accepted the action, and the 1 comes from person 1's own acceptance.

Check that if everybody accepts the action, each person gets a utility of 2, and if everybody rejects the action, each person gets 3.

It is now easy to verify that if players have the payoff functions just described, then properties 1 and 2 will be satisfied. Consider the case where the outcome is such that an infinite number of people have chosen the accept outcome. Clearly, this fact will not change whether or not one player (say k) changes the strategy. Hence, if any person switches from rejection to acceptance, this person will be better off and no one will be worse off. Next consider an outcome where a finite number of people have chosen accept. One person's change of choice clearly will not alter this fact. As such, if one person now switches from reject to accept, this person is better off and no one is worse off. Since all outcomes must be such that either an infinite number of people choose accept or a finite number of people choose accept, the above argument establishes property 1. QED.

Now I will prove property 2. Let S be the collection of all individuals in this society whose name is an odd number. Consider an outcome in which no one chooses to sign the contract. Now if all members of S change their decision and decide to sign the contract (that is, they choose accept), then clearly those outside S will be worse off. Each one of them faces a utility decline of 2 (= 3 – 1). Therefore, property 2 is satisfied. QED.

To see some of the policy dilemmas that can arise in this game, consider the case in which the payoff functions of the citizens of this society are as just defined. Now suppose each citizen is given the freedom to make his or her own choice. So this is like a game where each person has to choose accept or reject. It is obvious that this game has a unique Nash equilibrium, where all players accept the contract, which could, for instance, be a contract for a job that exposes them to sexual harassment. This is because no matter what others do, each person is better off choosing accept. And in the Nash equilibrium each person gets a utility of 2.

Consider now the outcome in the above game when there is a law that prohibits all individuals from choosing the contract (that is, everybody is forced to choose the action reject). Evidently, every player i will now get a utility of 3. By equation (1), player i is better off than in the Nash equilibrium of the original case. Hence, not only is the Nash equilibrium in a regime where there is no legal prohibition on choosing the action Pareto suboptimal, everybody in this society would be better off if the action were prohibited.

If we were deciding on whether or not to prohibit people from signing the contract, using *any* social welfare criterion that happened to respect the Pareto principle, we would have to prohibit it. Of course, if starting from such a prohibition we allowed one agent to sign a harassment contract, we would achieve a Pareto improvement, since that person would be better off and, according to property 1, others would be unaffected. If we started making such 'opportunistic' adjustments of the law to allow for exceptions whenever such an exception resulted in a Pareto improvement, we would end up in a state that is Pareto inferior to what would prevail in a regime of a total prohibition. This is a paradoxical-sounding result, where each step leads in one direction but a collectivity of such steps leads elsewhere. There are examples of such paradoxes in the world of art, particularly in the works of Maurits Escher and Oscar Reutersvard.[20] This artistic equivalence is used explicitly in Basu (1994a) and Voorneveld (2009).

This paradoxical result is also germane to the construction of a principle for banning sexual harassment and some other labor market practices, such as exposure to excessive hazards. I will return to the moral quandary that this gives rise to after discussing the case of a finite society.

It was demonstrated above that the moral status of each single act or contract may be different from the moral status of a class of such acts or contracts. Some may object to this demonstration on the ground that it was based on the existence of an *infinite* number of potential contracts. Indeed, some may consider the realism of the economist's model of competitive general equilibrium to be suspect because of the assumption that the action of each individual has no effect on market variables, such as prices, but the action of a collection of individuals does have an effect.[21]

I argue here that the problem of infinity is avoidable if we relax the usual assumption of human preferences being transitive, and allow individuals to have what in choice theory and mathematical logic is called a 'quasi-transitive preference relation' instead. A person's preference is said to be quasi-transitive if, whenever x is preferred to y and y is preferred to z, it is also the case that x is preferred to z. The important aspect in which the transitivity of preference differs from quasi-transitivity is that the latter does not require the indifference relation to be transitive.[22] Hence, a person with a quasi-transitive preference may be indifferent between x and y and between y and z, but prefer x to z. This cannot happen in the case of a person whose preference is (fully) transitive.

Though most social scientists are trained to believe otherwise, a little introspection shows that the transitivity of indifference is a remarkably unrealistic assumption.[23] As discussed earlier in the book, most people will be indifferent between a cup of coffee with 1 grain of sugar and a cup of coffee with 2 grains of sugar,; and, more generally, between a cup with n grains and a cup with n + 1 grains. But they will not be indifferent between 0 grains and m grains, for a sufficiently large number m.

Recognizing this is a good way to reconcile two standard assumptions of the competitive market model: that an individual's action does not affect another person's welfare and that the actions of a collection of individuals may well effect the welfare of someone not belonging to this collection.

I will use the assumption here of quasi-transitivity not in a competitive model but in a game model. Return to the same kind of setting as in the section above, but now assume that the set of individuals is finite. Let me for simplicity's sake assume that we have a society with three individuals. As before, each person has to choose between accepting some deal or contract, or rejecting it. Let me use 1 to denote accept and 0 to denote reject. So saying that a person chooses 1 means that the person accepts the contract. After all three persons make their choices, the outcome can be described by a triple, in which the first number describes person 1's choice, the second number describes person 2's choice, and the third number person 3's choice. The outcome $(1,1,0)$ thus means that persons 1 and 2 accepted the contract, while person 3 rejected it.

I will now assume that each person has a preference relation over all possible pairs of outcomes, and the preference relation is quasi-transitive. Let me now impose a couple of restrictions on individual preferences. First, I will assume, as before, that each person prefers 1 to 0 for themselves (no matter what the others choose). Further, it will be assumed that if two outcomes, x and y, differ only in the choice of person i, then person j (who is distinct from i) will be indifferent between x and y. This will be called property 3, and this simply says that one person's action has no externality on others. This merely formalizes the standard assumption of no externality in competitive markets and is a counterpart of property 1 in the above analysis.

Next consider a seemingly contradictory property, called property 4, which says that there are situations where if several individuals change their actions, then an individual who is not one of them can be affected, in the sense of being better or worse off. Property 4 is the counterpart of property 2 in the finite-population case. If individual preferences were transitive, properties 3 and 4 would not be compatible in a finite-population society like the one I am analyzing now. But with a quasi-transitive preference, the two properties become compatible, thereby giving concrete shape to Parfit's paradox.

Let me now analyze the possible outcomes of this 'game.' I put game within inverted commas to remind the reader that these are games with no payoff functions, but preference relations over the outcomes, in which the preference relations are complete and quasi-transitive. There is a substantial literature in economics on aggregating quasi-transitive individual preferences.[24] Yet there is little on games with quasi-transitive individual preferences. So I am about to conduct a somewhat novel exercise.

To see the kind of results we can get, consider the case where properties 3 and 4 are true in the following sense. If two people switch from action 0 to action 1, and the third person holds fast to his or her choice of action, then the third person is worse off, and if only one person changes the action, the other two people are unaffected by it. In addition to properties 3 and 4, assume the following is true: when other people's choices remains the same, each person prefers to sign such a contract (that is, prefers to choose 1 over 0).

In this game, the Nash equilibrium is clearly given by (1,1,1), since no matter what others do (as long as their actions are held constant), each individual prefers 1 to 0. We can think of individual preferences as being compatible with properties 3 and 4, however, which imply that each individual prefers (0,0,0) to (1,1,1). Let me assume that this is the case. Then (0,0,0) Pareto dominates (1,1,1). Hence, if a government committed to the Pareto criterion has to choose between imposing a law disallowing sexual harassment or prohibiting excessive workplace hazards (in whatever example we are considering), and having no such law, it should opt for having such a law.

But the matter does not end there. As soon as we consider other policy options, it leads us to a moral quandary. Suppose such a law is in place and so the outcome is (0,0,0). It is easy to see that (1,0,0) is Pareto superior to (0,0,0), (1,1,0) is Pareto superior to (1,0,0), and (1,1,1) is Pareto superior to (1,1,0).[25] This game has no Pareto optimal outcome. Therefore, we no longer have a compelling case that if a change is a Pareto improvement, it must be allowed, since, as we just saw, the repeated use of this criterion can have us end up with a Pareto inferior outcome.

One way of overcoming this problem is to override consumer sovereignty and work with what may be described as each consumer's 'subliminal preference'—that is, an ordering (a complete and transitive relation) that may be thought of as the 'true' preference underlying a person's *self-perceived* preference. Roughly speaking, a person's subliminal preference is an ordering created by converting as few as possible cases of perceived indifference into strict preference. If we maintain that social decisions ought to be based on individuals' *subliminal* preferences, then in the above example the Pareto deadlock gets broken. It is now easy to see that in the above example, given individual preferences as described, the only outcome that cannot be Pareto optimal under any subliminal preference triple (that is, for the three players) is (1,1,1). If in addition we prefer to treat players symmetrically, the game being fully symmetrical, the preferred outcome must be (0,0,0), justifying once again a ban on the contract, even though consenting adults may knowingly want to sign such contracts. It is worth emphasizing, however, that this entails overruling consumer sovereignty—the expression of individual preferences as perceived by the individuals themselves.

Acts and Rules

The games discussed in the above sections illustrate the conflict between 'act consequentialism' and 'rule consequentialism,' where the former refers to a moral system in which each act is evaluated in terms of one's consequentialist ethic before one takes a stand in favor of or against the act. Rule consequentialism, on the other hand, refers to a moral system in which one adheres to certain rules of action, where the rules are evaluated using one's consequentialist ethic. In other words, these are counterparts of the standard notions of act utilitarianism and rule utilitarianism. It should be stressed that these moral systems are all part of consequentialism, in the sense that the goodness of a behavior is judged in terms of its *consequences*—the kind of world the behavior brings about and how human welfares are affected in the world created by the behavior. This stands in contrast to deontological ethics, which evaluate actions in terms of how well they are in keeping with certain codes of behavior—one must never tell a lie, one must not eat pork, and so forth—*no matter what the consequences of such action*. For the most part, I will be concerned here with 'Pareto-inclusive ethics,' meaning moral systems that respect the Pareto principle to the extent possible.

Consider now the above three-player game, and assume that a moral agent (who is not a player and in that sense stands outside the game), committed to any Pareto-inclusive consequentialist ethic, has to recommend each player's choice of action or strategy. If this moral agent were an *act* consequentialist, he or she would recommend to each person seeking the agent's advice that the person choose action 1 over 0. This is because each such choice is a Pareto improvement. As such, the social outcome will be (1,1,1).

Now suppose that the moral agent, using the same moral principle as the above one but committed to *rule* consequentialism, has to choose between the following two rules. Rule 1: whenever persons face a choice between signing a sexual harassment contract (action 1) and not signing it (action 0), they should choose action 0. Rule 2: whenever persons face a choice between action 1 and action 0, they should choose action 1. Clearly, the moral agent will opt for rule 1, since this is the rule that leads to the Pareto superior outcome. Hence, the social outcome will be (0,0,0).

Since (0,0,0) is strictly Pareto preferred to (1,1,1), the above example shows that not only does rule consequentialism lead to a different recommendation from act consequentialism but it also can lead to a Pareto-superior choice. It is noteworthy that the argument for banning certain voluntary transactions is here founded in consequentialism (albeit *rule* consequentialism). There is no resort to deontological ethics, as is often the case when intervening in people's free choice.

The large numbers argument—namely, the ability to morally differentiate single acts and a large number of such acts (without abandoning the Pareto principle)—helps us analyze several practical policy matters.[26] It can provide a foundation for why we may wish to outlaw the yellow dog contract, as in the Norris-La Guardia Act of 1932. It could be claimed that if one worker prefers to give up the right to join trade unions in order to get a certain job that demands this of workers, then this may be a Pareto improvement. But if such yellow dog contracts are made legal, then lots of firms will offer these contracts, and the terms for jobs without a yellow dog clause may deteriorate so much that those who are strongly averse to giving up the right to join unions will be worse off in this world. Of course, we have to construct a model and show that this is true in realistic economic scenarios. All that I have done here is to demonstrate that this is logically possible, even in finite societies. Once this has been done, we can clearly distinguish between allowing a single worker and a single employer to sign such a contract, and legalizing such contracts in general.

To make my task harder, I have concentrated in this chapter on actions or contracts, which seem to make some people better off without making anybody worse off. But the large numbers argument can be carried over to other contexts as well. There was a debate raging in the United States over the last few years as to whether the state should legalize the use of torture to extract information from prisoners. In a recent newspaper article, Anne Kornblut presents the pros and cons of Charles Krauthammer's argument that the use of torture in limited situations should be legalized.[27] Krauthammer tries to persuade us by constructing extreme examples. A bomb, say, has been planted by a terrorist and it will kill a million people. The terrorist will not provide you with any information on how to defuse the bomb unless you torture the terrorist. Krauthammer maintains that it is morally incumbent on us to torture the terrorist. Many people would agree that this person should be tortured, because it is a case of one person's suffering versus a million persons' suffering.

One immediate difficulty with this contention occurs with a seemingly inconsequential alteration in roles. Suppose we live in a strange world where the bomb has been planted by a terrorist, but the only way to get the terrorist to reveal this information is to torture an innocent person who has no connection with the bomb or the terrorist. Through some magical connection, inflicting unbearable pain on this innocent person makes the terrorist speak. The numbers of those suffering pain and those being killed are unchanged but many more people will be uncomfortable with the above recommendation now.

But even ignoring this difficulty, the point that Krauthammer misses is that the fact that he can create examples where torture would be justified is not equivalent to a case for *legalizing torture*. Legalizing torture immediately refers to a *class* of situations. There may be plenty of reasons not to give torture the sanctity of legislative justification, even though this will mean that our hands are tied in some special cases where we may have reason to use torture.

Return to the case of sexual harassment in the workplace or the problem of hazardous work. To justify banning hazardous work, for instance, by using the large numbers argument entails a different kind of reasoning than what is popularly used to justify such bans. The case for a ban here does not rest on the fact that *the worker's* health will be harmed. If the worker is willing to take that harm for the extra money that will be earned, we have no moral jurisdiction over this to stop the worker. We must not treat the worker whose health is damaged as the victim and have the courts step in, although that is typically what is done. The large numbers argument points to the fact that many workers accepting such contracts may have a negative welfare impact on *other* workers—for example, those who have an especially strong aversion to hazardous work—and that becomes the real basis of why we may wish to disallow such contracts. This is not a standard case of externality since the signing of each such contract has no effect on other workers. It is only the signing of a *class* of such contracts that has this effect.

For economic theorists, it is interesting to note that, if we are to demonstrate this in a finite-population economy, then we have to allow for the fact that individuals may fail to satisfy the transitivity of indifference. While there is a lot of work on intransitive preferences in economics, modeling market equilibria with individuals who have quasi-transitive preferences is rare.

It should be clarified that I have not constructed a full argument for why voluntarily agreed-on sexual harassment contracts should be banned but instead have simply explained how such a ban can be justified even though we may be committed to the Pareto principle. To go further and assert that it is incumbent on us to ban such contracts we have to use some more moral axioms. For developing a transparent and *generalizable* criterion for banning certain voluntary transactions we need to have some prior normative rules for ranking preferences the same way that we rank actions—castigating some as bad and praising some as good.

We do not typically morally rank preferences, but it is arguable that we can and should.[28] If some persons say that they do not like people of a certain race, or that they prefer not to be friends with anybody who is overweight, most of us would consider these to be unacceptable preferences. We may not do anything about it, but we still consider such preferences to be morally wrong. Let me call all preferences that we do *not* consider morally wrong 'maintainable preferences.' Here are some preferences that I would consider maintainable, and I expect that most other people would agree.

"Jack prefers apples to oranges."

"Jane prefers not to work four days a week."

"Esther would rather be unemployed than face sexual harassment at work."

"Asmita considers it her right to be able to join a trade union and she prefers not to join a company that denies her this option."

Clearly we cannot have *moral* objections to these preferences. You may not wish to marry the person who plans to work three days a week or, for that matter, the one who does not share your passion for oranges, but surely you will not morally castigate these people for having these preferences.

Among maintainable preferences we need to separate out two kinds, though, and the rules for government intervention depend on this categorization. To understand this, observe that some preferences may be dysfunctional in the sense that they could hurt their carriers. Persons with the second preference above will clearly be poorer for working so little. So they have to pay a price for their preference.

Now we, as outside observers, may decide to take a stand on this 'price for having a certain preference.' We may consider certain preferences to be so understandable that no one should have to pay a price for having that preference. Many would consider the last two preferences and especially the penultimate listed above to be of this kind. Not only is the strong aversion to harassment a maintainable preference but most of us also would hold that no one should have to pay a price for having this preference.[29] Many would feel similarly about a worker's right to associate with other workers. Let us call a maintainable preference that has this property an 'inviolable preference.'

Notice that this is typically not the case with the first or second preference in the list above. It would be perfectly reasonable to tell the person with the second preference: "Yours is a maintainable preference—I have no moral objections to it; but you do understand that you will be poorer by virtue of having this preference. You surely cannot expect society to compensate you for your high leisure preference."

In other words, while the second person's love of leisure and the third person's strong aversion to workplace harassment are both maintainable preferences, only the latter is an inviolable preference.

Of course, being a normative matter, there is no hard-and-fast rule about where we should draw the line between these categories. It is also possible to see that what we consider inviolable may change through time and even across space. But in most of our minds, at this point in time, we can create a distinction between these categories.

I am now ready to construct an argument for why it may be correct to ban yellow dog contracts and disallow contractual sexual harassment in the workplace. Suppose we consider the fourth preference above to be inviolable and then consider the case of yellow dog contracts. Assume firms are permitted to demand that potential employees relinquish the right to join trade unions. This will give rise to two kinds of firms (for the same kind of work): some paying a lower wage and making no such demands, and others paying a better wage but requiring individuals to give up their right to join unions.[30]

Workers with strong preference for joining unions—the fourth type of preference in the above list—will now join the former firms. In other words, they will have to be reconciled to a lower income *by virtue of their preference*. But the inviolability of the preference for joining unions means that this should not happen. The way to ensure this is to have a law like the Norris-La Guardia Act that bans yellow dog contracts.

This is the crux of the argument about why certain rights may have to be made nontradable. Allowing the trading of such a right inflicts a cost on some people who have a strong preference for holding on to these rights, and if this preference is inviolable, then government is required to protect people from having to pay a price for having the preference. One way of doing this is to disallow anybody to trade or waive this right.

It is worth noting that the overall moral system being used here is neither pure welfarism nor deontological ethics. It is best described as a 'miscible moral system,' which uses welfarism and in particular Paretianism to first weed out certain options, and then permit the use of nonwelfarist considerations, such as dignity, autonomy, and agency, to further eliminate options.[31]

We may be able to carry this argument over to other matters: sexual harassment in the workplace, hazardous work, the well-being of laborers employed in export-processing zones where they may be required to give up some rights, and so on. Yes, individual freedom would at first sight seem to require that having given a person a right—such the right not to be harassed at work—we should give the person the additional right to trade this right. Given individual rationality, this can only benefit the individual. But the exercising of this latter right, the right to waive the basic right, could mean that others who attach a greater value to the basic right will now have to pay a price for that. If this is unacceptable, then the state needs to step in.

Multiple Equilibria

Another general argument for disregarding the PFC occurs in economies in which there are several equilibria. Consider, in particular, an economy that has two competitive equilibria. Based on the Invisible Hand Theorem discussed in chapter 3 of this book, we know that each of these equilibria has to be Pareto optimal. That being so, neither equilibrium can be Pareto superior to the other.[32] Keeping this in mind, consider imposing a ban that prevents a particular equilibrium from being realized and therefore deflects the economy to the only other equilibrium. In that case, the ban cannot be denied on the grounds that it will cause a Pareto worsening. This contention was used (Basu and Van 1998) to justify banning child labor in some situations.[33] It was first demonstrated that some economies are likely to have more than one equilibrium—in particular, one equilibrium in which wages are low and households send their children to work, and another in which wages are high and children do not work. In case the country is caught in the former equilibrium, a ban on child labor can be justified or, more minimally, a ban cannot be denied on grounds of the Pareto principle.

A single child not being allowed to work will of course hurt the child's welfare, since typically it is poverty that drives children to work, and stopping one child from working would have a negligible effect on adult wages and therefore on the households' poverty. But when a general legislative ban is put in place, all children will be forced to leave work. The unfilled demand for labor caused by this will push up adult wages, and it is entirely possible that in the new equilibrium children will be better off.[34] Once again, behind this is the large numbers argument. In general equilibrium theory we usually *assume* this—that one buyer or seller has no impact on prices, but that a collectivity does. The formal analysis sheds light on how we can actually achieve this in a finite or countable society.

This argument could potentially be taken to other matters of labor market regulation. But each case will have to be analyzed theoretically and empirically to see if the argument does actually apply to it. One ancient problem on which this has been used to shed light has to do with the statutory limit on work hours (Raynauld and Vidal 1998; Singh 2003). Should the law be used to set a limit on the maximum number of hours that a worker is allowed to work? At first sight the answer seems to be no, based on the PFC,[35] If an employer wants a worker to work for fourteen hours a day and there is a worker willing to work that many hours, there is no reason why the government should get in the way. But note that one reason why workers may wish to work so many hours is that the hourly wage rate is low. Workers could then be driven to work hard for subsistence reasons. A statutory limit on work hours can, by limiting the supply of labor, push up the hourly wage rate, and it is possible that at this higher wage rate people would not want to work that many hours. In other words, the labor market may have two or more equilibria, in which case banning the long work-hours equilibrium is fully compatible with a commitment to the Pareto principle.[36]

There are other problem areas within labor market intervention where it is not evident whether any of these assertions apply. But at least now we know what to look for if we are to ban some form of voluntary contract without abandoning the Pareto principle.

One such problem that is a source of some concern to the International Labor Organization and other activist groups is that, in some developing countries, workers who wish to work in an export-processing zone are being asked to give up their right to collective bargaining as a condition for being allowed to work for a firm located there. The principle of free contract seems to suggest that it is fine to ask workers to do so, as long no one coerces a worker to work in an export-processing zone. If a worker is willing to give up the right to bargain collectively in order to work in such a special zone, there must be other benefits that make this worthwhile to the worker.

At this stage this argument seems quite compelling. If we are to stop the use of such yellow dog contracts in export-processing zones, we cannot leave this to some arbitrary hand-waving justification or an opportunistic resort to some deontological ethic. We need to construct a formal argument founded on persuasive ethical principles. What this chapter has done is to highlight where those arguments may come from. We basically have to see if the large numbers argument or the multiple-equilibria one applies to this problem. If it does not, we will have to treat this as a case where free contracting has to be allowed. If this means that workers will be asked to leave their right to collective bargaining at the door of the export-processing zone, then we have to put up with that. To do otherwise would likely lead to a Pareto worsening, and this would hurt the very workers we are trying to protect.

Domains of Intervention

Market fundamentalists, who would leave it all to individuals pursuing their own interests in the belief that the invisible hand invariably guides society to some collectively optimal state, are getting both Smith and economic theory wrong. There are cases where one needs the visible hand of the state to stop market transactions. The standard justification for this in economics is externality. But what if there is no observable externality on uninvolved third parties? For many economists, this means that there is no further justification for collective or state intervention. Yet this leaves us with many difficult cases—voluntary slavery, sexual harassment where the possibility of this is made clear to workers before they sign up to work, hazardous work, and trade in body parts.

Faced with these troublesome questions, many clutch at whatever opportunistic rationalization is available—also known as straws. This is risky, especially in today's globalized world where we may wish to enact laws for distant nations or agree to collective conventions that are enforced on all countries. For many well-meaning activists, it is easy to err on the opposite side of the market-fundamentalist economist by seeking to ban a variety of labor market contracts that in the context of a developed nation, may well be justified. It is easy to forget that to stop poor workers from working in hazardous conditions may be to condemn them and their family to starvation, and that to legislatively ban child labor under all circumstances may risk pushing children into prostitution and causing malnourishment.

In the contemporary world of free-flowing capital and goods, interventions to stop contracts, exchanges, and trade that are voluntarily undertaken, with no obvious negative externality on others, need to be founded on appealing ethical principles. I would go further and argue that the Pareto principle, which says that between two social states of the world, if there is one called x where no one is worse off and at least one person is better off than in the other state, y, then x should be chosen over y, unless it can be shown that this principle is self-contradictory—that is, that the repeated use of this principle leads to a negation of the same principle. This chapter aimed to outline some fundamental criteria that could be used to decide if a particular contract should be allowed or not. In particular, the chapter demonstrated that there are some specific situations where the Pareto principle does indeed turn out to be self-contradictory in the above sense.

As described in this chapter, these criteria apply naturally to some specific problems, such as that of child labor, sexual harassment in the workplace, and the use of statutory limits on work hours. But there are other problems where they either do not apply or we do not as yet know if they do. These have to remain on our research agenda. By trying to base our interventions on well-founded underlying principles, we can at least hope to eliminate arbitrary interventions, and more important, the risk that small and powerful lobbies with their own selfish interests will hijack the policies of governments and international organizations.

CHAPTER 8

Poverty, Inequality, and Globalization

Governance and the Globe

The efficiency and fairness of a market economy are intricately connected to the nature of governance and institutions for collective action available to society. This was the subject matter of the opening chapters of the book. The emphasis is on the word 'intricately,' since this connection is far from obvious, and ideologues on either side of the debate tend to underestimate the complexity of it. On the one hand, we have the Invisible Hand Theorem, which shows how individuals going about serving their own interests can end up creating an efficient society that serves their collective interests. By drawing on some existing writings by economists and constructing new arguments, however, it was also demonstrated that this proposition hinges on several conditions—technical and conceptually substantial.

Once these provisos are recognized, it becomes clear that for society to attain efficiency, and, even more so, fairness and justice, we need appropriate governance along with social institutions and norms. For one, we need rules, *given which* a market can function effectively. In the absence of government or some form of collective action, it is likely that the market will descend into Hobbesian disorder, and inequality and poverty will prevail at levels that are intolerable.

One natural domain for studying the intricate link between market outcomes and governance is the globe itself. Since we do not have a global government, and the structures of global rule setting and organization are still rudimentary, the world as a whole is a convenient terrain for understanding how markets function in the absence of an overarching government. That is what the present and the next chapters set out to do. This chapter studies global inequality and poverty, and the special problems that arise from the fact that political globalization is trailing way behind economic globalization. I will argue that inequality in the world is high precisely because of this handicap of political globalization. This assertion will be used to enter into some normative and policy questions about what can be done within the current global polity. The next chapter studies the nature of politics and democracy spawned by the kind of globalization that has occurred thus far.

Since we are beginning to tread on some normative terrain, I want to stress that this book is not about the size of government. In my opinion, much of that debate has been a misleading one. As we saw in chapters 2 and 3, the state has a huge role to play in regulating a market economy and trying to redistribute some of its spoils. But if the government has been captured by a lobby or corporation, it is better to have less of it. If a nation happens to have a mature sense of social norms that leads to natural restrictions on antisocial behavior, then there may be less need for direct government action. As I tried to show in chapter 4, social norms can be a substitute for the law, which in the end is nothing but a set of beliefs in people's minds.

What I do believe—and since this is a normative *axiom*, it should be placed visibly on the table—is that poverty and inequality are 'bads.' The extent of poverty in today's world is unacceptable. The reason that the world does not erupt in dissent is because a huge amount of intellectual effort goes into making it *appear* acceptable. Of inequality and poverty, it is the latter that should be our primary target, and though economic inequality is also bad, we may have to tolerate some amount of it *in order* to control poverty. This normative stance is not being derived from something else; it is an *axiom*. I state this bluntly to prevent confusion. It will lead to some interesting policy positions. It may mean that *given the present system*, we may need to follow many of the standard policies that economists recommend concerning trade, tariffs, fiscal policy, and the money supply. This is compatible with directing energy into trying to conceive better worlds. I will address this in the closing chapter.

Inequality

That inequality in the world is large, we all know. Yet once we look carefully at the numbers and ponder them, the extent of it takes one's breath away. Much has been written about the world's wealthy people. The stories of the super rich—say, the top one hundred people—make for interesting reading. The super rich are a motley group. Some had inherited wealth, and some began poor; some have had alcohol problems, and some not; some live simple lives, traveling economy class and driving old sedans, and most do not. For those looking for tips to join these ranks, I should mention that one good first step is not to get much education. Among those classified as the world's ten-richest people in 2007 by *Forbes* magazine, at least five either dropped out of college or never went to one.[1] The information that does cause surprise is just *how* rich these people are. According to the latest estimates, the world's ten-richest people in 2007 had a combined wealth of $343.5 billion.[2]

What makes this otherwise-entertaining information tragic is the other end of the spectrum. Information about the poorest people is hard to get, but we know a lot about national averages. Consider Ethiopia. It has a population of over seventy million people and a national income of around $12 billion per annum. If we assume that the ten-richest people in the world earn a return of 10 percent per annum on their assets, then their combined annual income is virtually three times the annual income of all the people of Ethiopia. Since Ethiopia also has some rich people, the income gap between the poorest, say, 90 percent in Ethiopia and the world's richest people is hard to comprehend.

If we leave out individuals and turn to nations, the gaps shrink, but they are still striking. Take the richest and poorest countries (in terms of per capita income) in the list of the 152 nations for which detailed data are provided in the *World Development Indicators 2005* (World Bank 2005).[3] These countries are, respectively, Norway at the top, and tying at the bottom rank, Ethiopia and Burundi. Norway has a per capita income of $43,400, and Ethiopia and Burundi have a per capita income of $90. If we make purchasing power parity corrections on these figures, they get a bit closer, but the gap is still enormous. A person picked at random in Norway is expected to be sixty times as rich as a person chosen randomly in Burundi, even with a purchasing power parity correction.

I present these statistics in particular to draw attention to the fact that even though the debate on whether global inequality has risen or fallen in recent times may be unresolved, the *amount* of inequality is staggering; the *hiatus* between the richest and poorest people is *too large*, and the *extent* of poverty on earth (whether or not it has risen lately) is unacceptable. I like to believe that there will come a time when looking back at today's world, human beings will wonder how we tolerated this situation. It is often commented, by pointing to the staggering wealth of the rich, some of whom have made their money from scratch, that this shows the greatness of capitalism. But to praise capitalism for this in a world of so much poverty and destitution is like pointing to Genghis Khan's or Nero's fabulous power and wealth, and admiring the greatness of a monarchy.

From this observation, to answer the question, "What should be done?" turns out to be much harder than persons of action commonly suppose. Seeing global poverty, we frequently leap to conclusions such as how bad governments are in the developing nations to leave their citizens so poor or how mean governments are in the industrialized nations not to divert more money to poor nations. Once one takes account of the realities and constraints within which policymakers and politicians in poor and rich nations function, none of these propositions survive—at least not in any obvious way. There are many changes that a vast majority of us may want, and yet none of us are empowered to do anything about it. Indeed, there are rich people (admittedly not too many) who have expressed abhorrence for the economic system in which we live. Some have taken the line that "given that we *do* have this system, and since I have the talent to prosper in it, I will do so; but I wish that you had the sense to realize that we have a grossly unjust system that deserves to be altered." One can virtually see such a declaration in the statements and actions of some left-leaning millionaires, successful activist writers, and Hollywood radicals. Despite the fact that this may be no more than words, one is grateful for it, especially because it contrasts so sharply with the jaded plans and proposals, like the Washington consensus, that emerge from organizations representing the vested interests of rich countries and the elites of poor nations; the sole aim is to perpetuate the status quo. As Ha-Joon Chang (2002a, 2002b) argues so persuasively, these conservative proposals are really a disguise for kicking away the ladder after one has made it to the top.

The intellectual design problem of how to redistribute income and mitigate poverty is a difficult one; we do not have ready answers. But as soon as we admit that we live in a seriously flawed system that needs not just policy tinkering but rather a major overhaul, then at least a first step is taken. For major policy shifts, we have to begin by asking ourselves hard questions: What are the connections between inequality and poverty? Do we have to tolerate one if we wish to wipe out the other? If so, what should our priorities be?

The aim of this chapter is to answer some of these questions. I will begin by maintaining that today's inequality has some important connections with globalization. One reason why within-country inequality seems to be on the rise around the world—from Japan and Sweden, onetime bastions of equality, to the United States, China, and India—has to do with globalization, and the increased mobility of capital and highly skilled labor. The acceleration of *economic* globalization over the last half century while institutional and political arrangements have remained stagnant has given rise to some practical problems that will concern me in this and the next chapter. So let me begin by quickly reviewing some of the more interesting features of globalization.

Some Facts of Globalization

Has globalization led to greater inequality or less?[4] This question has greatly exercised the minds of many analysts. The reason why it has loomed so large in our debates is that for many ideologues, how we answer this question amounts to a verdict on globalization. I believe that seeking a verdict on globalization is a hopeless project. First of all, the term is too much of a catchall, and therefore it can be good and bad, depending on what aspect of it we are looking at, in which period, and at which location. It was a step in globalization when the Spaniards came into contact with the Incas in the early sixteenth century. And judging by the fact that the native populations of the New World rapidly declined under the combined might of the sword and new bacteria, clearly this globalization was not good. Even if it could be argued that the native populations are better off *today* than they would have been had they remained 'undiscovered,' it could still be argued that their welfare, aggregated over the last few centuries, has been adversely affected. On the other hand, when the British came into contact with the Chinese of Hong Kong, that was also a step toward globalization, and it could be maintained that on this occasion globalization benefited all the parties involved.

This diversity of experience suggests two things: that a single answer for the effect of globalization is too much to expect, and that globalization is *potentially* beneficial for all.[5] The latter suggests the need for policy design that can convert the potential benefit into an actual one, and that will indeed be the driving motive behind the policy analysis in this chapter. Globalization is the subject of virulent attacks nowadays and is equated with corporate control. I have no difficulty with an attack on the latter and in fact believe it is desirable, but globalization is much more than the rule of global capital, as it is often made out to be. Globalization leads to the intermixing of people, the flow of music and culture between distant lands, and it prepares the ground for the breakdown of narrow national and racial chauvinisms—all attractive properties. Even in terms of pure economic well-being, it has the *potential* to lift people out of poverty.

Still, the discussion of the normative qualities of globalization—for instance, whether it is good for us—which occupies so much space in public debates (and on which I will make some limited comments), is on one level a futile debate. Globalization is the unintended consequence of the actions of billions of individuals over the course of history, and it not apparent if anybody has the power to stall, let alone reverse it. Its inevitability makes it a bit like gravity. We can surely talk about the goodness or badness of grav-

TABLE 7

Levels of GDP Per Capita, 1500–1998 (in 1990 PPP Dollars)

	1500	1700	1913	1998
United States	400	527	5,301	27,331
Sweden	695	977	3,096	18,685
United Kingdom	714	1,250	4,921	18,714
Japan	500	570	1,387	20,413
India	550	550	673	1,746
China	600	600	552	3,117
Africa	400	400	585	1,368
Ratio of richest to poorest	1.8:1	3.1:1	9.4:1	20:1

Source: Madison 2001

ity ("how it pulls us all down"), but such conversations are unlikely to be of much value.

So let me move on to the facts of globalization and inequality. The rise of globalization, as measured by trade volumes and capital flows, has been written about extensively (Bhagwati 2004). The total value of exports all over the world in 2006 was $12,063 billion, up from $3,452 billion in 1990, and the total amount of foreign direct investment globally in 2006 was $1,352 billion, while it was $202 billion in 1992 (World Bank 2008).

As far as prosperity and inequality go, though there is scope for debate about whether global regional inequality has increased or decreased over the last two or three decades along with its relationship to growth, the trend, viewed over a long stretch of time and measured as the ratio between the richest and the poorest, seems to be an unequivocal deterioration.[6] According to Angus Madison's calculations (2001), displayed in table 7, if we track the per capita GDP of large regions of the world, the growing disparity is obvious. The richest region was 1.8 times richer than the poorest region half a millennium ago, whereas currently, the richest region has a per capita income that is 20 times the income of the poorest region.

What has happened in recent times remains more controversial.[7] The income gap between the richest and poorest nations seems to be climbing sharply. If we take the average per capita income of the twenty-richest countries and the average per capita income of the twenty-poorest ones, and look at the ratio of these two numbers, it was eighteen in 1960, but had risen to thirty-seven by 1995 (World Bank 2001; see also Pritchett 1997).

A more comprehensive way to measure inequality is to compute the Gini coefficient.[8] What do we find if we do this for nations? Interestingly, the answer depends critically on whether we use population-weighted or population-unweighted data, and a part of the controversy is caused by this difference. If we use population-weighted data, this means we pretend that all Chinese earn the per capita income of China, all Indians earn the per capita income of India, and so on, and then compute the Gini coefficient of the world. The use of unweighted data means that each country is treated as one person earning the per capita income of that country. So evidently both methods have their shortcomings. This problem is encountered in economics at various levels. Even within the household there is often a lot of inequality, and this is especially significant for households that have internal conflicts of interest (Basu 2006a; see also Alaka Basu 1992; and Agarwal 1997). But thanks to the inadequacy of data, we frequently are compelled to treat the household as a single decision-making unit.

If we go the route of using unweighted data for each nation, then we find that the Gini coefficient of intercountry inequality has grown over the last few decades (Milanovic 2002). On the other hand, if we use population-weighted data, we find that the Gini coefficient has been declining slowly but almost monotonically since the late 1960s, with the pace of decline picking up a bit in the 1990s (Melchior 2001; Melchior, Telle, and Wiig 2000). The latter is driven in large measure by the strong economic growth in China since the late 1970s and India since the early 1990s, since the population weights for these countries are high.

Thanks to improving data, we can now also compute the global, interpersonal Gini coefficient. Sudhir Anand and Paul Segal (2008) find that global inequality is huge by this measure, but that there is no significant trend one way or the other over the last three decades of the twentieth century. Global interpersonal Gini fluctuates between 0.63 and 0.69. To put this in perspective, virtually no nation has an inequality as large as this. The qualifier 'virtually' is important, because there are a few nations within which inequality is as large as in the world. Namibia, for instance, has a Gini coefficient of 0.74 (World Bank 2007).

It should now be clear that depending on exactly what one chooses to use as the measure, one can find almost any evidence. Is one measure clearly superior to another? If we are interested in *individual* well-being, as much of economics is, it may seem right that we use population-weighted data. To treat China and Canada as comparable units does not seem right. But there are two possible responses to this. Given the significance of the nation-state as a political unit, and given that our political perceptions are shaped by an awareness of intercountry situations, there may be a case for trying to find out what is happening to intercountry incomes. Second, if we are interested, ultimately, in the individual, instead of looking at either the population-unweighted or population-weighted intercountry inequality, we should look at global interpersonal inequality. This is because we lose vital information if we count all the people of China as one person or treat all the people of China as if they each earn the per capita income of China, especially since inequality in China has been growing. The same is true for India. Fortunately, this debate's resolution is not critical to what I want to argue here.

If I were to try to associate global inequality with globalization, I would take the longer-run view of what has happened, since globalization is a process that has been with us for centuries. Globalization has gone through some brief periods of retreat (Williamson 2002), but the long-run process has been a slow and steady one of the globe coming together. The long-term regional inequality (and I am not equating this to interpersonal inequality and poverty, though interpersonal inequality has probably moved in tandem with regional inequality) seems also to have increased over the extremely long run. But no matter what view we take of the trends, it seems easy to contend that there is reason for concern. First, while the Gini coefficient is important, the gap between the richest and poorest is important as well. If a sizable population feels increasingly marginalized because they find themselves becoming poor relative to global wealth, this is bound to stoke political volatility. We worry about individual decisions that are on their own tiny and imperceptible, but increase aggregate pollution to intolerable levels and lead to global warming. Something similar is true of global inequality and mass poverty. And like environmental degradation, they can cause political degradation, leading to insurgencies and violence that make civilized life impossible. Even if that did not happen, such yawning income gaps as occur today would seem to me to be normatively unacceptable. No matter what the trajectory has been, and no matter what its connection to globalization, the level of inequality that we see today, as cited at the start of this chapter, is far too large for complacency. Poverty, though, is even more intolerable than inequality, and we need to think through their interconnections before we think of crafting policy interventions. I will turn to that after the next section, which is a brief discussion of some possible fallouts of globalization.

Some Analytics of Globalization

To understand how globalization can have the negative fallout of marginalizing people, despite its *potential* to benefit all, consider the case where the world's markets for goods and services are suddenly and fully opened up for free movement. Given that a disproportionately large share of the world's GDP comes from the industrialized nations, it seems reasonable to predict that the prices of goods in poor nations will converge more rapidly toward the prices in industrialized nations than the latter converge toward the former. In other words, the international prices of goods and services will move to somewhere between the prices in industrialized nations and those in developing countries, but closer to the former.

Labor being less mobile than goods and services, it seems reasonable to expect that for sections of the labor force in poor nations, and especially for the illiterate and unskilled, who are unable to take advantage of new technology, wages will lag behind prices.[9] Hence, for some of the poorest people there can be a period of increased hardship before the benefits of opening up trickle down. This is one of the critical problems of rapid globalization. To a certain extent, the reported increase in inequality within poor nations (for India, see Banerjee and Piketty 2005) is a consequence of this.

Conversely, it is natural to expect that with globalization, the skilled end of the labor market in poor countries will benefit disproportionately. Their access to modern technology will increase their pay. Also, as their compatriots find jobs in developed countries and move out, the shortage of their skill in the home country will push the price for their work up and make them richer. Banerjee and Thomas Piketty's study shows that the group that has gained disproportionately in India over the last decade is the richest 0.01 percent of the population. It is not hard to show that as income stretches out in this manner for some, the poorer people are not just poorer compared to the richest; rather, their absolute welfare may decline because of the rise in the price of goods or because they are excluded from the 'market.'[10]

During a field visit to the village of Jakotra, in a remote corner of Gujarat close to the border of Pakistan, I found a palpable concern among the poor villagers about what globalization might do to them (Basu 2007e, chapter 11). The villagers of Jakotra earn their livelihood largely from handicrafts and mainly embroidery work on textiles. The villagers were concerned that their meager livelihood could get wiped out by competition from some international producer that decides to manufacture embroidered clothing in large factories and export to India. Talking to the villagers, I realized what a double-edged sword globalization is. On the one hand, they have benefited in the last decade because of globalization, and their ability to sell their product in faraway lands and cities.[11] On the other hand, they rightly fear that this prosperity may not last. These people are still poor enough, moreover, that the end of prosperity for them could mean acute poverty, destitution, and even starvation. When that happens, it would clearly not be good enough to point these people to the potential benefits of globalization. The right policy is to craft government interventions that provide a safety net for the poorest people during times of transition.

Something analogous is true for developed countries concerned with the problem of outsourcing. The overall benefits of outsourcing are apparent enough. When the U.S. automobile industry began eroding because of competition from Japan, if the U.S. government had thwarted competition by blocking Japanese cars from coming into the country, it is likely that there would be many more automobile workers in the U.S. today, but the country would also be poorer for this. In the early 1990s, it looked as if the Japanese economy would overtake the United States. But the openness of the information technology sector in the United States, drawing talent from all over the world, prevented this from happening.

There are analogues of this in the current outsourcing problem. Blocking outsourcing will mean that more people in the United States will be able to find jobs doing call center, data filing, and rudimentary software work, but it will almost certainly mean the loss of competitive advantage for the United States and an overall loss for the country. This is not to deny that there are people who are being hurt, certainly in the short run, by outsourcing. The right policy here, as in the case of poor countries facing competition, is not to stop outsourcing but to devise policies that soften the consequences of competition for the population that is hurt by it. In any case, outsourcing is in no immediate danger. On the contrary, the repeated attacks on outsourcing during the last U.S. presidential election coupled with the attacks on U.S. entrepreneurs who outsource as being unpatriotic—as expressed, for instance, on the popular Lou Dobbs show—has had the opposite effect. It alerted small entrepreneurs that were not outsourcing about the profits to be made in this area, and over the last three or four years there has been a sharp rise in outsourcing by small and medium firms. Advertising on U.S. television is expensive, and the small back office outfits in the developing nations would never have been able to afford it; the attacks did it for them for free.

A problem with globalization is the shrinkage of policy space for national governments, which is probably at the heart of the rise in within-nation inequality. It is often pointed out that the rich and the large corporations are treated with kid gloves. There is a lot of truth to this. The amount of subsidy that is given to the rich far outstrips what is given to the poor. Areas where the rich live are invariably better maintained by city councils. We fret about small vendor encroachment in the cities of developing countries. But if we measure the public space occupied, for example, in New Delhi by the cars of the rich, since they build their homes from wall to wall, leaving no space for their cars within their own privately owned space, this far outstrips the area occupied by the poor vendors.

Globalization also means that governments are unable to raise taxes on the rich and on corporations, for fear that they will move to another nation. During the last twenty years, the average corporate tax rates in Organization of Economic Cooperation and Development (OECD) countries have fallen from 45 to below 30 percent. From 2000 to 2005, twenty-four out of the thirty OECD countries lowered their corporate tax rates, and no country raised its rates (Weise 2007). The radical prescription to just raise corporate tax rates, and make the rich pay for their use of public space and property, may not be the solution. In today's globalized world it can drive corporations out of a nation, and push the rich and skilled people to other cities and continents. This can end up hurting the poor. This possibility is demonstrated formally below. So while we do need radical policies to 'solve' this problem, they are not the policies that first come to mind. The problem has to be attacked on a global level, and may call for an even more radical overhaul of the system in the long run than what is currently promoted by many radical groups.

The next two sections illustrate some of the policy dilemmas mentioned above and the risks of globalization. But I should emphasize that the message of this must not be read as one against globalization. The real danger is global corporate control and the oligarchy of the rich. The potential benefits created by the easier flow of goods, services, software products, and labor are enormous, and to stop these would be a gross error. At the same time, the fear of these getting stopped must not lead us to praise all aspects of globalization. By pointing to its negative fallout, this book hopes to encourage policies to counter it and better distribute the spoils of globalization. This should not only be seen as a moral imperative; to ignore the marginalizing groups is to risk political instability and war in the long and maybe even not so long run.

Inequality and Poverty: The Quintile Axiom

As is already evident from the above discussion, poverty and inequality are different qualities of a society (Sen 1997; Subramanian 2006). One of these can go up while the other declines. This is in fact what has been happening in India since at least the 1980s. The percentage of people whose consumption is below the poverty line is declining slowly but fairly steadily. On the other hand, because the rich are becoming so much richer, the inequality in society, no matter how it is measured (in terms of the gap between the richest 10 percent and the poorest 10 percent, or the Gini coefficient), is rising. I take the view that the extent of inequality that is necessary *to curb poverty* is the amount of inequality that should be tolerated. I will formalize this below. But two words of caution are in order. It is often said, usually by market fundamentalists, that as long as poverty is declining, there is nothing to complain about. I want to clarify that the rule I just stated for 'tolerable inequality' is not the same as this. It is quite unbecoming that when the rich are making such huge gains in India, the poor should be asked to be grateful as long as they get any positive gain. Second, the extent of inequality necessary to minimize poverty can be quite different under different institutional and economic systems. We will probably need quite a bit of inequality in today's system, but the hope is that we can in the future move to a system where the inequality that we will have to tolerate in order to minimize poverty will be small.

But we need to give a little more sharpness to these abstract principles of policy.   In designing policy it is important to try to clearly spell out our ultimate objectives. A new tax, subsidy, or new restriction on trade is seldom good *in itself*. The goodness or badness of such action depends on what it does to what we value ultimately for society. There may indeed be philosophical difficulties in spelling out, once and for all, ultimate or basic value judgments, as Sen (1970) has argued. New situations and new policy conundrums may compel us to abandon some judgments that we earlier held as fundamental.[12] But keeping in mind that new situations and new choices may make us want to mold our objectives, we must ask what it is that the policymaker should try to maximize.

I have elsewhere suggested a simple normative rule, which has attractive properties, not least of which is simplicity, and which is particularly helpful in situations where poverty and inequality are pitted against one another. Where traditionally we associate each country's main objective with its per capita income, the normative criterion that I have proposed elsewhere and am going to maintain here would require us to associate it with the per capita income of the poorest 20 percent of the population. I call this the 'quintile income' of a country.

What I am proposing is that in evaluating a country's well-being, we should focus on the country's quintile income. Henceforth, this normative principle will be referred to as the 'quintile axiom.'

The quintile measure should not be confused with a poverty measure (or the inverse of a poverty measure) of a society. Hence, the objective of raising the quintile income of a country need not coincide with that of lowering poverty. This will certainly be so if we use an absolute measure of poverty (which can become zero and so leave no further target unfulfilled, whereas that can never happen with the target of maximizing quintile income) and may not be true even for most relative poverty measures. The quintile axiom I am recommending is an *overall* normative target in the spirit of John Rawls's famous maximin criterion (1971).

At first glance this indicator may seem arbitrary, but as a rule, any single indicator for measuring a nation's well-being is arbitrary until we get used to it. We could focus our attention on an even smaller segment at the bottom end of the income distribution, but data at that end, as also with the very rich, become somewhat undependable. The bottom 20 percent is simply a practical cutoff. All that this axiom tries to capture is the need to concentrate on the badly off people in society. This is what the enterprise of economics should be mainly concerned with.[13]

There are ways in which the quintile axiom or the general idea behind it can be generalized. We could, say, give weights to the incomes of people at different levels of poverty, with the poorest people getting the highest weights, and then look at the weighted per capita income of society. But I am interested here in developing a measure that is simple and easy to understand. The quintile axiom is a suggestion in that spirit.

It is worth seeing how evaluating an economy using the quintile income not only makes a large difference to the absolute numbers, as is only to be expected, but also can change the rankings sharply. Table 8 provides the per capita incomes and quintile incomes of a selection of nations. As expected, Norway and Japan move up the ranking ladder sharply, and the United States moves down it. At the poorer end Romania, India, and Bangladesh make relative gains. The sharpest losses caused by shifting attention from per capita income to quintile income occur in Peru, Guatemala, and Sierra Leone.

The quintile income measure, viewed as an equity-conscious measure of welfare, has several normative advantages. Unlike a policy that tries to minimize poverty or inequality, the objective of maximizing the quintile income has a natural dynamism because it is a moving target. In a country with gross inequalities, this measure will suggest that we focus on the conditions of the poorest people. If the better-off people are ignored totally and for too long, though, they will soon be a part of the bottom quintile of the society and so deserve attention. If there is full equality in society, this measure does not allow the policymaker to sit back. Since in such a society the quintile income

TABLE 8
Quintile Income of Nations, 2006

Country	Per capita income, international $, PPP (constant 2000)	% of income accruing to poorest 20%	Quintile income, international $, PPP (constant 2000)	Year income share reported
Norway	37,667	9.59	18,064	2000
United States	38,165	5.44	10,373	2000
Switzerland	32,775	7.55	12,381	2000
Japan	27,992	11.00	15,396	1993
Finland	30,420	9.62	14,632	2000
Sweden	30,392	9.12	13,858	2000
South Korea	20,572	7.91	8,131	1998
South Africa	10,338	3.47	1,796	2000
Trinidad and Tobago	14,708	6.00	4,412	1992
Malaysia	10,091	4.37	2,205	1997
Russian Federation	10,350	6.15	3,181	2002
Romania	8,722	8.07	3,521	2003
Peru	5,725	3.73	1,067	2004
China	6,621	4.25	1,407	2004
Guatemala	4,150	2.93	608	2002
India	3,308	8.08	1,336	2004
Bangladesh	1,916	8.60	824	2000
Sierra Leone	753	1.00	38	1989

Source: Computed from World Bank 2008.

coincides with the per capita income, the aim now will be to raise the per capita income.

Also, a focus on the quintile income does not mean that the growth rate should be ignored. It is simply that the growth rate should be measured in terms of the growth rate of the per capita income of the bottom quintile of society. This new measure has the advantage of directness. Instead of saying or claiming that we should aim to increase income growth, and then expect the benefits to reach the poorest sections, this measure says we should aim to increase the growth rate of the quintile incomes.

It is true that, unlike the UN Development Program's Human Development Index, the quintile income ignores the nonincome aspects of development. My defense against this criticism is twofold. First, what I am recommending is not that we ignore nonincome aspects of development but that where we would have focused on per capita income, we now concentrate on quintile income instead. Second, I would conjecture that in general, quintile incomes will have a closer relation to a nation's various standard-of-living indicators, like infant mortality, life expectancy, literacy, and so on, than per capita incomes. This is something that would in fact be interesting to investigate later.

The focus on quintile income also suggests how we should view inequality. In general, I believe that inequality is undesirable, but that poverty is the greater evil. So the amount of inequality that we should tolerate is the amount 'necessary' to minimize poverty, which will here be equated with maximizing the quintile income.[14] It is, for instance, probable that a society of perfect equality (at least given our contemporary values and preferences) would be crushingly poor. Hence, the focus on quintile income will steer us away from attempting perfect equality.

This quintile income criterion enables us to decide what the 'right' amount of inequality is in each society. This is illustrated formally in the next section. The formal model will also show how this may depend on the level of globalization. This naturally gives way to the idea of having to coordinate policies across nations, which is what the last section of this chapter will explore.

Poverty-Minimizing Inequality, with or without Globalization

In this section, I develop a simple, highly stylized model to capture some of the principles discussed thus far. In particular, the model will depict how the quintile axiom may imply that we have to tolerate a modicum of inequality, and how globalization weakens each nation's ability to control poverty and thus directs our attention to the need for the intercountry coordination of policy.

Consider a world with 'many' identical countries. Each country has a certain population. And of these people, half are 'rich' and half are 'poor.' What I mean by rich and poor is simply that in the absence of any government or community intervention, the rich are individuals who have an income of a thousand dollars and the poor have an income of zero. The somewhat-contrived assumption that someone lives at zero income is made only for reasons of algebraic simplicity. If this seems troubling, suppose that income is defined to be what a person earns over and above subsistence earnings. We can use a standard neoclassic economics assumption about the rich being more innately productive than the poor or the rich being the more educated people, or we can alternatively assume that this is a discriminating society and the rich are the favored lot. The exact explanation does not matter for the limited purposes of what I am setting out to explain here.

Let me now introduce a minimal government into the picture. All this government does is to tax the rich and transfer that money as a direct subsidy to the poor. Suppose the government sets the tax rate at t. That is, a fraction t of the income of the rich is collected by the government as tax. Let me denote the pretax income of the rich to be $Y(t)$, with the t in the bracket being a reminder that the pretax income depends on how high the tax is. As t rises, it is reasonable to assume that $Y(t)$ will either remain unchanged or fall. This is because as t becomes high, it is likely to dampen a person's zeal to work hard and earn more. So if the tax rate is t, then the rich person's posttax or disposable income will be $(1-t)Y(t)$.

Let me assume that up to a tax rate of three-tenths or 30 percent, there is no negative impact on a person's earning zeal. In other words, $Y(t) = 1,000$, as long as t is less than or equal to three-tenths. So if the tax rate is 30 percent—that is, $t = 3/10$—then a rich person's disposable income is seven hundred dollars. Since all the tax collected is distributed by the government to the poor, and the number of poor people is the same as the number of rich people, each poor person will receive three hundred dollars. Each poor person's disposable income is thus three hundred dollars. To sum up, if this society uses an income tax rate of 30 percent, there will still be some inequality, with the rich earning seven hundred dollars per person and the poor earning three hundred dollars per person.

Suppose the government is interested in pushing toward greater equality. Then in this simple framework, there is only one thing to be done: raise the tax rate even further. I will suppose that this will impair the drive of the rich to earn money, however. Let us assume that the income that the rich gets begins to decline as the tax rate grows, and in particular, if the tax rate is set at 50 percent, each rich person will then earn an income of four hundred dollars (instead of the thousand that they earned when the tax rate was less than or equal to 30 percent).[15]

We now have enough material here to raise some critical policy questions. Clearly, what tax rate a government chooses will depend on the welfare criterion that the government uses. To start with, suppose that the government is 'utilitarian' in the sense that it is interested in maximizing the total national income without regard to who gets how much. Then clearly the tax rate will be set somewhere between 0 and 30 percent. Since in this entire range the incentive to work is unchanged, the per capita income in this society remains at five hundred dollars (and the national income is five hundred multiplied by the population). Any such tax rate will make the rich work the hardest and ensure that the national cake is as large as it can be. Since a whole range of solutions (namely, t from zero to three-tenths) is compatible with the utilitarian welfare criterion, it may be convenient to think of some simple 'tiebreaking' assumption. Economists often do this to make the solution unique. In some contexts (and this is one of them) this is harmless. One such assumption is to suppose that the government has a 'lexicographical' preference in the sense of being utilitarian, but among two policies that create the same total income, it prefers the one that leads to a better distribution. In that case, the government would set t equal to three-tenths. Another harmless tiebreaker assumption is to suppose that when the tax is zero, people get a small extra joy that makes them a little more productive. So at $t = 0$, the rich produce an income of eleven hundred dollars (instead of one thousand). As soon as t becomes positive, the income drops to one thousand dollars and then the behavior follows exactly as described above. Let me call this the "boost at zero" assumption for later reference. With this assumption, clearly the utilitarian government would set the tax rate at zero.

To keep the discussion simple, let us assume for the time being that for some technical reasons (say, the limited computational ability of the audit department), the government has to choose between tax rates of zero, three-tenths, a half, or any higher rate.

Next consider a government that is focused on the poor and wants to maximize quintile income as discussed above. This government will clearly choose t to be three-tenths. At this tax rate, the poor have a disposable income of three hundred dollars. None of $t = 0$, ½, or higher gives the poor as much income.

Finally, consider a government that is totally focused on inequality minimization. Such a government will set the tax rate at t *at one-half*. At this point, the rich and poor have the same disposable income—namely, two hundred dollars each.

The reader can check, using the $Y(t)$ function described in the above footnote, that this result is more general than it is made out to be above. Let me allow for greater generality and assume that the government can choose any tax rate that lies on the grid of ten—that is, t has to be one of 0, 10, 20, or 30 percent up to 100 percent. To make the analysis a bit more stark let me from now on make the boost at zero assumption.

It is now easy to verify that if the government is utilitarian, it will set the tax rate at zero. If the government follows the quintile rule, it will set the tax rate at 30 percent. In this example, the quintile rule coincides with Rawlsianism (or more accurately, the leximin extension of the Rawlsian rule).[16] Hence, Rawlsianism also leads to a tax rate of 30 percent. But if the government is committed to total equality, it will raise the tax rate even higher, to 50 percent.

Notice that to get to this point, however, the poor are made poorer than they would have been with a lower tax on the rich. That is, from a tax rate of 30 percent, which optimizes quintile income, if we raise the tax rate to 50 percent, inequality declines but this happens at the expense of greater poverty, since the poorest people become poorer. This is the sense in which poverty and inequality can entail trade-offs. I take the view that in a situation like this, the inequality that occurs at the point where the poor people are made best off is worth tolerating, because this is the inequality needed to maximize the well-being of the poorest sections. This is the idea of tolerable inequality discussed above.

It is worth clarifying that it is not always the case that the poverty-minimizing tax will be less than the inequality-minimizing tax, as in this example. If this does not happen, then of course there is no quandary between poverty minimization and inequality minimization. Also, all the analysis here assumes that we have an economy that runs along fairly usual neoclassical lines. I believe that it is in principle possible to have altered human norms whereby people will not resent having to make contributions for the less fortunate of the world and will continue to work hard even if their incomes are taxed to transfer income to the poor. This leads to more radical policy prescriptions, which will be discussed in the closing chapter.

The shrinkage of policy space that occurs with globalization, and also how globalization may contribute to greater inequality *and* greater poverty, can be illustrated using the above model as well.[17] To see this, let us now suppose that workers can move from one nation to another, and that they prefer to go where they can get the highest disposable income. But when a worker decides to migrate, he or she needs permission (a work permit or visa) from the destination nation before the worker can actually manage to migrate. I will also assume that if all countries have the same tax/subsidy rates, then each person stays in the home country. That is, when indifferent between migrating and not migrating, a worker will choose the latter.

In reality, with globalization, movement between nations can occur for corporations, goods, and services. But since this is a simple model, I assume that labor is the only factor that can migrate. The instrument that governments have for attracting skilled labor is the tax rate. So effectively, what I am describing here is a model of 'real tax competition' (Atkinson 2005).

The problems of domestic policy in the event of globalization of the kind just explained can be illustrated in many different ways. Let me here consider the case where each country aims to maximize its quintile income. In other words, each country has a good government, genuinely concerned with raising the standard of living of its poorest citizens. If the boundaries of nations were exogenously closed (that is, no labor movement were allowed), we have seen that each nation would set the tax rate at 30 percent.

Now let globalization remove the exogenous hindrance to labor movements. Note that each country setting the tax rate at 30 percent is no longer an equilibrium. If one country lowers t, then clearly all productive people from other nations will want to migrate to this country. If the government now decides that it will allow some of the rich people to come in and not allow any poor person to enter, it will certainly be able to increase the income subsidy per capita that it gives to its poorest citizens. And for this reason it will be in each national government's interest to cut tax rates a little. So the tax rate of 30 percent cannot prevail in an equilibrium. To use the language of game theory, every government setting the tax rate at 30 percent is not a Nash equilibrium.

From the above analysis, it should be evident that there is no tax rate t greater than zero that will prevail in an equilibrium. If all other nations charge t, a government can lower taxes a little, attract the rich, and use the tax collected to subsidize the poor citizens of the nation. Hence, in an equilibrium every country will set $t = 0$. Real tax competition in a globalized world results in the erosion of taxation, and in an equilibrium we will have all rich and poor people earning as if there is no government. Each country ends up behaving *as if* it were interested in maximizing the national income with no concern for poverty or equity. In other words, globalization erodes each national government's power to have an equity-conscious policy. The mobility of labor (and in a more realistic model, the mobility of capital) compromises a nation's policy efficacy.

Evidently we need to coordinate antipoverty policies on the international level. This is not to deny that redistributive and more aggressive antipoverty policies by individual governments are possible, and one must not let governments off the hook totally. At the same time, as globalization progresses, there is an increasing need to coordinate policies across nations.

When we see the enormous poverty in Ethiopia or Tanzania, we tend to blame the governments in these countries. While most governments have room to improve their performance, it would be wrong to overlook that how much control Ethiopia has over Ethiopian poverty or Tanzania has over Tanzanian poverty depends in part on what happens in Kenya, India, China, and the United States. One also sees this being played out within India. The state of West Bengal has had a democratically elected, prolabor government headed by the Communist Party of India (Marxist) for the last thirty years. On first being elected, the government made it clear to the corporations and big industries that if they did not provide workers with decent wages and working conditions, they could leave the state. This was a reasonable demand to make given how poorly Indian workers are paid. But the trouble was that the workers of West Bengal did not get employment on better terms. They did not get employment. The region just faced deindustrialization. I do not think that the aim of the government was wrong; its assessment of reality was faulty. The same government is now wooing industry by offering lavish terms. In the current global situation, this is the right thing to do. There is no other option. Indeed, it is essential to strive toward a major overhaul of global governance.

Policy Implications

It is no easy task to move from the theoretical construction in the last section to real-world policy. Countries are at different levels of development, and the policy instruments available to a government are more varied than choosing tax rates and immigration rules. How can countries coordinate policies in such a world? Do we need a central coordinating organization, like we have the International Labor Organization (ILO) for labor policies and the World Trade Organization (WTO) for trade policies, for crafting and coordinating antipoverty and greater-equity policies? We can only speculate about such matters, marshaling the insights gained from abstract theoretical models and the wisdom gleaned from empirical studies, and combining them with common sense, intuition, and guesswork.

Much has been written about the nature of pro-poor growth in developing countries (see, for instance, Klasen 2004) as well as the specific problem of pro-poor growth in the context of globalization.[18] Instead of going over the same ground, I will comment briefly here on two policy suggestions that seem to have few antecedents in the literature. Both of these are discussed further in chapter 10. These interventions and some other ones explored in the closing chapter provide different forms of taxation for the rich, especially in rich nations. A question arises about the feasibility of such policies since giving up on a part of one's wealth or income is never directly an incentive-compatible action for the individual. This is where some of the theorizing earlier in the book is relevant. As was pointed out in chapter 3, all human beings engage in actions that are not in keeping with their narrow self-interests. Pressures that come from social norms, habits that make us not even consider actions that, if used, could yield us benefits, and the pervasive power of culture can make us give away many individual advantages and not even think twice about it. So while giving up some of our spoils for the larger interest of the world may not be in our self-interest, it is possible to have people make those sacrifices and not even look on them as such. But habits, norms, and culture take time to evolve and settle in as part and parcel of society. Before that can happen, a tax on wealth as well as the resources one commands, consumes, and treats as a virtual inalienable right will be viewed as a tax, and so resisted. It will therefore require the hand of the law, the state, and international governance. Fortunately, as seen in chapter 4, once a law is enacted and announced, in developed nations it has a tendency to be obeyed and quickly become focal.[19] This is because the anterior laws—that is, the laws that require the agents of the state to enforce them (for example, punish drivers going faster than the speed limit, whatever the speed limit is)—are usually well established in industrialized nations. Hence, the ideas of policy action on the part of the government and international organizations discussed in this and the next chapters, while they certainly ought to be subjected to analysis and careful scrutiny, are not ones that can be dismissed out of hand as being incentive incompatible.

My first suggestion concerns workers around the world. One way to counter the problem of sections of workers losing out because of globalization, whether they are workers in developed countries losing work to outsourcing or laborers in poor countries losing jobs to low-cost high-tech imports, is to give workers a claim to a fraction of corporate equity income.[20] I do not mean profit sharing in the firm in which the worker works but more radically, that a fraction of equity earnings from all firms should be given to workers in all firms, including laborers who are currently without work. The full details of this would be complex and would have to be carefully worked out, but the broad idea is that a fraction of equity in firms should be owned by the government or some governmental organization on behalf of people in the poorest category—for instance, the bottom quintile. Presumably workers belong to this category and so will be able to partake in the profits earned by firms.

So when work is outsourced and some workers lose their jobs, a part of the extra profit generated by the outsourcing should be earned by the workers by virtue of their owning equity. This could be an important policy guarding against the excessive marginalization of workers. Moreover, it could help diminish some of the antagonism that exists among workers in developed and poor countries toward globalization. If it is true that over time the share of labor income will decline, which I believe is the case, then this scheme would have the advantage of automatically softening some of the impact of this on workers, because a part of what they lose because of dwindling employment and labor income will be returned in the form of higher equity income.

My second suggestion is to urge the need for a new international organization or a new division of an existing international organization that helps coordinate intercountry antipoverty policies. As we have seen above, achieving greater global equality and reducing global poverty may require the use of policy interventions that are *coordinated across countries*. A unilateral effort by one country is likely to cause the flight of capital and skilled labor from that country, impoverishing those who stay behind. Hence, we may get into a Prisoner's Dilemma type of situation where each country would like to take steps to curb inequality or help the poorest, but would not be able to do so.

The theoretical possibility of this happening was illustrated in the last section. This is also a real problem in today's globalized world. Inequality *within* China, India, and several other developing countries is on the rise. As argued above, this is closely connected to globalization, and probably explains why China and India—two of the fastest globalizers—are affected in a big way by this problem. Yet there is no institutional arrangement or even infrastructure for countering this. The fact that the income gap between the richest and poorest people in the world as a whole is greater than the gap that occurs inside any country is a reflection of the fact that we have no global political institution to address this. No government would be able to tolerate this kind of hiatus within its region of control.

It is well recognized that there may be coordination problems in trade, and we have the WTO to help mitigate such problems. We also know that labor market policies need coordination and have the ILO to address this situation. For environmental problems, we have the UN Environmental Program or the Global Environmental Facility. Yet there is nothing comparable to these for antipoverty and anti-inequality policies. As demonstrated in the previous sections, however, this is an area where the coordination problem may be no less acute. There is thus clearly a perceived need for a coordinating agency. This is not to deny that there are frequent announcement of targets, such as the Millennium Development Goals, but these are usually nice sound bites, with little teeth. Further, they do not recognize the centrality of the strategic coordination of policies across nations. This also ties up with the objective discussed above of giving workers an equity stake. In an ideal world, these stakes should cut across national barriers. This will once again create a need for a global coordination agency.

These policy questions are related to the larger topic of global governance and global democracy that especially arise in this age of globalization. These are the subject matters of the next two chapters.

CHAPTER 9

Globalization and the Retreat of Democracy

Democracy in Deficit

Wars are often waged in the name of democracy and freedom. This happened recently in Iraq, and it happened earlier in Vietnam. But when one accounts for the human toll of the firepower used in some of these theaters of war, it takes a handsome amount of gullibility to believe that wars are indeed in the interests of freedom and democracy in the nation being bombed. A unique data set collected by the U.S. military gives us what is arguably the most comprehensive account of the bombing of Vietnam. Here is a summary.

> The Indochina War, centered in Vietnam, was the most intense episode of aerial bombing in human history: "the United States Air Force dropped in Indochina, from 1964 to August 15, 1973, a total of 6,162,000 tons of bombs and other ordnance. U.S. Navy and Marine Corps aircraft expended another 1,500,000 tons in Southeast Asia. This tonnage far exceeded that expended in World War II and in the Korean War. The U.S. Air Force consumed 2,150,000 tons of munitions in World War II—1,613,000 tons in the European Theater and 537,000 tons in the Pacific Theater—and 454,000 tons in the Korean War" (Clodfelter 1995). Thus, the Vietnam War bombing represented at least three times as much (by weight) as both the European and Pacific theater World War II bombing combined, and about thirteen times the total tonnage used in the Korean War. Given the prewar Vietnamese population of approximately 32 million, U.S. bombing translates into hundreds of kilograms of explosives per capita during the conflict.

The above paragraph, including the quotation from Michael Clodfelter, is taken from Edward Miguel and Gerard Roland's work (2005). These numbers, from the database of the U.S. military—in particular, the Defense Security Cooperation Agency (DSCA), housed at the U.S. National Archives in Record Group 218—were obtained by Miguel and Roland from the Vietnam Veterans of America Foundation with authorization from the Defense Security Cooperation Agency.

It would indeed be an act of huge credulity to believe that this unprecedented amount of bombing on a vastly smaller and poorer nation, Vietnam, was done in the interests of democracy and freedom for that nation, or to put it differently, for the people being bombed. In truth, the bombing occurred not to promote democracy but rather because of a lack of democracy. The United States perceived some distant threats to its own interests and tried to obliterate that risk. Within democratic nations, individuals and groups often face distant threats from others. Your enemy's growing wealth can constitute a long-run risk to you. Some group's growing membership can make you feel that in the long run, your group may not be safe. Some Iraqis under Saddam Hussein felt that way about the Kurds. But that does not allow us to attack and drop bombs on those groups, because a democratic government does not allow such aggression based on conjectured apprehensions; the extent of aggressive action that a democratic government is able to take against one of its own states, no matter how antagonistic, will be much more limited than what it will be able to take against another nation that is equally antagonistic. Moreover, even normatively, it is not as if any aggressive action is justified as soon as one perceives any threat to oneself. Much of the wars and political instabilities of the world are illustrations of what happens when there is no democratic government at the helm, which is in fact the case at a global level. This is the utopia that some economists believe comes from actors being left completely free with no government intervention.

The global economy is an excellent place to study this. Thanks to technological breakthroughs over the last two millennia, with the pace picking up greatly over the last fifty years, *economic* globalization has been a part of our lives for some time now. This has meant a greater and greater flow of goods, services, and capital across nations. But this has not been accompanied by any comparable degree of *political* globalization. This is a dangerous brew that can destabilize the world, and for the academic economist, it underscores the vital need for government and governance.

We have seen above that individuals or groups left entirely to their own devices, and free to pursue their own selfish ends, far from leading to social optimality, can plunge a nation into Hobbesian chaos. This is what is tending to happen at the global level, since our institutions of global governance are so weak.

I want to begin by highlighting an important implication of this. One concomitant of globalization and technological progress, which has either gone unnoticed or been dismissed by those who did notice it, is that it has a natural corrosive effect on global democracy. As a consequence of this phenomenon, even if individual countries become democratic, the aggregate of global democracy may well be on the wane. The purpose of this chapter is to advance and defend this hypothesis, comment on its consequences, and suggest antidotes.

Globalization is often presented by economists as the coming together of economies. In other words, through the rise of new travel and transmission technologies, and the gradual dismantling of trade and capital flow barriers, it is now easier and cheaper to send goods, services, and capital from one nation to another. This has huge advantages and can potentially cause great improvements in standards of living. Indeed, many people around the world, such as in China and India, have gained by this. By a simplistic appeal to the Invisible Hand Theorem, we could take this kind of globalization to be completely good, but that would be wrong. A somewhat mechanical and popular use of the Invisible Hand Theorem would go as follows. The theorem tells us that if competitive markets are allowed to function without curbs on individual freedom, then the outcome of the economy is (Pareto) efficient. The global economy, we all know, is not really a single economy because of the numerous artificial barriers to the movement of goods and services that nation-states have erected. Globalization is a move toward dismantling these barriers through the creation of new technology and changes in government policy, while inching toward a single global economy. Hence, it is a move toward a world where the Invisible Hand Theorem would apply, and so it raises hope for global efficiency.

The potential advantages of globalization are undoubtedly large. Yet this argument has several flaws, including the well-known one, referred to in the literature as the second-best theorem, which says that even if a free market competitive equilibrium is optimal, it is not the case that every move *toward* it takes us closer to optimality. In other words, there may be nonmonotonicities involved, whereby being slightly closer to the competitive equilibrium may be worse than being further afield. But even if we leave out this second-best argument, there is a more practical problem. How an economy actually runs is never simply a matter of individual choice and rationality. Governments invariably play a role—providing public goods, enforcing contracts (a key foundational element for markets to function), and keeping inequalities from getting out of hand. The reader may wonder about this, given that it was claimed in chapter 4 that a government is nothing but an artifact of the beliefs of individual citizens. What nevertheless needs to be kept in mind is that this does not make it any less real, nor any less important.

A key difference between our emerging global economy and a single economy, such as that of the United States or India, is that the former has no government, since political globalization is clearly trailing behind economic globalization. The problem I am about to discuss stems from this anomaly.

One consequence of this is an erosion of democracy and the tolerance of global inequalities at levels that would not have been tolerated in any economy under a single government. The latter was discussed in the previous chapter, and the former is the subject matter of what follows.

Democracy entails many things, including the existence of a variety of political and legislative institutions, avenues for citizens to participate in the formation of economic policies that affect their lives, and in the ultimate analysis, a certain mind-set (for a discussion of this, see Sen 1999). Yet at the core of it and in its simplest form, democracy requires that people should have the right to choose those who rule them, and the principle that the vote of each person should count as much as another person's vote. Even this basic principle runs into paradoxes and puzzles, as Lewis Carroll, in his original incarnation as Charles Lutwidge Dodgson, well knew, and Arrow's trailblazing work (1951) demonstrated.[1] But the simplicity of these requirements has the advantage that we can easily check whether a society satisfies them.

Next, note that greater globalization, almost by definition, means that nations and people can exert a greater influence on other nations and the lives of citizens in other nations. Moreover, what is not true by definition but instead is a fact is that this power of one nation to influence another is by no means symmetrical. The United States, for instance, can cut off Cuba's trade lines. It can do so not only by curtailing its own trade with Cuba but also by threatening punitive action against those who trade with or invest in Cuba. This is not just a hypothetical possibility; the Helms-Burton Act of 1996 in the United States is testimony to how this can actually happen. Cuba, on the other hand, can do little to hurt the U.S. economy or polity. Likewise, China can do things to Taiwan or Singapore, which Taiwan or Singapore can in no way reciprocate. It is likely that the welfare of an Iraqi depends more on the outcome of U.S. elections than elections in Iraq.

In the early 1970s, the question of who was president of the United States was a life-and-death matter for ordinary Chileans. When on September 4, 1970, the Popular Unity candidate, Salvador Allende, won the election in Chile by a plurality of votes, and then on October 4, in the runoff election in Congress, he handsomely defeated his rival, Jorge Alessandri, and became president of the nation, this was an important event for Chileans. But no less momentous, and perhaps more so, for them was the event of Richard Nixon becoming president of the United States—a matter in which they had no say. This democratically elected Chilean government initiated far-reaching reforms to transfer wealth out of the hands of the wealthy and the big corporations to the poor. No matter what view one takes about whether this policy helped the poor in the long run, there can be no doubt that the Allende government had the mandate of its people. But soon U.S. president Nixon set up his infamous "Committee of 40" to promote covert action in Chile, buying up radio stations, bribing newspapers to encourage acts of sedition, and ultimately, on September 11, 1973, engineering a violent military coup in which thousands were killed or declared "disappeared." Inside the presidential palace, La Moneda, Allende spoke for the last time to the citizens of his nation on a crackling radio, with the sound of gunfire in the background: "Radio Magallanes will surely soon be silenced, and the calm metal of my voice will no longer reach you. It does not matter. ... Other people will overcome this gray and bitter moment where treason tries to impose itself." Shortly after that, the coup leaders broke into La Moneda and Allende was killed. On September 13, a notorious army commander, Augusto Pinochet, became president of Chile. A national democracy stood brutally crushed.

As the world shrinks, and powerful governments develop a variety of instruments and ways to influence the lives of citizens in other nations, it is no longer enough for people to be able to choose the leaders of their own nations. Since democracy requires the ability to choose the leaders who have influence over your life, in a globalizing world like today's, citizens, especially those from weaker nations, need to be able to vote in the elections of the rich and powerful nations. When Hans Blix, onetime UN inspector and Swedish national, was asked by Deborah Solomon of the *New York Times* about the U.S. presidential race, he replied, "I think maybe we foreigners should have the right to vote in your next election, since we are so dependent on you."[2] Since such transnational voting does not happen, globalization is bound to cause a diminution of global democracy. This is my 'basic proposition.'[3]

Transnational voting, even as a hypothetical suggestion, sounds naive and not something that at this stage of world history, can be proposed without inviting the charge of absurdity. Such a system also has its pitfalls and disadvantages. Not surprisingly, transnational voting is not what I am recommending. Still, that should not prevent us from recognizing that in its absence, the world is as much of a democracy as the United States would be if its electoral rules were such that only the residents of the District of Columbia were allowed to vote to elect the president of the whole country.

What this implies is the need for thinking of other ways to shore up global democracy. Much of this will entail the creation of new global institutions, agreements, and systems of international law, and also some innovative restructuring of existing international organizations. I shall turn to some of this later in the chapter.

Globalization and Influence

The big and the powerful have always considered it natural to encroach on the sovereignty of others. This is best exemplified by the story, no doubt apocryphal, that used to do the rounds in India of the Indian diplomat in Moscow showing a map of South Asia to Joseph Stalin. Stalin, who was believed to be quite ignorant of the world beyond the USSR and its immediate neighbors, looked surprised and observed, "I didn't realize India was such a big country." Then, suddenly noticing Sri Lanka, he asked, "What is the name of this little Indian island?" "This is not an Indian island, sir," the Indian diplomat responded, "This is Sri Lanka, a sovereign nation." Legend has it that Stalin's response was: "Why?"

Fortunately, in today's world, to have influence in the affairs of another nation, it is no longer necessary to occupy the other nation's land or to go to war with it (even though, at times, it is the cheaper and therefore more tempting option). Furthermore, even when there is war, unlike those of yesteryear, it is less a battle over territory than an act of reprisal or a punitive action to make nations conform to certain kinds of behavior. And given the march of technology, the stronger nations are able to take this action with little direct confrontation and loss of lives. A simple statistic captures this changing nature of war. If we take the ratio of the number of dead civilians to the size of military casualty in armed conflicts, we find that this has risen almost relentlessly, from less than one in the first decade of the twentieth century to more than five in the 1990s (Dreze 2000). This at least in part reflects how powerful nations can take action against others with minimal military casualties in their own ranks.

More important is the fact that military action, even of this arm's-length kind, is now often unnecessary. Thanks to globalization, there is a variety of economic instruments that nations can use to influence outcomes elsewhere. Foremost among these is money. Thanks to the ease of instantaneous electronic links and the improving system of global guarantees, capital has flown across national boundaries like never before. It is true that in the heyday of imperialism, capital did go from one nation to another, but this almost invariably took the form of money moving between the territories of the imperialist nation and its colonies. In other words, the presence of the army in (or direct control over) another territory was a prerequisite before money went there. That is no longer the case. With a gentle tap on a mouse, one can today move funds to lands with which one may have little tangible contact. And capital has flown to distant lands at unbelievable rates. In 1969, the World Bank, for instance, gave out a total of $1.8 billion worth of loans. By 1999 this had grown to $32.5 billion. The private sector capital flow has grown at an even faster rate, and by 1999 World Bank lending had become a miniscule 2 percent of the total private sector lending to developing nations.

A rapid withdrawal of such capital can have devastating effects on the debtor nations, as we saw in 1982 in Latin America and in Asia in 1997, when the Asian superperforming economies succumbed to financial crisis. A sudden stoppage or cutback in trade can likewise bring nations to their knees.

Like capital, international trade (after a slowdown in the years between the two world wars) has risen steadily. Between 1990 and 2004, the total global exports and imports rose by over 200 percent. These global linkages have fueled unprecedented growth rates for national incomes (during the first six years of this century, China grew at around 10 percent per annum and India by 7.5 percent), but they have also created new vulnerabilities. Governments and international organizations can now use the threat of disrupting these flows (or the lure of releasing greater flows of money or goods) to enforce conformity to certain kinds of behavior. This is the idea of barter that textbooks tell us was a thing of the past, yet as this book argued earlier, it is very much a part of contemporary life. Individuals and firms are forever exchanging favors, and even more than them, nations and governments use the barter of favors, concessions, and treaties all the time. And with barter comes the scope for using threats. If you do not do x, I will not do y.

Such threats are frequently used. International organizations have given money while insisting that the developing countries fulfill certain conditions, many of which have had nothing to do with ensuring repayment. These conditionalities have, at times, even been contradictory, such as requiring the debtor nation to practice democracy and for it to privatize certain key sectors, unmindful of the fact that this was against the collective wishes of the people. Some of these conditions have been blatantly in the interest of the donor nation. In 1998, during the Asian crisis, the rescue package put together with money from several industrialized nations, most prominently Japan and the United States, had clauses that required Korea to lift bans on imports of certain Japanese products (which Japan had for a long time been trying to sell to Korea) and open up its banking sector to foreign banks (an item that had long been on the bilateral agenda of the United States vis-à-vis Korea). These were such surprising clauses that even a cautious magazine like the *Economist* commented on their obviously donor-motivated raison d'être. Some of these demands may well be good for the borrower, but that is not the issue here. From the point of view of assessing global democracy, what is relevant is that people of the weaker nation have little say in the imposition of these policies.

It is once again these same features of globalization that have made it possible for some nations, usually the powerful ones, to use sanctions to bring other nations into compliance.[4] In addition, nations have sought to leverage these sanctions by threatening action not just against the nation that it seeks to punish but also against other nations that do not join in the punishment. The classic example of this is the Helms-Burton Act, mentioned earlier, which seeks to take punitive action against companies and governments that trade and invest in Cuba. Clearly this act had a profound effect on the lives of Cubans (and some of the nations doing business with Cuba, such as Italy and Canada). Yet Cubans had little say in the matter, since they have no say in the choice of a U.S. president. There is some evidence to believe that Bill Clinton was a reluctant signatory to this contentious act, which has been challenged by some European nations and Canada. But he realized that signing this act would shore up the conservative side of his image, and since Cubans and Canadians have no say in his being or not being president of the United States, there was no substantial voter constituency that would have responded negatively.

Given that the benefits of democracy are ample, this erosion of global democracy must have negative fallouts. When segments of a nation become poor and marginalized in comparison to the rest of the nation, governments typically try to intervene through taxes and subsidies to counter this. This may happen because of a genuine ethical concern but also to keep the peace, because of the knowledge that when people are so marginalized that they have little to lose, they become dangerous and so even the rich have an interest in aiding the marginalized groups. Indeed, it is likely that the rise in global unrest and instabilities are a manifestation of this retreat of democracy. The lack of a global government means we do not have the institutions or instruments for controlling global inequalities, which as discussed in the last chapter, are now at an all-time high. And some of the inchoate demands of the protesters on the streets of Seattle and Washington, DC, may be founded in an intuitive perception of this erosion of democracy and the marginalization of large swathes of humanity.

Dollarization and Democracy

The lack of global democracy is also holding back some important necessary changes for a more efficient functioning of the world economy. One consequence of the freer flow of capital from one country to another that has received less than adequate attention is that it has led to an intertwining of different markets. Thus, a fall in the Thai housing market can cause a collapse of the Thai baht in a way that could not have happened before. Likewise, a fall in the Indian rupee can today cause a meltdown of the Indian stock market in a way that was inconceivable even ten years ago.

The reason for this is the large presence of overseas investors in any nation. Suppose you are a New Yorker who wants to buy shares, perhaps through some foreign institutional investor or mutual fund, on the Mumbai stock market. To do so, your dollars will first have to be converted to rupees and then used to buy the shares. Your aim, like that of virtually all overseas investors, is not to hold rupees but rather to make some money, and then eventually convert that back to dollars (basically, any globally accepted currency) to spend on clothes, housing, and so on in the United States. Now suppose the Indian exchange rate begins to fall. As a foreign investor, you will have good reason to sell the Indian stocks and take your money out of India, because even if the stock prices remain unchanged, your earnings in dollars will be smaller if you leave your money in India with the rupee falling. So while a fall in the exchange rate with no decline in stock prices gives the Indian investor no reason, ceteris paribus, to take money out of the stock market, the foreign investors will have good reason to get out of India. But if there are a sufficient number of foreign investors, and they all begin to sell their stocks, the stock prices will begin to decline, and *then* there will be reason enough for Indian investors to sell the stocks as well. And so now the stock market will be brought down too.

Likewise, if the Thai housing market begins to collapse and this in turn hurts the profitability of Thai companies, this may cause the stock prices to fall. If Thailand had no foreign investors, that would be the end of the matter. But if there are foreign investors, after selling their stocks, they will change their bahts to dollars since they had gone into Thailand originally for the Thai stock market. Hence, now the exchange rate will start collapsing.

These linkages between domestic markets in a developing country and the exchange rate are new, and played a larger role in the rapid spread of the 1997 east Asian crisis from one country to another as well as from one market to another than has been recognized by economists (for a discussion on this, see Basu 2003b). Governments and citizens have already been aware of this at the level of intuitive perception, and this has given rise to demands for currency unions and dollarization. Indeed, there are gains to be had from groups of countries coming under single currencies, and ultimately converging into a one-currency world—something that Stanley Jevons had recommended, prematurely, in 1878.[5]

The main advantage of dollarization for a developing country is that it will delink the various domestic markets. The housing market suffering losses will be less likely to disrupt international trade, for example. To dollarize, somewhat surprisingly, is the equivalent of compartmentalizing the bellows of a hovercraft, so that one puncture does not bring down the whole vehicle.

The main disadvantage of dollarization is the loss of autonomy.[6] By coming under the control of the U.S. Federal Reserve Board, a nation would lose control over its own monetary and to a certain extent even its fiscal policy. Most nations will consider the cost of coming under another's central bank control too big a loss of autonomy to contemplate, though there have been times, such as in the case of Ecuador, where the instabilities were so great that this loss of economic sovereignty may well have been worthwhile.[7] The only way that the advantages of common currencies will be feasible and more widely acceptable is if we can think of central banks as being answerable to all the nations that use the common currency. The European central bank does have this feature of multicountry democracy, and that is the reason why the euro, despite its recent instability, is expected to be a net gain for all the nations that have it as their currency.

Unfortunately, global democracy is so underdeveloped that currency unions for countries that need them most—namely, the developing nations—remain a distant fantasy. Not only can we not think of a global democratic government (an idea that Bertrand Russell had campaigned for) with a global central bank, the main international financial institutions that we do have, such as the International Monetary Fund (IMF) and the World Bank, remain largely answerable to the industrialized nations. Even when such organizations work for the poor countries, it is the *industrialized nations'* perception of the poor nations' well-being that is catered to.

Democratic Global Institutions

What can be done about the erosion of global democracy? Since in the social sciences political correctness demands optimism, it may sound strange to respond with a "not very much." Yet that is true, at least over the next one or two decades. Utopian schemes such as a global government or bank that is answerable to all nations in the world are a distant dream. Can we conceive of some minimal global justice even in the absence of global government? These questions have been debated by philosophers.[8] My aim here is the much more limited one of investigating some practical ways of filling the caveat of global government, especially in the context of economic policymaking.

Let alone achieving *global* democracy, trying to transplant democracy within a nation that has not had a history of it can be treacherous. It can lead to war or comedy. Nowhere is the latter as vividly illustrated as in Rory Stewart's riveting account of Iraq at war. In August 2003, Stewart, who is British, was appointed the deputy governor of Amara in southern Iraq as part of the Coalition Provisional Authority to help rebuild civil society and democracy on the ruins of Saddam's dictatorship and George W. Bush's war. After he took office he had to play host to an "American democracy expert," who had flown in to the lawless marshlands to explain democracy to the local clerics and warlords. "On a white board he drew an oblong on its side, to represent the council, and then beneath it four vertical oblongs, to represent its subcommittees. 'He is drawing a dog,' said a sheikh" (Stewart 2006).

There can be little doubt that the process of globalization will course on, and intercountry democracy will continue to get bruised. It will be some time before this will bring us to the question of global governance and banking. In the meantime, we can strengthen the democratic structure of global institutions, such as the World Bank, the IMF, and the WTO. These are small measures, but extremely important ones, for they can contribute to global stability and even as an end in itself they are morally desirable. The lesson, ironically, is quite different from what the protesters in Seattle and Washington, DC, and also some archconservative groups in industrialized nations, want—to wit, the dismantling of these organizations. On the contrary, we need to restructure these organizations and recognize that they have an especially critical role to play today. In the previous chapter I argued that there is an urgent need for an organization that allows for the coordination of national policies for combating poverty and inequality.

The process can of course be hijacked, so that these institutions become batons in the hands of the powerful nations. On the other hand, it is naive to believe that by removing these institutions, the powerful will be defanged. We need these mitigating institutions, but those committed to global democracy will have to be ever vigilant. There is enough evidence that powerful politicians in powerful nations like to think of international institutions as valuable only to the extent that they can use them to their own advantage. On January 20, 2000, Senator Jesse Helms, arguably the most important congressional voice in the United States, told the council members of the United Nations: "If the United Nations respects the rights of the American people, *and serves them as an effective tool of diplomacy, it will earn and deserve their respect and support*. But a United Nations that seeks to impose its presumed authority on the American people, without their consent begs for confrontation and—I want to be candid with you—eventual US withdrawal" (emphasis added, but it is also my hunch that Helms would want it this way).[9] Helms later expressed distaste for "supranational institutions," including the international criminal court that had just been created. What is most damaging about this kind of remark is that any organization that meets with Helms's approval immediately becomes suspect from the point of view of the world as a whole. The last thing that a credible international organization will want now is Helms's blessing.

What we need to work on is to give nations, rich and poor, equal say, at least in international organizations that are supposed to play a mediating role in world economics or international relations. This horizontal equity is violated in most organizations through at least one of two routes. First, there is the open channel, which gives a larger share of votes to the nations contributing more to these organizations. This is certainly true of the IMF and World Bank. The second route is through the lack of transparency in decision making. One can see the importance of this for democracy by looking at policymaking within a country. If the decision-making process is, to some reasonable degree, visible to all, it becomes difficult for any group or lobby to hijack the agenda. Big business and the military, which are usually close to government, are able to push through their interests much more in Pakistan than in India, and the reason is simply that the government is more open to scrutiny in India. The same holds true for international organizations. Big and powerful nations, by virtue of contributing senior personnel and money to these organizations, have much greater access to them. So if decisions occur behind opaque walls, big and powerful nations are much more likely to divert the agenda to suit their own interests. Take the case of the WTO. While it does follow the important principle of one country, one vote, it is widely perceived as a preserve of powerful and rich nations. This is because of what some analysts call the "green room" effect—that is, what goes on behind the scenes (Schott and Watal 2000). In the green room, the agenda for what will appear on the table for all member nations to discuss and vote on gets set, and a lot of the end results get determined at that stage. If the WTO is to become a more democratic institution, it must not allow its green room to be commandeered by a few.

This problem is nowhere more obvious than in the drafting of international labor standards. These standards are ostensibly designed in the interests of the workers of developing countries. But ironically, the biggest opposition to such standards has come from the poor countries, and not just from their governments but also from the trade unions and grassroot workers. The apprehension in the developing world is justified. The form that these standards are tending to take—and the increasing talk of using trade sanctions to impose these standards—is close to what protectionist lobbies in industrial nations seek. This is not surprising given the greater access that the lobbies of rich countries have in the corridors of power in international organizations.

Many are surprised by this criticism of global institutions. The fact that the questioning of the practice of richer nations (which contribute more funds) exercising more voting power in these organizations sounds outrageous simply shows how far we still are from global democracy. It does not at all seem outrageous that Bill Gates does not have multiple votes in U.S. elections on the grounds that he contributes more to the government coffers. In fact, the suggestion that he could have more votes sounds outrageous. This is because democracy within a nation is a much more settled idea. But it is time to give serious thought to how we can ensure more equal voting power to different nations, irrespective of their wealth.[10] Money itself confers a lot of advantage; one of the basic tenets of democracy is that we should not compound this advantage by giving the rich extra voting power.

In the same Security Council address mentioned above, Helms complained that while the United Nations "lives and breathes on the hard-earned money of the American taxpayers," UN officials had the audacity to declare "that countries like Fiji and Bangladesh are carrying America's burden in peacekeeping."[11] Plainly, he was piqued not because some individual UN official had said something that may have been inaccurate but rather because it was minor nations like "Fiji" and "Bangladesh" that were being accorded such significance. The notion that each country should have an equal say is as yet unacceptable even as an idea.

Fortunately, opinions change. Multinationals nowadays talk in terms of environmental responsibility and the importance of respecting labor standards, even when that implies having to take a cut in profits. This seems to violate age-old beliefs and also the textbook descriptions of multinational corporations. When the "one person, one vote" idea first came about, the rich feudal landlords must have been shocked, and cried foul at this blatant injustice and the chaos in the process of decision making that it would cause. But this democratic principle *within a nation* no longer seems strange.

With the call for restructuring international organizations ringing out from the streets of Seattle and Washington, DC, and also congressional committees, such as the one headed by Allan Meltzer some time ago, this is a good time for us to think through some of these issues not just from the perspective of economic efficiency and greater cost-effectiveness but also from the point of view of representation of the poor. For the sake of global stability, economic efficiency, and also morality in international relations, we must try to impart a greater democratic structure to our international organizations. This may not be in the interest of every state, individually, but it is certainly in the collective interest of all states. And it will be one small step toward spreading the idea of global democracy as an eventual goal.

CHAPTER 10

WHAT IS TO BE DONE?

Interpreting the World and Changing It

What is to be done? In answering this question, I have to disappoint the reader. This is a book that, in keeping with Marx's famous and slightly pejorative description of philosophical works, tries to interpret our social and economic world, not change it.[1] It tries to lay the groundwork for a manifesto, but cannot pass for one. If it seems radical, that is only because so much of what passes for interpretation and description of the world in the social sciences is a Panglossian justification for the current system, the distribution of power as it presently is, and the status quo of wealth. On some topics, where to justify the status quo would be too blatant, we have a conspiracy of silence; we say nothing in the hope that our attention will drift to less dangerous topics. All I have tried to do in this book is to describe, as truthfully as I could, the functioning of the economy, how it produces goods and services, and how it distributes these among individuals. All academic disciplines rely on assumptions, and economics is no different in this regard. But there are two kinds of assumptions: those written up explicitly and at times enshrined as axioms, and those that are built into the woodwork and thus hidden from view. While the explicit assumptions of economics have received a lot of scrutiny, those in the woodwork have largely gone unchallenged. Through force of habit many professionals have ceased to view them as assumptions, and regard them instead as immutable facts. The aim of much of this book has been to challenge these hidden assumptions. As soon as this is done, it becomes evident that the justifications for the status quo are much weaker than normal economics or social science seems to suggest.

When it comes to everyday policymaking, my own position is not far from what legions of economists will tell you. Individuals should have freedom in signing contracts, and they should be able to rely on them. Individuals should have the latitude to make their own decisions, when these do not have negative externalities on others, without meddlesome intervention from the state.

In general, trade is good, and it is desirable to keep an economy open; fiscal deficits should be kept small; the money supply ought to be kept under control; and individuals should be rewarded for their efforts as well as for creating new wealth, technology, and ideas. In designing payment systems, we should be attentive to individual incentives. Borrowing a term from the methodology of science literature, I will call this 'normal policy'—that is, the kind of policy that we would want to implement *within* the current system. When it comes to normal policy, mainstream economics does not do too badly. The fact that in an ideal world we would have different policies does not mean that in everyday life we should adopt those policies.

But there is a catch in the adjective 'everyday' used above. Given the everyday decision problems that we face in the current system, all this is sensible advice. Where I take issue with the mainstream is in its belief that this is the only viable system, that everyday is the only possible kind of day. The less productive individual has to make do with a barely subsistence income; the corporate manager has to earn one hundred times what a worker earns; and free market capitalism is the only system that can work. To treat this as the only viable system is a nice way to blight the chances of the dispossessed and the deprived. This thesis is far too convenient for those who currently control the wealth and power. I do not think this is a premeditated conspiracy of contemporary social thought but it is in effect a conspiracy all the same. It is consciously or unconsciously perpetrated by all of us, like the minions in Kafka's *The Trial* who through their individual actions unwittingly perpetuate a system.

I have tried to argue that there are enough cues in the present world that a better and vastly more equitable society is viable, that there is enough evidence as well as a priori reasons to believe that human beings are capable of not exploiting every opportunity for personal gain. We do numerous acts simply because we are supposed to. This raises the hope that we can create a world where individuals will work even when they know that much of the fruit of their labor will go to those who are less fortunate. Marx's ([1875] 1959) morally resonant appeal, "From each according to his ability and to each according to his need," cannot be dismissed out of hand as mere sloganeering. Even though all that is being claimed is that a radically better society is *in principle* possible, and even though we do not have a road map for how to get there, this is an important assertion.

We know from previous attempts to build better societies that while passion is a necessary ingredient, it is by no means sufficient. Many of those who have tried just by their heart have blundered. I cannot deny a certain admiration for those who have yearned for such a society, and those who have actually tried to achieve it—Karl Marx, Mao Tse-tung, Martin Luther King Jr., Che Guevara, Fidel Castro, Ho Chi Minh, Allende, and Gandhi. The fact that most of these experiments failed, and some of the initially idealistic leaders took perverse paths and created draconian systems, is not because their target was wrong but rather because they took to an impossible path. There is also the problem of trying to create an idealistic society in a small pocket of a globalized world. The chances are that such experiments will either peter out because the leadership gradually becomes like any conservative government, or become perverse as the leaders battle against the corrupting influence of other powerful nations that try to block and derail such experiments. I am aware that of the revolutionaries just named, several are hated figures, and only a few are generally admired. It is interesting, though, that the ones who are generally admired are those who never actually got to govern. This fits in well with what I am asserting here.

What does it mean, critics may ask, to say that a better and fairer world is possible, but not to know how to get to such a world? Is that a meaningful construct? This is a legitimate question, but the criticism implicit in it is not a valid one. To elucidate this I can do no better than fall back once again on the master observer of the human condition: Kafka. This time we have to draw on his other posthumously published novel, *The Castle*.

K arrives one snowy night to the village outside the castle where he has been summoned to be a land surveyor. But who exactly has summoned him, and how does he reach that person? He knows of the magnificent castle; people speak to him about it. But how does he actually get there? He takes up lodging at the village inn to wait his turn, whenever that may come. But all his efforts to reach the castle turn out to be in vain. We know it exists, but there are no obvious roads or bridges to take him there.

The Castle has been interpreted, variously, as expressing human anguish in the face of a surreal and meaningless bureaucracy, the ambiguity of meaning, and above all, the yearning that human beings feel for that elusive better world. It is interesting that we know even less about the protagonist of this novel than what we do about Josef K. in *The Trial*. For instance, we do not know his first name. This sparseness of description is deliberate; K could be Kafka himself, or he could be any of us.[2] As Roberto Calasso (2005, 11) observes, "Compared to all other fictional characters, K is potentiality itself."

K's desperate and ill-conceived attempts to get to the castle lead him to grief and misery. For Kafka, there are lessons in this. That something is feasible is an important enough claim even if we do not yet know how to achieve it. At least it opens up the quest for change and teaches us not to acquiesce to our present state. At the same time, we have to be careful not to jump to ill-conceived action. In the heat of passion, it is easy to get the targets wrong. Take, for example, the widespread protests against globalization. I believe that this is a misguided manifestation of the legitimate grievance against global corporate control and avarice. Powerful global corporations, with the huge amounts of resources that they can commandeer at the drop of a hat, their disdain for the governments of poor nations and the environment, and their power over the media, which they frequently own, are a daunting force. We have reason to be wary of them. But the common tendency to equate this with globalization is a mistake. There are huge benefits that globalization can confer, such as enabling poor people to be better off, enriching our cultures through the infusion of ideas, arts, and music from other cultures, and bringing people of different geographies closer to one another.[3]

Restless though we may feel, we need to garner more information, theorize, analyze, and cogitate before we resort to action. The world has seen insurgencies and revolutions, many of which, though noble in intent, have ended up making matters worse or led us to a society that was eventually no different from the one that was dislodged. In a sense, the Russian Revolution of 1917 was of this kind. It began full of idealism and promise, but ultimately led to the creation of new czars and a new bourgeoisie.[4] I believe Saramago was right when he suggested that the fall of the Soviet Union was not a collapse of socialism but rather of capitalism, for the late Soviet regime was in fact a capitalist economy in disguise.[5] The demise of the USSR is thus an indictment of a perverse brand of capitalism, not of socialism.

Radical writing has occasionally argued that all capitalism—be it in poor nations or rich—is prone to crony capitalism. I believe there is some truth to this, and one can see this not only in the manner in which private corporations cornered contracts in Ferdinand Marcos's Philippines or Anastasio Somoza's Nicaragua but also in the behavior of large business lobbies that operate barely beyond the precincts of governments to bring pressure on policy and corner lucrative business deals in the capitals of rich nations. The only mistake with this observation is the risk of the failure to realize that even socialism runs the risk of crony capitalism. In fact, under socialism, so much of the booty tends to be gathered under one roof—the roof of the government—that this becomes an obvious target for loot. Groups form, as they did in Russia, to corner, consume, and plunder these resources under the control of one central government. In constructing ideas for a better world, we have to be aware of this risk and construct careful safeguards against it.

If we are ever to switch to a fairer economic system, the nature of activism will have to be different from—and in many ways, more radical than—what we have managed thus far. To develop such a blueprint, one will need analysis and the best of scientific thought. The aim of this book is to urge us toward such radical research and activism, and provide a theoretical foundation, however rudimentary. It is also possible that the construction of a better society is not a matter of sudden action and huge policy initiatives but rather slow evolution with some deliberate inputs from the sidelines. There is reason to be restless about the present economic system. Yet there is reason to be cautious about subversive action. An ill-conceived plan can lead to perverse consequences. There is a risk that the tyranny of a few will be replaced by the tyranny of another few.

In strategizing change, another common mistake—widespread in extremist thinking—is to cast individuals into categories of good and evil. It is true that the rich benefit from the current system, but it would be a mistake to assume that they are all complicit in its persistence. It is heartening that among those who demand change, no matter how inchoately, some are rich and influential people—that is, those who have clearly done well by the system. One of the most famous examples in history is Friedrich Engels.[6] He ran a flourishing business, and used much of the money he made from this to ensure that others in the future would not be able to make so much of it or would be forced to part with the bulk of it in favor of those who were less fortunate.

The defenders of the status quo often attack the recommendations for radical change that come from the rich or otherwise successful as hypocrisy. How can we trust George Soros's recommendations for a more equitable world when he himself has done so well by the skewness? Surely Ted Turner cannot be in favor of better-distributed wealth since he has so much of it? Can his well-known friendship with Castro be anything more than a fashion statement? Can someone as successful as Michael Moore or George Clooney really be serious about his radical views?

The aim of the conservative media is to discredit such views, which is a clever strategy from its point of view. Suppose we take the stand that one must not talk of radical changes like eradicating poverty, abolishing inheritance, and redistributing wealth from the rich to the poor until one gives up one's own above-average wealth, then those with above-average wealth face a dilemma. They will have to either give up their wealth or not talk about radical change. Given that hardly anybody will want to give up his or her wealth *unilaterally*, this is a smart recipe for leaving the present system unchallenged and thus unchanged.

It is an entirely consistent view to take that if the world is hugely unequal, I would rather be at the rich end of the spectrum, but at the same time I wish that the world were not so unequal. It is good to have people who despite their own advantage in the present system, are willing to admit to its gross inhumanity. While it is entirely possible that some among them do not really believe in what they say, to silence these people is to dampen the hopes for change. Moreover, our aim should be to evaluate the validity of an argument or a proposition on its own strength, and not because it comes or does not come from a particular person.

Before turning to a few actual prescriptions for action, it bears pointing out that there is a troubling intellectual quandary in deciding what to agitate against. It is foolish to deny that there are some systemic wrongs in life that we have no choice but to live with. As noted earlier, if we come to believe that gravity is unfair, for it keeps pulling us down, no one will dispute that agitation is not the right response to this. Likewise, and hard though this may seem to some demagogues, there are social wrongs that unlike gravity, arise out of the actions of us individuals but are so linked to the collectivity that for each individual, it is almost as immutable as gravity. So there are some collective wrongs that we may simply have to live with. But there is a fine line here, and I believe that there are individually futile actions that we should nevertheless urge individuals to undertake. There are many contexts in which each individual's efforts would be futile and even counterproductive, but if a large group could collectively make the effort it would yield desirable results. This was spelled out in chapter 7 as the large numbers argument. I am suggesting that this can lead to a quandary not just for the self-regarding individual but even for morally motivated persons. I have already discussed the problem of intranational inequality. This seems to be on the rise everywhere in the world, and may well have a connection with globalization. For an individual nation, perhaps not much can be done to stall this process or at least stall it without causing some other grave damage to the economy. If there can be coordinated global action, though, the process can be stalled. I also discussed in earlier chapters how being trustworthy may not be, individually, a wealth-enhancing trait, but when a group comes to acquire this trait the whole group may do much better than it would in the absence of this quality.

One reason why it is worthwhile pointing to the ills of society that no individual can cure is that as argued chapter 3, human beings have the public good urge—that is, the urge to do the things that, *if* done by everybody, lead to a reward for all. In other words, as observed earlier, if a person knows that no one throwing litter on the street makes the city clean and the person likes the city to be clean, then that knowledge itself is likely to give the person the urge not to litter the street. My claim was that this public good urge is hardwired into us. Hence, it is not always a futile exercise for the analyst to point to desirable changes that can be brought to fruition if, and only if, all or a substantial number of people strive toward them. This recognition can itself spark action and bring about desired changes.

The need to look beyond our current system to create a better world, where those who have managed to wrest control of a disproportionate amount of the world's resources and wealth are disengaged from their possessions, and where people get rewards according to their need and work according to their ability, is one such massive collective agenda. The path to this remains unclear, and thus we have a large project ahead of us. But that does not mean that there is no scope for action in the interregnum. There are other less radical changes that we should strive for even within the current system. The next section is devoted to a sampler of a laundry list of such prescriptions.

The 'Environmental Case' against Inequality

There are changes in the interregnum that are worth striving for. They are *relatively* small changes, hard but not infeasible. The basic thought that picks up on ideas introduced in the early chapters of the book and underlies this section is that there is more inequality in the world than can be morally justified. While a certain amount of inequality is inevitable and even necessary for the successful functioning of an economy as well as for development, what we have today is, by a wide measure, beyond such a level.

The argument is best understood through an environmental analogy. It has been a hard-fought battle, but there is recognition now that we cannot continue to guzzle global resources at the current rate.[7] Among other things, it is unfair to future generations, those not yet born to stake a claim.

There is a horizontal counterpart to this contention that has received much less attention. Just as future generations would suffer if we continue to use up resources, warm up the globe, and pollute the atmosphere at the rate at which we are doing so now, if the rich in today's world continue to consume and use resources at the present rate, it is probably inevitable that a large segment of the world's population has to be destitute. There are limits to the world's resources that make this inevitable. The world has enough resources to eradicate poverty, but probably not enough for this to be possible without some cutbacks in the consumption of the wealthiest people on earth.

One reason there is so much discussion of the intergenerational problem, but so little of the horizontal one, that is, across regions and across people, is our subliminal awareness that the latter is dangerous. The ones who are deprived are present, and to make them aware is to risk that this will not be a mere academic discussion. A premise of this book, however, is that this question of horizontal inequity cannot be postponed endlessly. To try to look away from this is not morally prudent, nor good for our own well-being. The political turmoil and economic distress that we see in today's world are manifestations of these underlying injustices, which we may not admit to, but that we cannot write off either. The few practical policy suggestions that follow, in contrast to the bulk of the book, which is meant to be interpretative, stem from this urgent awareness.

Property, Possession, and Inheritance

In the current setting and arguably even in future ones, we cannot conceive of a functioning economy that does not uphold large domains of individual property rights. For individuals, as we currently know them, to strive and be productive as well as innovative, they need the assurance that once they have acquired something, they will be able to keep and use it, without having to organize a private army to guard it. But property rights to what you have earned is one thing, and property rights at birth to what someone else has earned is another. One does not have to be utopian to question the ethics and economics of inheritance. This was once a subject of much discussion, but it has deftly been removed from public discourse. A large part of the unacceptable inequality in the world occurs through the channel of inheritance, for it allows the rich to amass not just what is possible through one lifetime but rather through multiple lifetimes and dynastic lineages that can span centuries.

Further, the legislative structure that makes inheritance possible by granting one the right to will away property after one's demise, and therefore ensures that some people will be born poor, often close to starvation, and some rich, at times so rich as to be beyond the comprehension of most ordinary people, is like having a legally mandated caste system or state-supported apartheid. There has to come a time when looking back at this arrangement, our descendants will wonder how human beings could have tolerated such an unfair system. The reason why so little is said about this is precisely because the unfairness of *this* system of private property is so blatant that people with a vested interest in it realize that the only way to keep it safe is to not let it come into the domain of public discourse. This is a classic case of the conspiracy of silence. This inequality, as discussed above, also has an intertemporal dimension, as today's rich use up a disproportionate amount of our common resources, and risk bringing our progenies into a degraded environment.

Intelligently dismantling the current system of inheritable private property—or realistically, at least a part of it, by having a large, say, 50 percent, inheritance tax or estate duty—will not solve all the problems of poverty but can make a substantial dent in global poverty, inequality, and the general unfairness of our contemporary economic life. I am discussing this under the category of "smaller initiatives," fully aware that that is so only in relative terms; the interests that will resist change even after the conspiracy of silence is disrupted are formidable. What offers hope is that among the rich in the world, there are those honest enough to admit that while the current system of inheritance benefits their progenies and so is good for them, it is morally wrong and ought to go.

The hurdles and practical complexities that will have to be handled if we are to dismantle the laws of inheritable private property, even in partial measure, are numerous. First and foremost, every time we think of a new law or a change in the law, we have to anticipate the people's and the market's response. Most governments have a tendency to clutter up the economy with too many laws, each of which may be well-meaning, but the net effect of many of those laws, after the market has responded and the has dust settled, may be questionable.[8] Many governments have tried to control the economy beyond their capacity, and the result has been a dismal backlash.

Turning to the question of disallowing inheritance, imagine, as an opening gambit, that we enact a law whereby each person's wealth at the time of their death accrues to the state—for instance, to some fund that is collectively owned by all citizens.[9] It is important to recognize that this does not mean that what people currently pass on to their children or loved ones (or in the event of there being no such persons, to some foundation) will, under the new regime, go to the state—that is, the collective fund. This is because people will surely respond to the new law by giving away a lot of their wealth to their children and loved ones *before they die*. How much a person can transfer by this method is, of course, limited by the fact that they cannot predict the time of their death. In deciding how much to give away while alive, one will therefore have to balance the risk of living long years after giving away one's wealth to loved ones, who may turn out to be not so loving in return, and being caught dead before being able to give away much. So there will be some circumventing of anti-inheritance laws, but not all of them. A part of this leakage can be blocked by limiting the amount of gift one can give away or by having a gift tax, but this in turn may discourage charitable giving. Moreover, for every new law being contemplated, we must be wary of overlegislation, something that the world already suffers from. In the end, we have to think of a simple anti-inheritance law, and then live with the fact that some leakage and economic distortion will be its concomitant.

Let me add that a policy of this kind ought to be accompanied by a plan to promptly distribute what accrues to the government in the form of estates of the deceased back to the larger population, and in particular the needy, since it is not a good idea to have the state control large funds and run commercial ventures. The state is usually not good at this, and such a wealthy state also risks becoming the target of capture by powerful groups, as happened in the Soviet Union before its collapse.

In the longer run, we also have to worry about an international dimension to this problem. If all persons' wealth at the time of their death goes to the state, this will not do anything to intercountry inequality, at least not in any direct way. Morally, it is not clear why, with the death of individuals, their wealth should be shared by all citizens of only their own nation. This may be better than the wealth going to only their children, but it is still not good enough. If inheritance is viewed as a caste system, then even after inheritance is disallowed and money flows into a national coffer, some of the problems of the caste system remain, since the people of a poor country remain doomed to poverty. Ideally, there should be a system of transferring a part of this inheritance fund from rich to poor nations, but this raises a host of philosophical questions about the meaning and status of the nation-state and the rights of people across national boundaries, and also the political feasibility of such transfers.[10] At first blush, this may seem like an unworkable idea.[11] Why will rich nations agree to transfer funds? The same question would have arisen before the age of taxation. Why will rich individuals allow themselves to be taxed in order to provide support and welfare to the poor? The fact that they do, does not make this an easy policy option, but it shows that it is not impossible.

Global Policy Coordination

This takes me back to the subject of policy measures needed to fill the gaps that have arisen by virtue of rapid economic globalization without comparable advances in global governance, discussed in the previous two chapters. For now, we have to work with stopgap measures, until such a time comes when we have a common global polity and are able to institute truly global policies—an idea that has, in different forms, engaged some of our most powerful minds, like Bertrand Russell, Stanley Jevons, Leon Trotsky, and the poet Rabindranath Tagore. The idea of global governance is both controversial and utopian. But it is not as impossible as it may appear. Currently, the world has over two hundred national governments, and it must seem that having one government to replace them all and take charge of the mammoth population globally is quite infeasible. Another way of viewing the current situation, though, is to note that one-sixth of the world's population is already under a single government—I am referring to China here. For that matter, another one-sixth is under another single government, India's. If the world consisted only of Africa, which has fifty-three nations and close to nine hundred million inhabitants, and we asked ourselves if so many people and so many countries could ever come under one government, the skeptic would say it is an impossible dream. But that cannot be right, because it has already happened in China and India.

Let me nevertheless leave aside the subject of global governance. As suggested above, and discussed at length in chapters 8 and 9, what we need minimally but urgently is the ability to coordinate better between national economic policies. For some kinds of policies, we do have organizations or treaties for global, intercountry coordination—again, the ILO for labor market policies, the WTO for trade policy coordination, and others for the environment, nuclear nonproliferation (which may alternatively be described as the maintenance of nuclear inequalities), and so on. Yet there is no organization for coordinating policies for the control of poverty and inequality. There needs to be two kinds of policy activism to ensure this: the first, involving the transfer of resources from rich to poor nations, and the second, helping to coordinate the effort of each country to control its own poverty and inequality.

As I pointed out in chapter 8, what each nation can unilaterally do to control inequality and, to a certain extent, poverty within its own boundaries is severely limited. In today's globalized world, with capital easily moving in and out of nations, and with skilled labor, top managers, investment bankers, and scientific personnel also fairly mobile across countries, it is difficult for nations to control their own inequality without creating a negative backlash on the economy. We have seen some of the mechanisms through which this works. So the way to curb inequality and divert greater effort to the eradication of poverty is for several nations to simultaneously adopt policies that will prevent one nation from benefiting from another's effort to control inequality or mitigate poverty. To start a global agency for the coordination of antipoverty and inequality-mitigation policies—say, by coordinating tax rules, such as corporate tax rates, which, left to atomistic, nation-based decisions, invariably get set too low—will not be an easy task but it is not impossible either. Similar efforts have had a modicum of success elsewhere. Consider the Comprehensive Nuclear Test Ban Treaty. Each nuclear nation on its own would have no interest in giving up the right to test its nuclear bombs. But nations realized that it was in their *collective* interest to do so, and after a lot of toil and struggle, a ban came into existence in 1996. The same is true of the Kyoto Protocol, which is an environmental treaty for controlling greenhouse gas concentrations. Its existence is testimony to how nations can solve hard coordination problems, and the fact that the United States under Bush refused to ratify it, and we are only now once again trying to get back to a global agreement based on the Copenhagen summit, shows the vulnerability of these global arrangements.

What is good for the world and what we should collectively aspire to may at the same time be what we would not advise any individual nation to implement *unilaterally*. It is fully understandable why each European nation has moved on a trajectory of secular decline in the corporate tax rate, even though they may all collectively regret this. Many Asian nations fret that Malaysia with its low corporate tax rate is drawing international capital away from other Asian nations. Still, one cannot fault Malaysia for doing this. What we need is a collective, international decision and enforcement agency to plug this drain.

'Colonization of the Future' and Equity for Workers

I turn now to a final and even trickier prescription. Earlier chapters have discussed how large masses of people have lost vital resources or wealth to other groups, at times under compulsion but also on occasion voluntarily. The indigenous people of the Americas lost their land to the settlers, often through deals, contracts, and treaties, each of which at that time may have seemed advantageous to both sides, yet taken together amounted to a near total disenfranchisement of a people. This is once again a version of the large numbers argument that we encountered in chapter 7. I will refer here to these processes of history as "Escher's stairway," whereby a sequence of short, upward-moving steps eventually takes one to the bottom of the stairway (Basu 1994b; Voorneveld 2009). Unlike in the case of the large numbers argument, in these long historical processes there may be the additional complication of the eventual losers not fully comprehending the meaning of the transaction they have undertaken. In the Americas case, as I tried to show in chapter 1, the natives, not accustomed to having land treated as a matter of individual property and exclusive ownership, did not fully comprehend what a land sale meant. Likewise, the high noon of colonialism was made possible by colonies going under imperial control with little fight, and frequently through a series of 'trades' and 'exchanges' that seemed fine at each stage, but in total amounted to subjugation and large-scale poverty.

Is it possible that such processes are currently in motion, that there are people who are on Escher's stairway, making voluntary decisions in the belief that each one is making them better off, while the totality of such decisions is moving them toward penury and destitution? The answer, in all likelihood, is yes. These kinds of processes have been with us for centuries, and they keep taking new forms and so are not easily recognizable. Trained researchers may try to guess as to what these processes are, but to most ordinary citizens they become evident only in retrospect. I would hazard that the process of colonization that is currently happening is best understood as the colonization of the future. As society has progressed, human beings have become adept at more and more sophisticated contracts, spanning large tracts of time, such as: I will take your money and buy a house now, and pay you back slowly over the next thirty years. I will think of a clever idea that can help people make money, but all those who use my idea will have to pay me a certain sum. I will buy shares in a company, and that little piece of paper will ensure that I earn a fraction of all future profits of the company. Recently, there have been entrepreneurs offering to invest in the education of smart students in the form of equity—a natural and innovative idea once one thinks about it. That is, the firm or entrepreneur will fund a student's higher education, and then, through the student's life or maybe some predefined length of time such as fifteen years, take a certain percentage of student's income. The contracts are often fine-tuned, exempting the students from having to pay anything if they earn less than a certain amount. Companies offering such investment include CareerConcept in Germany, and My Rich Uncle and Direct Human Capital in the United States.[12]

These are just a few examples of the complex contracts with long-run future claims that are becoming available now. There is no denying that many of these ideas are useful and can help people. At the same time, one cannot be unmindful of the fact that most people do not understand the implications of such contracts. Every now and then, we have credit crises precisely because a segment of the population has signed on to contracts the full implications of which they do not grasp, or because the collection of these contracts are not together consistent.[13] In the case of the most innovative and extremely long-run contracts, it is probable that the full implications are not known to anyone, and will evolve through future disputes, litigations, and judgments. But one implication of this is clear enough. Human beings of our generation are laying larger and larger claims to the output of tomorrow. This is happening on a level never seen before in human history, which is not surprising given that we now have mechanisms of long-term contracts and that their enforcement is better than ever before. Most ordinary people, not just in poor nations, but even in the United States, Japan, and Europe, have little idea of the modalities of property rights on ideas. So they are shocked to learn that there are approximately 6 million patents currently in effect worldwide. Hence, there are around 6 million ideas, which are *owned*; if you want to use one of those ideas, you are strictly supposed to pay the person who owns it. In China, the mushrooming of Harry Potter titles, which were not written by J. K. Rowling but ghostwritten by Chinese authors, to cash in on the Potter mania illustrates this confusion. Some of these fake books, such as *Harry Potter and the Chinese Empire*, may well be produced by publishers aware of the violation of copyrights law. But that some of these publishers do not even understand that they are violating someone's intellectual property is clear from observations like those of Wang Lili, editor of the Chinese Braille Publishing House, which put out *Harry Potter and the Chinese Porcelain Doll*. She explained the decision to publish such a book by saying, "Harry Potter was so popular that we wanted to enjoy the fruits of its widely accepted publicity in China."[14] In a lecture in Calcutta on January 9, 2007, Stiglitz mentioned how the publisher of a pirated Chinese edition of one of his books asked him to write a foreword to the "new edition." Evidently, the idea of intellectual property, as developed by a small global elite, is poorly understood by most people. It is therefore easy for the few who are conversant in these matters to take advantage of other people's confusion, the way the early settlers in the New World took advantage of the native people's incomprehension of the concept of land sales.

All this also means that when tomorrow arrives and people go about their daily chores, working in factories and farms, and producing goods and services, of the total goods and services produced—that is, of tomorrow's GNP—a large (and increasingly larger) portion will be claimed by the previous generations. People will use their slips of paper denoting long-term contracts such as shares, patents, and copyrights to lay claims on the output. The flip side of this is that for those who do not have these claims from a previous period, either because they did not sign farsighted contracts or were born with no inheritance, there will be a relatively small share of output to lay claim on. Workers, for instance, will have a smaller pie from which to earn their income, and the aggregate wage bill can even decline, since a large part of the output will have claimants from previous generations as well as those possessing technology or property rights in ideas. So what is being colonized now are claims on future output. And those who are at the receiving end of this process are not concentrated geographically, as in the old colonization story. When these workers and other large masses of people, who get impoverished by this process, wake up, it will be too late for them, like it was for the colonies that lost land gradually over the centuries. What is happening today is thus the colonization of the future. Those who are steadily losing out through this process do not realize it, just as Native Americans did not fully realize that their land was being colonized until after it happened.

My expectation is that this process of the colonization of the future will cause a steady deterioration in the conditions of the working class. As the share of the output in each period available for distribution to workers shrinks, wages will see a relative decline and rates of employment will fall. There are enough unexpected shocks—from nature and the collective implications of individual actions—to our global economy that this trend will not be immediately visible. But it seems likely that this will be the long-run trend. Some early signs of this process are already apparent. The oft-heard complaint about jobless growth in industrialized and some developing nations, along with rising inequality, are symptoms of this. For poor nations, this crunch may be some distance away, since despite the shrinking aggregate of jobs and wage bills, workers in poor nations, with a little intelligent policymaking by their governments, should be able take advantage of their relatively low wage and hold on to their jobs. So the trend will begin with the working classes in industrialized nations feeling the squeeze before people in other nations do. They will resist this through political means, and this in turn may cause some global strife and tensions. One already hears this in the frequent complaints that poor nations are stealing the jobs of the industrialized countries. Each time a firm outsources work to a developing country in order to increase its profits, this move is treated as one worker getting the better of another. All this is made worse by our propensity to exploit our environment and degrade the world's natural resources.

It is not necessary to view this as a worker versus worker problem, however. Each such act of outsourcing causes profits to rise. So this may equally be viewed as a capital versus worker matter.[15] The firms that earn greater profits by shifting some of their operations to developing nations can, in principle, pay the workers in the industrialized nations a part of the profit to compensate them for their job losses. Nonetheless, as the share of the wage bill shrinks, our tendency is to overlook this and point a finger at the poorer workers who find employment.

What does one do to stall the process of the colonization of the future with its attendant negative economic and political fallout? This brings me to the policy suggestion. One small step that we can take is to give the working classes and the poor, in general, an equity stake in our profits. So each time workers lose out because jobs are lost, or wages get lowered or do not keep pace with prices, and the profits rise, the workers get back a part of what they lose from their equity share of the profits. I call this a small step, fully aware that even this seemingly small change of policy regime has pitfalls galore, and will need a lot of detailed thinking and political jockeying for it to be realized.[16] The threat of insurgency and the subversion of the economy from the poorer classes can nevertheless make the rich more amenable to such radical policies. I believe that such action on the part of the poor would be understandable.

Let me elaborate a little on what I am proposing. In a nutshell, I am advocating that all human beings below a certain level of income should have a claim to a share of the *aggregate* profits. Hence, instead of giving workers just a fixed income guarantee, as in the standard welfare system, we need to couple such a minimum guarantee with an equity stake in profit. So, if in the long run, the share of profit rises and the wage bill falls, the incomes of workers need not fall and certainly will not fall as greatly as the decline in wage earnings. Further, as entrepreneurs turn more sophisticated, and extract more and more profit out of the productive system, they will have to be reconciled with 'leakages' to the poor and the working class. This will be countered, of course, by taking money that will not be shown as profit, such as salaries for CEOs and major shareholders for fictitious work done. This also will introduce some distortions in the system. But as in the case of the inheritance tax, there are limits to how innovative individuals can be. If the scheme is worked out carefully enough, and adjusted every now and then to respond to newer methods that CEOs will discover to beat the system, the benefits should outweigh the costs of distortion.

Once again, we have to encounter the problem of intercountry profit. If these schemes are confined within national boundaries, they will still be desirable, but the unfairness meted out to those born in poor nations will remain largely unresolved. This takes us back to the problem of economic globalization having progressed at a pace that is in excess of political globalization, and consequently, to the need for putting global governance structures in place.

Despair and Hope

While trying to implement changes that are *relatively* small and therefore more feasible, like the ones discussed in the previous section, it is important to keep alive hopes for more sweeping reforms that will eradicate poverty from the world (something that is technically already feasible, given the enormous riches of today's world economy) and bring inequality down from the incomprehensible heights that prevail today to more tolerable levels.[17] Such a world would be not merely efficient, as free market economies are purported to be, but also fair, and so there would be less room for disgruntlement as well as fewer reasons for the political turmoil and instability that so plague our times.

Peace in such a world will not have to rely on brainwashing the masses into believing that their poverty and deprivation are justified, and that they are ordained to their condition by some immutable law of the economy.

A central message of this book is that the form of capitalism that so much of the world either relies on or aspires to is a grossly unfair system. The belief, popularized in so many books and by so much journalese, that all we need to do is to work toward perfecting this system and all will be well, is a myth perpetrated, at times deliberately and at times unwittingly, in the interests of those who gain from the persistence of this unjust system. It is the same kind of myth, propagated and actually believed in over long strands of history in India, that the caste system was the way things were meant to be, and the pain and deprivation suffered by the *dalits* and other disadvantaged groups were part of a divine plan, as just punishment for their sinful previous lives. It is the same kind of belief fostered in the United States in the age of slavery and lynching that the public humiliations and torture that were inflicted on blacks were the right treatment for lesser lives. It is the same kind of belief that makes people feel that "redistributing the wealth" is wrong because the current distribution is somehow the right one, forgetting that the current distribution itself is, in part, an outcome of grasping, lobbying, and the bartering of favors as well as the accumulation of wealth that has occurred through inheritances passed carefully down dynastic lineages.

So persuasive were these beliefs that even the people bearing the brunt of these morally skewed systems did not question the fairness of the system. Indeed, the persistence of these societal arrangements was predicated on the widespread acceptance of there being fairness in the desserts dished out to people. Practices that look so grossly unfair in retrospect or at a distance— lynching, apartheid, the acquisition of lands of indigenous peoples by guile and force, and castigatory and vindictive action directed at selected racial groups—look different when one is living in a society that embraces them. We are somehow made to believe that those who gain from such practices do so rightly. Some have of course dissented against these injustices, but by and large the oppressed have, over long periods, simply acquiesced. This is no doubt caused by the psychological need of the oppressed to somehow believe that they deserve what they are getting, for the alternative is to live with levels of rage and anger so great as to be self-destructive.

Cut to contemporary times. Consider the prototype free market system that prevails in some form in all industrialized nations and is aspired to by other states. In this system, what is collectively owned by human beings with shared rights is shrinking, and the world's resources are increasingly cut up and partitioned, with each slice of the partition possessed as property by some individual. Usually, it is a small fraction of the population that gets to own these bundles of property and the right to income streams extending into the distant future, and these rights come with the right to bequeath them to whoever one wishes, usually one's progeny. This means that in this system, there will be persons born in ghettos or slums with no inheritance, and there will be those born with large inherited wealth, with the best of education provided almost from birth. As such, there is just no competitition between these two classes of people. The former will stand virtually no chance of 'making it,' while the latter will find it difficult *not* to make it. Those born poor are blighted from the start, their condition made that much more dire by the fact that the common resources available to future generations born without inheritance are shrinking thanks to the inexorable dynamic of individuals establishing private and excludable rights over them, and bequeathing these to their children.

We, including the losers, do not question this system because we are a part of it. But if we could distance ourselves from the system and then contemplate it, we would have no difficulty in realizing that the society that we inhabit is, in a significant sense, alarmingly close to the most casteist and exclusionary society that we can think of throughout our histories. In addition, a small segment of the population overuses resources, thereby depriving others in the contemporary world and ensuring that future generations will arrive in an environmentally depleted world. Some people do not stand a chance simply because of where they are born. Those people born poor have as many disadvantages in contemporary capitalist society as the *twice born* have advantages in a caste-based society.[18] If these inequities are allowed to persist and grow, a time may well come when the poor decide that, just as society considers it fine for the rich to outwit the poor, it is fine for the poor to outhit the rich.

To hold down the poor in their current state would be comparable to burning down "to the ground" schools for black children, as Alice Walker poignantly writes, "by local racists who wanted to keep ignorant their competitors in tenant farming" or evicting "sharecroppers, like my parents, . . . because they attempted to exercise their "democratic" right to vote."[19] Consider one of the big slums of the world—Kibera in Nairobi or Dharavi in Mumbai. If a young person from one of these slums who lives a life of abject poverty—with no decent clothes, no health care, and the sight of their children growing up into beggary—comes to one of the gated areas of the city where the rich live in opulence, splendor, and wastefulness, and feels the urge to bring this inequity to an end by robbery or revolution if need be, should an outside observer find this baffling?

The outside observer who understands this sentiment may still have reason to dissuade this person from taking sudden action on the ground that that is likely to be futile in the long run. It may even worsen the situation by instilling fear among people, and so leading to lowered investment and innovation. On the other hand, the threat of the widespread use of such insurgencies could compel the rich and powerful to devise policies for distributing the world's aggregate wealth better. What this book urges is that instead of waiting for the pressure of insurgencies and revolts to build up, we should work toward radical policy shifts that take from the rich and give more to the poor. We should strive for a society in which there is neither outwitting nor outhitting. Given the ingenuity that some bring to outwitting, we may have to think of blunt policy measures like placing a cap (which can be some multiple of society's per capita wealth or income) on how much wealth a person can amass, or how much income a person can earn and keep, with accruals beyond these limits being acquired by the state and redistributed among the masses. This will no doubt dampen the incentives of even those who are engaged in legitimate activities that yield benefits for society at large. But by setting the cap sufficiently high, costs can be kept to a minimum, and this minimal cost may be the price we have to pay to stop those who are engaged in building up wealth through exploitation.

The urge for a major overhaul would have to be declared as futile if there was an immutable law that our current system—maybe with minor improvements—is the best that we could hope to have. But this is where the other argument in this book becomes relevant—namely, that vastly better systems of society than what prevail today are, in principle, possible. The 'in principle' is a qualifier that tempers the claim somewhat. Nevertheless, it is an important claim in the sense that it tries to dislodge the accepted doctrine that only outcomes that are incentive compatible with the interests of selfish individuals are sustainable.

What a large part of this book argued is that we humans have the capacity for and ways of tempering our selfish proclivity and for not working relentlessly to pick up every advantage that comes our way. This proclivity does not always get vented; societies can get caught in an utterly selfish equilibrium. There are in life a thousand things that each of us can do to enhance our own welfare, but for reasons of social norms, culture, our sense of integrity, and biological and social hardwiring, we do not even consider many of those actions. In many nations, you can leave your valuables out on your lawns unprotected by walls and no one will touch them. This was not always the case; these countries have, through processes that we do not fully comprehend, managed to develop these norms. In most cultures today, we do not resort to physical violence to get what we want and what we could easily get by delivering a quick punch or a kick. A couple of millennia ago, this nonuse of a strategy that is technically feasible would have been unthinkable. In Japan, in the middle of the night, when there are virtually no cars on the roads and no police in sight, it is common for pedestrians to wait for the appropriate signal before they cross the street. In India, it is not common to do so in broad daylight, with flowing traffic and police in uniform on duty.

It is possible to argue that once a norm gets established, it is not in an individual's interest to violate it and so it is 'rational' for the individual to do what they do. But as I have pointed out earlier, this is a purely semantic matter about what we call rational. The important observation is that a behavior that looks incompatible with individually rational behavior in today's society may well be so in another society where the culture and norms are different.

Hence, a better society—for instance, one that relies on human beings not taking from a freely available common pool beyond what they need, or one where people work hard even though everybody gets the same income no matter what they do—may be feasible despite not being individually incentive compatible in the textbook sense. We can come to have norms where behaving otherwise is met with so much social disdain or self-loathing that no one does so. And in the long run, the norms can become so much a part of us that we end up following them not for any reason but rather because that is our instinctive behavioral response.

Those who have therefore been left in poverty and deprivation through no fault of their own, which is the vast majority of the poor, have every right to call the bluff perpetrated by some public analysts, politicians, and advocates of the status quo, who contend that their poverty is a measure of their productivity and essential to create the incentives that enable the world to attain a higher *average* income. In turn, this creates hope that those who have, through generations of exploitation and the use of inheritable rights, established control over large tracts of the world's resources and wealth, will ultimately be compelled to part with their spoils, and we will have a world to which we can all lay claim as equal citizens and into which future generations can arrive without finding themselves in the midst of a wasteland.

NOTES

PREFACE

1. Sister Wendy Beckett, *Sister Wendy's Odyssey: A Journey of Artistic Discovery* (New York: Stewart, Tabori, and Chang, 1992), 22.

CHAPTER 1. IN PRAISE OF DISSENT

1. This was not uncommon in other parts of the world either. Kiran Desai's descriptions of the law courts in colonial India (2006, 62) in her novel *The Inheritance of Loss* is quite realistic: "He heard cases in Hindi, but they were recorded in Urdu by the stenographer and translated by the judge into a second record in English, although his own command of Hindi and Urdu was tenuous; the witnesses who couldn't read at all put their thumbprints at the bottom of 'Read Over and Acknowledged Correct,' as instructed."

2. This gets some confirmation from Christopher Columbus's report to the court in Madrid: "[The Indians] are so naïve and so free with their possessions. ... When you ask for something they have, they never say no." And he concluded the report by assuring "their Majesties" that he would bring them "as much gold as they needed and as many slaves as they ask" (cited in Zinn 2003, 3).

3. It is worth inserting the caveat that this is not the only way to measure inequality. There are, in particular, measures that are not unmindful of what happens to the distribution of incomes of the 'middle group'—those who are neither too poor nor too rich. I am not making claims here about these other kinds of inequality. A more comprehensive discussion on inequality occurs in chapter 8.

4. Reported in the *Economist*, October 11–17, 2003, 13.

5. In fact, we buy more than that. Richard Fuld, the longtime chief of Lehman Brothers, earned forty-five million dollars in 2007, while the company was being driven into the ground. As the columnist Nicholas Kristoff observed in the *Week* (October 19, 2008, 80), "That amounts to roughly $17,000 per hour to obliterate a firm."

6. I have shown (Basu 2010a) how through clever design, Ponzis can be camouflaged into regular economic transactions, causing prices to deviate from values and leaving a trail of destitutes in their wake.

7. This is different from religious determinism that implies the hand of someone behind all that has happened and is to happen. Moreover, the normative implications of determinism are easy to misconstrue. I have discussed this at some length in Basu 2000.

8. While for this reason 1776 is often treated as the birth year of modern economics, it is interesting to note that this idea of how the free market can help coordinate the diverse interests of individuals was already there in a lecture that Smith delivered in 1749, and that survives today only in fragments (Rae 1895).

9. It is further arguable that in modern human society, there is coordination among strangers that goes beyond the market, and some would contend that this has biological and evolutionary roots (Seabright 2004b).

10. Smith's own perspective was not, I should clarify, godless. In his *Theory of Moral Sentiments* (1759), for instance, he makes it clear that in his view, the harmonious order that naturally prevails is guided by God. The reference to divinity, however, all but disappeared by the time he came to writing *The Wealth of Nations*.

11. It was nearly lost to a group of gypsies, who kidnapped Smith when he was three years old. But the boy was rescued a few days later. I will leave it to social psychologists to speculate about what this experience may have done to Smith's development, and through it, the development of capitalism in the world.

12. As Jacob Viner (1927, 212) put it so eloquently after describing Smith's theory of how laissez-faire works, "The foregoing is familiar matter. What is not so familiar, however, is the extent to which Smith acknowledged exceptions to the doctrine of a natural harmony in the economic order even when left to its natural course. Smith himself never brought these together; but if this is done, they make a surprisingly comprehensive list."

13. This remark has to be qualified by pointing out that there is a growing recent literature on Smithiana that recognizes this (Rothschild 2001; Dougherty 2002, Foley 2006). Indeed, if one evaluates Smith by going beyond the *Wealth of Nations* to his earlier book of 1759, *Theory of Moral Sentiments*, it becomes evident that Smith viewed economics as embedded in the larger fields of morality, politics, and sociology. These various Smiths—in particular, one describing the "economic man" and crying out for formalization, and the other recognizing the larger embeddedness of human beings— and the consequent claims on Smith by different schools of thought are discussed well in Evensky 2005a, 2005b.

14. For discussions of slavery, forced labor, and bonded labor, see Engerman 1973; Ellerman 1995; Genicot 2002; Bardhan 2005; Bakshi and Bose 2007; Lilienfeld-Toal and Mookherjee 2008.

15. The two understandings that I am talking about have parallels with the ancient ideas of *techne* and *episteme*, but are at the same time distinct from them. Xenophon, a contemporary of Socrates, when not busy fighting wars as a mercenary soldier, wrote about history, political philosophy, and the goodness of horses. In discussing Socrates, he drew a distinction between techne, which refers to the kind of knowledge that is associated with craft or some particular skill such as that of playing the harp, and episteme, which is close to our usual idea of knowledge. He did not consider the distinction of much value; that emphasis would come later with Aristotle. The two understandings being discussed here are really further categorizations of episteme, though my 'intuitive knowledge' may be viewed as the kind of knowledge that underlies techne. Even in the study of human intelligence there is the need to recognize the role of intuitive intelligence. For an engaging inquiry into this, see Gigerenzer 2007.

16. The beautiful expression "trained incapacity" to describe the idea of the incapacitating effects of overlearning is usually attributed to Thorstein Veblen.

17. Ronald Coase referred to this idealized, constructed world as "blackboard economics" in more than one place (see, for instance, Coase 1991).

CHAPTER 2. THE THEORY OF THE INVISIBLE HAND

1. Or as captured, with some poetic license, in a clerihew by Subramanian in the *Newsletter of Royal Economic Society* in 2009:

> For Vilfredo Federico *Pareto*
> It's true from Sicily to Soweto
> That x is socially the best
> If it's best for me, and the rest.

2. I am urging the reader to be like the playwright Simon Gray. Harold Pinter once wrote this elegant ode to the cricket legend Len Hutton: "I saw Len Hutton in his prime/Another time/another time." He sent it to Simon Gray, his friend, and later called him to check if he had received it. Gray replied, "Yes, but I have not finished reading it" (Gussow 1994, 13).

3. For a scholarly account of the trajectory of the invisible hand proposition from Smith to recent times, and in particular, its role in the debate on free markets and state intervention, see Medema 2009.

4. The reader should be warned that much of what we know of Pythagoras's life and work is speculative history. It is not even certain that it was Pythagoras who proved the Pythagoras theorem.

5. Typically, the assumption is that there is a 'continuum' of individuals—that is, there are as many individuals in an economy as real numbers on the number line.

6. In intertemporal settings in particular, even this 'necessary but not sufficient' view of the Pareto principle runs into difficulty, raising a host of deep analytic and ethical questions (for a capacious commentary on the subject, see Hockett 2009).

CHAPTER 3. THE LIMITS OF ORTHODOXY

1. This is because the same final distribution of goods, without the violence, is Pareto superior. Of course, one can complicate this further by raising questions of feasibility. If the actual use of violence is the only way to make someone part with his or her property, then again violence need not be Pareto suboptimal. I am grateful to George Akerlof, whose questioning about some aspects of my work on household decision making drew my attention to the problem of violence.

2. The meaning of what constitutes 'greater freedom' is riddled with matters of contention, both technical and philosophical (see, for instance, Pattanaik and Xu 1990; Sen 1999; Arrow 2001; Foster 2010). Fortunately for my present purpose, there is no harm in staying clear of this controversial subject.

3. Gifts, for instance, in tribal societies or even industrial ones are often matters of exchange. As Paul Seabright (2004a) points out, from this perspective gifts are as venal as regular commerce.

4. This is not to deny that there can be perverse affects and that companies can actually lose money because competition drives them to overadvertise. There is, for instance, evidence that when tobacco companies were stopped by law from advertising on television, their profits rose.

5. This term is used by children in Calcutta to describe a kid who they reluctantly have to allow to join in some ongoing game. An elé belé is not an actual player but rather someone who is allowed to go through the motions of play and have the delusion that he or she is actually playing. When I was a child in Calcutta, and a kid was thrust on me and my friends by a doting mother, the cruel art of whispering elé belé into one another's ears could be extremely handy. All NGOs and grassroots activists that respond with verve to the invitation of governments and international organizations to participate in democratic decision making would do well to be cautious that they are not elé belés (Basu 2007d). An analysis of a similar process occurs in Michael Buroway's (1979) account of how capitalism survives and thrives by creating the illusion of choice to workers who may have little choice. A lot of gender discrimination takes this form, in which women are deluded into the belief that they are empowered.

6. For a trenchant critique of the strategic control of popular media, see Chomsky 1991.

7. See also Alfred Marshall 1890. Marshall noted, for instance, how "the more pictures or books a man has, the stronger is his taste for them likely to become. ... The virtue of cleanliness and vice of drunkenness alike grow on what they feed upon" (94).

8. An effort to use a Veblenesque premise to show that full rationality on the part of human beings may actually be *logically* problematic occurs in Pagano 2007. The argument is based on the construction of an infinite regression, where to solve each decision problem requires solving a prior decision problem.

9. See Pattanaik 1970; Fishburn 1970; Suzumura 1983.

10. There is also a line of argument that posits that human preference depends not merely on the goods and services a person actually consumes but also on the set of alternatives from which a person chooses the consumption vector. This is not a line that will be pursued here, especially because there is already an ample literature on this (see Sen 1999; Alkire 2002).

11. I mean this in a deeper sense than what could be captured simply by allowing for uncertainty and the use of expected utility. One way of capturing ill-definedness is to assume that human preferences or utility functions are 'fuzzy,' in the technical sense of the term. This approach, which was in vogue at one point of time (for a survey, see Salles 1999), does make for some leeway, but as is now evident it brings about no fundamental change.

12. A sign of his alienation was the 'office hours' card that many professors paste on their doors, specifying the hours each week when students are encouraged to drop in for discussion. One particular year Veblen's card read, "Mondays 10:00 to 10:05 a.m."

13. The 'herd mentality,' widely noted in the literature, can work through individuals seeking information from other people's choice, or because they get direct utility from belonging to a group by virtue of shared behavior or preferences (Leibenstein 1950; Basu 1989; Banerjee 1992; Bikhchandani, Hirschleifer, and Welch 1992).

14. See, for instance, Leibenstein 1950; Basu 1987; Young 1998; Warneryd 1990; Basu, Bhattacharya, and Mishra 1992; Kandori, Mailath, and Rob 1993; Platteau 1994, 2000; Solow 1995; Schlicht 1998; Harrington 1999; Aoki 2001; Blume 2002; Conlin, Lynn, and O'Donoghue 2003; Emerson and Souza 2003; López-Calva 2003; Karni, Salmon, and Sopher 2007; Fisman and Miguel 2007; Smead 2008. The new literature in behavioral economics, including a lot of experimental research, also impinges on this. This is discussed in chapter 6.

15. In his comprehensive study of the causes of development, Justin Yifu Lin (2009) refers to this as the "culture hypothesis." I take the view, however, that culture and social institutions are malleable qualities that can be nurtured or dampened.

16. For an interesting and unusual analysis along these lines—on how some people do not "succeed" simply because they do not have the "capacity to aspire," see Appadurai 2004.

17. I am not considering the third kind of society where when after one has taken the money and then the time comes to deliver the goods, one does not decide, one just instinctively does *not* deliver, because such a society is unlikely to exist. No one will ever cut small deals and make advance payments if it is known in advance that one will invariably lose one's money in that situation.

18. In fact, at times one encounters the reverse phenomenon. I have to admit to encouraging our neighbors, Bob and Jean in Ithaca, New York, to believe that my property ended short of where it actually did, so as to mislead them into mowing a part of my lawn.

19. It is in the same spirit that I once wrote an essay titled "On Why We Do Not Try to Walk Off without Paying after a Taxi Ride" (Basu 1983). For an ingenious answer to that question, see Myerson 2004. An interesting recent paper on the same subject (Guha and Guha 2010) realistically allows for the existence of individuals who are incorrigibly honest—they pay what they are supposed to without further thought, even though the majority of the population may be opportunistic (the way economics textbooks take all individuals to be) and do what is in their self-interest at each point in time.

20. The observations in this paragraph indicate the possibility of some interesting new research directions that can be pursued in understanding the evolution of societies, and particularly their rise and fall. Since some of the norms, such as that of not breaking a promise and working hard even when not being monitored, are efficient from a society's point of view and aid economic development, it is useful for a society to be endowed with such norms. Consider a society that somehow comes to acquire these norms. It is likely to prosper and develop economically. But of course, the individuals in such a society are vulnerable to mutants who do not share those norms and are able to take advantage of the 'normative loopholes' of this society. These mutants can, for instance, take advantage of other people's penchant for keeping promises and break their own for financial gain. Over time, they would destroy the norms of the existing society and cause its breakdown. Some such reason must underlie the easy capitulation of some well-developed societies to 'invasions' or the mere arrival of other groups that have been witnessed in history. The very norms that allow a society to be well developed and prosper economically, when it is relatively isolated, can become its source of vulnerability when there is an infusion of new peoples and cultures. While I do not go into any of the implied dynamics of this analysis in this book, some of the 'chemistry' of the coming together of different cultures will be studied in chapter 6.

21. Social norms do not always take this form. I distinguish between three different kinds of norms (Basu 2000). The one that has been popular in economics, because it does not tread on the individual rationality assumption, is called the equilibrium-selection norm. What I am discussing here is what I call a rationality-limiting norm.

22. Such texts were considered renegade writings in their times, and their authors were widely condemned, as was the case with Aquinas.

23. There is a Machiavellian caveat to this, which, in the interest of truth, we have to face up to. "Thou shalt not steal" is a development-friendly norm when used in all social interactions, but if we could develop a more nuanced norm, which allowed us to use one kind of norm for interaction with a group of "insiders" and another with "others," then adopting the nonstealing norm when dealing with the former yet not with the latter may be even better for the development of the society of insiders. As we saw above, the settlers in North America used such a norm, whereby different standards were set on what they could do among themselves and what was permissible vis-à-vis the natives. The old imperial powers, when they went to their colonies, often managed to use different norms of behavior among their own personnel and when their officers interacted with the people of the colonies. From the point of view of economic progress for a group of people, the best norm is therefore "Thou shalt not steal from your own people." This leads to some crucial and complex questions of identity, which I will address in chapter 6.

24. I do this by using an idea from Lindbeck, Nyberg, and Weibull 1999. See also Besley and Coate 1992; López-Calva 2003.

25. See also PROBE 1999.

26. This is not to suggest that this is always the right way to go. Some norms may be so deeply entrenched that it may be cheaper not to try to change them but rather to simply change behavior by fashioning appropriate incentives of rewards and punishments.

27. See Hurwicz 1960; Myerson 1983; Maskin and Sjostrom 2002. For a recent survey, see Sen 2007.

28. A disproportionately high number of letters to Tim Hartford seeking 'economic' advice in the *Financial Times* pertains to incentive problems. See, for instance, "Fair's Fair" and "Storytime Split," *Financial Times*, June 21 and July 5, 2008, respectively. Most of Hartford's answers use incentive-compatibility considerations, with a dose of common sense, which goes to support what I argue below. There is some writing that takes the incentive-compatibility models further so as to recognize the role of 'unusual' goods and incentives, such as the incentive of being awarded a title or prize that consists of no material gain but simply an honor. This gives rise to interesting problems about the creation of such goods (Besley and Ghatak 2008; see also Basu 1989; Ellingsen and Johannesson 2008).

29. For an interesting analysis of how incentive theory would be enriched by taking account of our innate prosocial behavior and preferences, and the need for esteem, see Ellingsen and Johannesson 2008.

30. In an ideal construction, one would want to bind together the social norms that constrain all human beings, and the rationality that propels and motivates them. This is not an easy task (see Gintis 2007).

31. There is also evidence that there are a variety of ways in which informal peer monitoring takes place among workers, thereby placing curbs on individual shirking (see Freeman, Kruse, and Blasi 2004).

32. Some new research has shed interesting light on how language can be a vital determinant of development (see, for instance, Ku and Zussman 2009; Clingingsmith 2009).

33. The remainder of this section draws and expands on Basu 2006c.

34. While the urge to act in one's collective interest is innate, the particular collectivities that one identifies with are often social constructs. A person's national or

religious identity is in all likelihood a social construct, whereas identity with one's off-spring and immediate family is probably biological. The fact that people are frequently willing to die for their nation or coreligionists shows that the strength of socially constructed ties are not necessarily weaker than the biologically preordained ones.

35. Whether our empirical research should be confined to this has been a matter of some debate (Banerjee 2005; Bardhan 2005; Kanbur 2005; Mookherjee 2005; Rodrik 2008), though in my own contribution (Basu 2005a) I went beyond this focus. The remainder of this chapter draws on this earlier work of mine.

36. The philosophical foundations of probability have a history of confounding not just philosophers and statisticians but also economists, most famously John Maynard Keynes. Indeed, it may be Keynes's early encounter with probability theory that led to some of his sharply negative views on the empirical method of the kind that Mookherjee (2005) discusses.

37. "We Sceptics follow in practice the way of the world, but without holding any opinion about it" (Bevan 1950, 52). Interestingly, this amounts to a critique of behaviorism. But I take behaviorism to be an easy target, summed up (no doubt in somewhat of a caricature) in the observation, allegedly made by Russell, that there is no way to tell the difference between a mathematician asleep and a mathematician at work.

38. The limitations that I discuss for empiricism should not be read as an endorsement of theory as the instrument of choice for understanding the way that the economy works. Theory can help us sort certain deductive complications, but may not be able to do much more (see Basu 2000, appendix). For excellent and persuasive essays on skepticism in the context of theory, see Rubinstein 2006a, 2006b.

39. The fact that human beings have a propensity to pick up patterns beyond what is actually there has been documented in psychological experiments (see Tversky and Kahneman 1971). Amos Tversky and Daniel Kahneman report on several other interesting findings on the mind's tendency to misread nature and find more regularities than what nature is endowed with. It could be argued, though, that this tendency on the part of human beings may have evolutionary survival value.

40. For centuries, human beings had faith in Aristotle's science as the basis of knowledge. We now know that while it had other intellectual appeals, such as poetry and the stimulus for thought, it was not science. In Arthur Koestler's words (1972, 111), Aristotle's science was instead "pure rubbish."

CHAPTER 4. THE ECONOMY ACCORDING TO LAW

1. Kafka died in 1924, and *The Trial* was published in 1925. The first English translation appeared in 1937. Kafka had given Brod the unfinished manuscript of *The Trial* in 1920 because he was going away to a sanatorium after learning that both his lungs were affected by tuberculosis.

2. Another similarity between Kafka and Saramago, which can be somewhat forbidding for the reader, is the relentless length of their paragraphs, which makes their books unputdownable for reasons that go beyond their arresting prose.

3. In terms of a broad agenda, clearly this has a lot in common with the New Institutional Economics (NIE). Unsurprisingly, I find the NIE's aims commendable,

but believe that its analysis has some critical weaknesses. Some of these are discussed in Basu, Jones, and Schlicht 1987. The mode of analysis adopted in the present chapter is quite distinct from the NIE.

4. For a philosophical account of the foundations of law and economics, see Dworkin 1986, chapter 8. For a lucid survey of the different schools of thought that have provided the methodological foundations of contemporary law and economics, see Mercuro and Medema 1998.

5. This telling will not explain why the game is called the *Prisoner's* Dilemma. For those curious about the original parable, any early game theory textbook will have the account.

6. The kind of game being talked about here is close to Ken Binmore's concept (1994, 2005) of 'the game of life.' In that game, what a player can do is given by everything that is open to them. That game cannot be affected by uttering some magic words or writing down some sentences on paper.

7. For similar views of the role of law, see also Basu 2000; Mailath, Morris, and Postlewaite 2001. The focal point has been used to interpret law, though in a somewhat different context, by McAdams 2000; Carbonara, Parisi, and Wangenheim 2008. The recognition of strategic behavior on the part of those staffing the legal system is explored at length in Lopucki and Weyrauch 2000. For the connection between social norms of the kind discussed in chapter 3 and the law, see Eisenberg 1999. See also Sugden 1989.

8. Kafka also had a clear sense of this metaphysical nature of law. He suggests this in his novels discussed elsewhere in this book and is explicit in his essay "The Problem of Our Laws" (Kafka 1970), where he refers more than once to the nonconcreteness of the law: "perhaps, these laws that we are trying to unravel do not exist at all."

9. This is also the claim that underlies the elegant, theoretical model in Mailath, Morris, and Postlewaite 2001. The use of a focal point to understand the more general idea of political power is developed in Myerson 2008. This model is founded in a Humean view of the state. The fact that political systems in the end have to stabilize on outcomes that are self-enforcing in the sense of Nash is also central to Avner Greif's historical studies (see, for instance, Greif 1998).

10. On Indian roads, when traveling by taxi, I am always impressed by the sight of stop signs whizzing past my car window.

11. Among game theorists, there is disagreement about whether the Nash equilibrium is the best positive theory of what occurs in a game. While the language used here suggests a belief in Nash equilibrium as the best positive theory, this is not necessarily so. Whenever in this chapter there is a reference to the Nash equilibrium, readers can replace this with their favorite equilibrium concept.

12. Rachel Kranton and Anand Swamy's provocative analysis (1999) of how the arrival of the law to enforce the repayment of loans in colonial India actually made matters worse rather than better is related to this. See also Berkowitz, Pistor, and Richard 2003; Aldashev, Chaara, Platteau, and Wahhaj 2008; Hoff and Stiglitz 2008. For the view that state formation has to contend with the problem of multiple equilibria in game-theoretic contexts, see Hardin 1989.

13. This is part of a larger claim that even without the law, many of the controls of the law can be replicated in society through nonformal means. See Ostrom 1990; Ellickson 1991; Dixit 2004; Mansuri and Rao 2004.

14. For some insightful heterodox positions on freedom of speech and the media, see Chomsky 1991; Fish 1994; Fiss 1994.

15. For a pertinent contemporary example, see Iversen and Raghavendra 2006.

16. Given the increasing corporatization of the press that is happening in India, India which once had this advantage, may soon lose it.

17. This is not to suggest that the law was not used during the McCarthy persecutions. There were occasional references to the Taft-Hartley Act of 1947—in particular, to the sections that prohibited trade union leaders from expressing a belief in Communism. The Smith Act of 1940, which was originally meant to target Nazi sympathizers, was also used, but it got redirected to those with left-wing ideologies. Yet it seems fair to claim that the law played a minor role, and more important, that the same laws *could have* remained on the books and that the United States could have gone through that period without the McCarthy purges and harassments. The same laws are compatible with different social outcomes.

18. For some illustrative descriptions, see Basu 2000; Mailath, Morris, and Postlewaite 2001.

19. By filling in a little more description of how players would play in other contingencies—that is, if Sai played music at levels A and C—it can be shown that the behavior just depicted can be part of an even more demanding concept of equilibrium—namely, a subgame perfect equilibrium.

20. The distinction between different kinds of rules of a game is discussed by Binmore (1995). Self-imposed restrictions can also be achieved by the internalization of social norms, which can affect a person's 'character' (Cooter and Eisenberg 2001). This is a subject of plentiful writing in law and economics. See, for instance, Sunstein 1996; Cooter 1998; McAdams 2000; Posner 2000.

21. See Sunstein 1996; Cooter 1998; McAdams 2000; Carbonara, Parisi, and Wangenheim 2008. Amir Licht (2007) makes the interesting argument that the rule of law itself is a social norm in some societies. That is, it can be a kind of metanorm that leads people to prefer legal rules over the rules of tradition or custom.

CHAPTER 5. MARKETS AND DISCRIMINATION

1. A similar set of experiments recently conducted by Erica Field and Patrick Nolen (2005) with South African children—blacks, whites, and coloreds—found similar results, especially for boys. Of course, race, unlike caste, is visible. So an announcement of race is not as revelatory as the announcement of caste. So what Field and Nolen do is to consider situations where no mention is made of race and situations where the atmosphere is 'charged' by making use of questionnaires on race. Recent experimental tests show that identity and, in particular, the priming of it can also influence a person's attitude to risk and time preference (Benjamin, Choi, and Strickland 2009).

2. It remains a bit of a puzzle as to why this does not happen for children who live with their guardians instead of their biological parents. It is possible that when asked if their parents talk to each other, children whose parents do not live with them gave erratic answers.

3. It is interesting to note that the Gounders were not always considered an elite group. In the early part of twentieth century they were treated as a "backward caste" group. But over the years, through identity-based striving, their station in life

has improved. For a long time they were exploited severely by the money-lending caste groups; then they learned from their tormentors, and many of them are now moneylenders.

4. For a fascinating recent study of how caste characteristics interact with individual productivity, see Anderson 2007. In this study, higher-caste groups refuse to trade with the backward castes even though there are large gains to be made from the trade. This means that the productivity of the same backward caste group can be different depending on the nature of the other caste groups that it happens to be situated within.

5. This may seem too obvious a question, but a few students, alarmingly, did think the answer was "yes."

6. This was the only question for which no child got the right answer, which is (to the extent that IQ questions at all have right answers) 1234.

7. Sandesh, as all Calcuttans know and for the love of which they are willing to risk diabetes, is a delicious milk-based sweetmeat.

Chapter 6. The Chemistry of Groups

1. The recognition that an individual has interests that extend to society does not in itself contradict methodological individualism. But once we permit the group feeling to be ephemeral—a feeling that can come and go, that can be associated differently with different groups, and depends on the character of the group to which one belongs—then this wider notion of a person's interest does conflict with methodological individualism. We cannot start from the individual as a fully described entity and then build up to the behavior of the collectivity. We need to know something about the collectivity and the nature of the groups before we can characterize the individual.

2. See, for instance, Luhman 1979; Hoffman and Spitzer 1982; Dasgupta 1990; Gambetta 1990; Fukuyama 1996; Knack and Keefer 1997; Barrett 1999; Khan 2002; Bowles and Gintis 2005; Ben-Ner and Putterman 2009; Gintis 2007, 2008.

3. See Bardhan 1997; Akerlof and Kranton 2000; Deshpande 2000; Durlauf 2001, 2006; Fershtman and Gneezy 2001; Loury 2002; Darity, Mason, and Stewart 2006; Bowles and Sethi 2006; Sen 2006; Horst, Kirman, and Teschl 2006; Perez 2007; Subramanian 2007; Lindqvist and Ostling 2007; Appiah 2008; Dasgupta and Goyal 2009; Esteban and Ray 2009; Gray 2009.

4. For a discussion of some of the early philosophical controversies, see Goffman 1959; Tajfel 1974; Chatterjee 2002. See also Beteille 2006; Lin and Harris 2008.

5. We do not as yet have a theory to explain which social categories will become significant. A true understanding of this must lie in part in our cognitive ability and need to categorize. For an interesting preliminary investigation into this, see Fryer and Jackson 2008.

6. A similar moral line is taken in several essays in Martha Nussbaum and Joshua Cohen (1996), and especially the opening essay by Nussbaum, which draws on some remarkable lectures by the poet Rabindranath Tagore, arguing against nationalism.

7. See, for example, Sporer 2001; Meissner and Brigham 2001.

8. This may not be a particularly good example because the Hutu-Tutsi distinction is one of those constructed differences that arguably have few biological or distant-historical markers.

9. The literature in behavioral economics that recognizes other-regarding behavior as an innate characteristic of human beings has grown in recent times. For a sampler, see Fehr and Gachter 2000; O'Donoghue and Rabin 2001; Dufwenberg and Kirchsteiger 2004; Hoff and Pandey 2005; Karna Basu 2009; Falk, Fehr, and Zehnder 2006; Benabou and Tirole 2006; Andreoni and Samuelson 2006; Hoff, Kshetramade, and Fehr 2007; Bruni and Sugden 2007; Messer, Zarghamee, Kaiser, and Schulze 2007; Rubinstein 2008. An early study that attempts to formally reconcile actual human behavior founded on limited powers of computation and sensitivity to framing with rational choice economics is Rubinstein 1998.

10. It is in any case hard to separate these two empirically or experimentally (see Farina, O'Higgins, and Sbriglia 2008). To me, the assumption of some amount of *innate* concern in human beings for others seems intuitively the more plausible assumption.

11. The analysis can get more complicated because the Pareto principle can, in some situations, be self-contradictory, in the sense that its repeated use can lead to its own negation, as will be demonstrated in the next chapter. But that does not seem to happen here, and so we can ignore the complication for now.

12. There is now a small literature on product boycotts (Davis 2005; Becchetti and Rosati 2007; Arnab Basu, Chau, and Grote 2006; Grossmann and Michaelis 2007; Baland and Duprez 2009; Basu and Zarghamee 2008), and how we answer this question has enormous implications for the welfare stand we take on this.

13. Polanyi [1944] 1957; Granovetter 1985; Elster 1989; Ensminger 2000; Platteau 2000; Basu 2000; Francois 2002; Swedberg 2003.

14. On the Ultimatum game, see Heinrich et al. 2004; Bowles 2004. On the Traveler's Game, see Basu 2000; Capra et al. 1999; Zambrano 2004; Rubinstein 2006a; Halpern and Pass 2009.

15. It is useful to note that the Prisoner's Dilemma is no real dilemma, since what is best for one player does not depend on what the other player does.

16. It should therefore be clear that despite the different numbers and symbols, this is the same game as the Prisoner's Dilemma described in chapter 4.

17. That people do more for one another than would be dictated by purely selfish considerations is widely noted from various walks of life. Laborers typically work harder than can be explained purely in terms of their direct self-interest (Fehr and Gachter 2000; Minkler 2004). Caregivers often give more care than they are required to in terms of their job (Zelizer 2005). It is arguable that the commons problem is not as relentless as it is made out to be in classical economics because of this.

18. This refers to a much larger problem—namely, that of interpreting the payoffs in a game. We can of course write down the number that each player will earn, but there is no easy way of representing what this means to the player, who may 'correct' the number psychologically to account for fairness, altruism, and so on. Not surprisingly, this problem arises more seriously in sociological games, and one of the earliest discussions of this problem occurred in Bernard (1954); see also Swedberg 2001. Weibull (2004) encounters the same situation when analyzing the problem of interpreting results from experimental games.

19. In a paper focused wholly on this subject, we would distinguish between two kinds of other-regarding behavior. When a person makes a sacrifice for their child, for instance, it is likely that this behavior is an extension of a person's selfishness, since a child's welfare is often internalized by us. But when one makes a contribution to

some social charity or helps a person one does not know, this probably entails personal sacrifice. One does it not to gratify oneself but rather because one believes that one *should* do this. Behaviorally the two cases may look the same, but they are prompted by different internal processes and thus would be evaluated differently when we normatively compare the outcomes. In this book, I am considering the latter kind of model for other-regarding behavior.

20. See Weibull 2004; Battigalli and Dufwenberg 2005. Sen (2006, 21) discusses the standard question that economists ask, "If it is not in your interest, why did you choose to do what you did?" and goes on to observe, "This wise-guy skepticism makes huge idiots out of Mohandas Gandhi, Martin Luther King, Jr., Mother Teresa, and Nelson Mandela, and rather smaller idiots out of the rest of us."

21. Henceforth, a reference to payoff will mean effective payoff. And when I want to refer to a person's direct well-being (that is, the kind of numbers shown in table 6), I will speak of dollars or utility.

22. Despite a large literature, a formal definition of trust and trustworthiness remains elusive. The essential idea is that trust involves choosing a course of action that leaves oneself vulnerable to abuse or exploitation while also expecting that the other person will not take advantage of this.

23. The value of this to the individual would, of course, depend on how trustworthy others in society are.

24. That this is an intriguing and difficult subject is amply demonstrated in Cipriano, Giuliano, and Jeanne 2007. One folk wisdom on the subject is that these values are transmitted from one generation to another. The carefully constructed experimental study cited here involving African American and Hispanic families pretty much destroys this belief.

25. This is where the large size of population comes into play. Because the population is so large, knowing your own type does not affect your calculation of the probability of the type of an unknown player with whom you are to play the game. In contrast, if the population was small, say two, and you knew that half the population is type A and half is type B, then as soon as you got to know your own type, you would be able to deduce the type of your opponent.

26. To formally outline the conditions under which the total unraveling of cooperation occurs would require the use of an equilibrium idea that combines the work of Nash with Thomas Bayes. I have discussed this elsewhere (Basu 2010b) and will not go into it here.

27. This ambivalence carries over naturally to patriotism, since one attribute of patriotism is discrimination in favor of one's in-group, defined in this case in terms of shared nationality (Nussbaum 2008).

28. An approach that is different from the one taken here, but that also allows for the characterization of groups that may or may not be pitted against other groups, is the one developed by Robert Sugden (2000), where the group itself can be thought of as being endowed with preferences.

29. See Glaeser et al. 2000; Luttmer 2001; Eckel and Wilson 2002. There are several anthropological studies of how small groups form close-knit units of trust and mutual support. One study (Landa 1995) describes nicely how the Chinese middlepeople in the rubber trade in Singapore and West Malaysia are almost invariably of Hokkien-Chinese ethnicity, and how they form an in-group that can trust and rely on one another.

30. I checked into what used car advertisements look like these days in Delhi. Much to my surprise, there seems to be no mention of South Indian owners, which leaves me wondering if South Indians have over time become like North Indians, as mainstream economics would predict, or if political correctness is at last catching up on India.

31. See Tajfel 1974; Turner 1999; Akerlof and Kranton 2000; Basu 2005b; Sen 2006; Dasgupta and Goyal 2009.

32. Regrettably, this is not the only way to create division among the oppressed classes. There is evidence that by lowering the general standard of living, individuals can be made to turn against one another. This may be hardwired in us, as biological creatures, as experiments with rats show. In a celebrated experiment, Michael Sheard, David Astrachan, and Michael Davis (1975) demonstrated how rats in confinement when subjected to moderate amounts of electric shocks begin to inflict aggression on one another.

33. This was widely reported in newspapers and on the Web. See, for instance, http://www.gather.com/viewArticle.jsp?articleId=281474977294564.

34. Moreover, a subgroup's effort to subvert the group can be foiled by a sub-subgroup bent on subverting the subgroup.

35. As a digression on attribution, note that as discussed earlier in the book, though modern social scientists treat the invisible hand as the central message of Smith's *Wealth of Nations*, it is in reality a surprisingly small part of that book.

36. The importance of internalizing prosocial preferences and the need to inculcate such preferences have been stressed as well as formally modeled by Avinash Dixit (2009).

37. Models of corruption control in economics routinely assume not just that the citizenry may be corrupt but also the "corruptibility of the supervisors" (Mishra 2002, 166; see also Basu, Bhattacharya, and Mishra 1992; Garoupa 1999).

38. It is conceivable, though, that in experimental and examination-like situations people give the answers they feel are expected of them, and so these findings merely reflect the disciplinary training of economists, and that in reality, the behavior of economists probably would be no different from that of others.

39. The feedback from a group's aggregate behavior to an individual's preference or norms-guided behavior has been the subject of important inquiry in economics, and demonstrates the limits of methodological individualism (Leibenstein 1950; Basu 1987; Lindbeck, Nyberg, and Weibull 1999).

40. For a more detailed analysis, see Basu 2005b. Conflict between different ethnic groups is also modeled and studied by Joan Esteban and Debraj Ray (2009).

41. This general point that the payoffs that are explicitly displayed may not be the actual payoffs perceived by the players, even in a laboratory setting (let alone life), has been discussed in the literature (see, for example, Weibull 2004; Andreoni and Samuelson 2006). This recognition can throw a wrench into the traditional learning literature, since what constitutes 'success' is difficult to define in a game where an observer sees only the visible part of the payoff earned by the player.

42. Rush Limbaugh is a name that easily springs to mind. As the newspaper columnist Deborah Mathis perceptively observed (*Ithaca Journal*, October 17, 2003, 10A), Limbaugh owes his fame "to a generic, free-floating policy of zero-tolerance, which [he] has regularly applied to almost *any person unlike him*" (emphasis added).

43. Throughout this analysis we need to distinguish between the beliefs one holds about oneself and higher-order beliefs—beliefs that one holds about the other player's belief and the other player's about oneself and so on. There is a tradition in sociology that emphasizes the role of these distinctions (Troyer and Younts 1997).

44. For a general analysis, see Basu 2005b. The logic of the cascade described here occurs in a different context in Baliga and Sjostrom 2004.

45. Strictly, it is enough to bring even one of them into existence.

46. To check this out formally, suppose a player of type 2 believes that q is the probability that the other player will play A. Then, using the payoffs in the basic game, it can be seen that if the player of type 2 plays A, the expected payoff is $2q + 9(1-q)$. If the player plays C instead, the expected payoff is $(\frac{1}{2})q + (9\frac{1}{2})(1-q)$. The player will thus play A if, and only if, $\frac{1}{4} \leq q$. Since we already know that the other player will certainly play A if he or she is of type 3, and the probability of the other player being of type 3 is one-third, it must be that $\frac{1}{3} \leq q$. Since $\frac{1}{4} < \frac{1}{3}$, a player of type 2 will play A for sure. This completes the proof.

47. This model bears a striking similarity to the analyses of Timur Kuran (1988) and Ashutosh Varshney (2002).

48. At times the infiltration is less than perfect. At one stage the KGB presence in the United States was so deep that it was advised that if you suspected anyone of being a KGB agent, you should immediately call the CIA headquarters. But as a late-night talk show host warned, "Do not be surprised if the same person answers your call."

Chapter 7. Contract, Coercion, and Intervention

1. The significance of this comes out clearly in the books of Landa (1995) and Fukuyama (1996), and was discussed at length in the previous chapter.

2. While economists typically value this principle as a key instrument of economic progress and efficiency, one can think of other, philosophical justifications for adhering to this principle, such as equating a contract with a promise and maintaining, a priori, that it is immoral for promises to be broken (for discussion of some of these alternative justifications, see Kaplow and Shavell 2002, chapter 4).

3. This is one of the questions raised in Basu 2003a.

4. The standard form, as with yellow dog contracts, discussed below, or boilerplate contracts or contracts of adhesion, has been the subject of some debate. Alan Wertheimer (1996) has discussed this in the context of the *Henningsen v. Bloomfield Motors* (1960) case. See also Korobkin 2003; Choi and Gulati 2005.

5. He later took a more sophisticated line (Mill [1859] 1971) to rule out voluntary slavery contracts. For an interesting discussion of long-run child labor contracts, see Iversen 2004.

6. For more examples, see Kanbur 2004; Satz 2004; Fukui 2005. For further analysis, see Gaertner 2008; Singh 2009.

7. It is not that I wish to deny the use of all nonwelfarist moral principles. I simply maintain that nonwelfarist principles should not be used to violate the Pareto principle. We may use nonwelfarist criteria to choose between two Pareto noncomparable states (Basu 2003a). Hence, this approach, despite the centrality it grants to welfarism, is compatible with that of individual rights. Also, giving *lexicographical* primacy to the

Pareto principle and using possible nonwelfarist criteria only after that enables us to escape possible logical contradictions (Kaplow and Shavell 2002). For a construction on the impossibility of universal welfarism, see Hockett 2007a.

8. Sen (1970), for instance, demonstrates that if we wish to hold on to even a minimal form of individual liberty, we may be compelled to abandon the Pareto principle. For further discussions of this question, see Gaertner, Pattanaik, and Suzumura 1992. There are special problems that arise when we try to impose the Pareto principle on questions of sustainability and decisions that entail the well-being of all future generations (see, for example, Basu and Mitra 2003, 2007; Asheim and Tungodden 2004; Banerjee and Mitra 2007; Dutta 2008; Hockett 2009).

9. An outcome is Pareto optimal if for every feasible change there is at least one person who becomes worse off.

10. If torturers feel no innate pleasure from torturing, but use it only to extract money or other benefits from the torturee, then even the Pareto optimality principle would not justify torture. This is because, as noted in chapter 3, a society in which torture occurs is Pareto dominated by one in which the same concessions that are earned through torture are earned without torture (for a discussion of this in the context of domestic violence, see Basu 2006a).

11. For a lucid essay that recognizes the importance of the free market, but constrains it within the requirements of fairness and justice, see Sunstein 1997.

12. Nor do I find a compelling definition of coercion in the existing large literature, mostly outside of economics (see, for instance, Nozick 1969, 1974; Macpherson 1973; Zimmerman 1981; Cohen 1987; Trebilcock 1993).

13. An alternative way of viewing this is to say that we have a prior sense of the 'correct' assignment of property rights, and that coercion entails a forced (and therefore illegal) alteration of these property rights. To the extent that an assignment of property rights is a normative act, this interpretation is essentially the same as the one described above. But given that property rights must here mean an assignment of rights over all possible actions, there is the possibility of ambiguity that is discussed below.

14. See Akerlof 1976; Ziesemer 1997; Deshpande 1999; Basu 2000; Naqvi and Wemhoner 1995; Hatlebakk 2002; Villanger 2004, 2005.

15. For a demonstration of why this is credible, see Basu 2000; Hatlebakk 2002.

16. Nozick (1974, see especially 263) argues that there cannot be coercion if each agent acts "within their rights." What I have just demonstrated is that even if people choose *within their rights*, by making their choice conditional on what someone else does ("I will trade with you, provided you have boycotted the worker"), it is possible to exercise what on dispassionate analysis should be regarded as coercion.

17. See also Neeman 1999; Fukui 2005; Gaertner 2008. An unwitting use of the same idea occurs in Genicot 2002. Results of unexpected reversals in a game-theoretic context are discussed in Voorneveld 2009.

18. For an application in the context of globalization, see Dinopoulos and Zhao 2007. Analogues of this problem also occur in the management of environmental standards; see Solow 2009.

19. In general equilibrium theory, we do encounter examples of this kind where each individual's choice has no impact on others but a collectivity of such choices can have a perceptible effect. But these are usually formalized for economies with

an uncountable set of individuals. What I am about to demonstrate is the possibility of this happening in countable societies. Later in this section, I will show that similar results can be obtained even in finite societies, provided that we are willing to relax the assumption of transitivity of preference. To me it is more realistic to think of finite societies with intransitive preferences than uncountably infinite societies with each person having transitivity preferences. A more detailed treatment of this occurs in Basu 2007a.

20. The game described above has the clearest analogy in Escher's famous painting *Waterfall*, in which a steady stream of downward movement nevertheless ends up on a higher perch. For some similar paradoxes and deep insights into how to resolve them, see Arntzenius, Elga, and Hawthorne 2004. All the examples in the work just cited, however, entail infinite choices and therefore differ from what I am about to illustrate in the next section—to wit, that similar paradoxes can occur even in finite decision contexts.

21. For an interesting discussion of the philosophical basis of this assumption, especially its relation to methodological individualism, see Bhargava 1993; Arrow 1994. The philosophical objections to the use of infinity to model 'large number' were stressed to me by the philosopher David Lewis (personal communication with the author, January 15, 1990).

22. To make this explicit, let me repeat the definition of transitivity introduced in chapter 3. A person's preference is transitive if it is quasi-transitive, and in addition, whenever the person is indifferent between x and y and indifferent between y and z, the person is indifferent between x and z.

23. There is a small literature that points this out. See, for instance, Majumdar 1958; Fishburn 1970.

24. See, for instance, Sen and Pattanaik 1969; Pattanaik 1970; Fishburn 1970.

25. In the first case, this is because person 1 prefers (1,0,0) to (0,0,0), and since an individual's action has no externality, others are indifferent between these two alternatives.

26. It also sheds light on an important individual decision problem that was emphasized by Schelling (1985). There are situations, he argued, where one needs to have "rules for oneself." We can think of rules such as the following: I should not have more than two drinks; or, I must not wade further than ten yards into the shark-infested sea. Schelling contended, without formalizing it, that there are situations where a tiny bit more may always be desirable, but n tiny bits more may not be. At first sight this is a paradoxical claim. But the algebra of my analysis can be viewed as a possible formalization of this assertion.

27. See Kornblut (2005).

28. These ideas were proposed and developed in outline in Basu 2000, 2007b. See also Hayashi 2008. The case for a moral evaluation of preferences—the idea of "objectionable" preferences—was also argued for in a similar context by Howard Chang (2000).

29. That is—just to remind the reader—we do not morally disapprove of this preference the way we disapprove of someone's racism preference. This is a rather obvious point.

30. A standard market arbitrage argument leads to this conclusion. But in reality, one often finds that those workers with the least rights and working under the most

hazardous conditions are also the poorest. Hence, the theories of "equalizing wage differentials" may deserve further empirical and theoretical investigation.

31. For an even stronger critique of welfarism, see Hockett 2007a.

32. Once we move away from the competitive market to strategic environments, one equilibrium can indeed Pareto dominate another. One may be tempted to presume in such economies that individuals will naturally choose the Pareto-dominant outcome. But introspection suggests and experiments show that in games with large numbers of players, it is quite common to get trapped in the inferior equilibrium (see Bohnet and Cooter 2001). In that case, the justification for legal intervention (for instance, that of taxing or banning the inferior action) is immediate.

33. While I prefer to remain within a welfarist-consequentialist framework in addressing the possibility of legislative bans on child labor, for some deep and intriguing arguments that go beyond welfarism, see Satz 2003.

34. It should be emphasized that it is not being claimed here that this will always happen. For several reasons, such as the possibility of adult wages not rising sufficiently in response to a ban, or because prices rise and negate some of the impact, a legislative ban on child labor can actually leave children worse off.

35. The U.S. Supreme Court took this view in the *Lochner v. New York* (1905) case.

36. In the presence of multiple equilibria that do not Pareto dominate one another, a different justification for intervention, based on justice and fairness, is to make rules for moving from one equilibrium to another equilibrium depending on the context. A society may decide that on sunny days the outcome should be one in which player 1 gains the most, and on rainy days the outcome should be one in which player 2 gains the most. Justice, by this argument, is a method for selecting between different equilibria (Myerson 2004).

Chapter 8. Poverty, Inequality, and Globalization

1. Bill Gates dropped out of Harvard; Sheldon Adelson never graduated from the City College of New York; Li Ka Shing was forced to leave school at fifteen; Amancio Ortega had no formal education; and a Web entry for Ingvar Kamprad under education says "peddled matches, fish, pens," which I take to be a euphemism for "no higher education." Lakshmi Mittal, with his bachelor's degree in commerce from Calcutta, stands out for being comparatively overeducated.

2. See *Forbes* magazine, available at http://www.forbes.com/lists/2007/10/07billionaires_The-Worlds-Billionaires_Rank.html.

3. The list is comprehensive if one is interested in countries that have populations of more than one million. It therefore omits some really small nations, like Lichtenstein.

4. This and the next sections of this chapter draw on Basu 2006c, although I present the formal model differently here.

5. A *potential* benefit for all does not seem to me to be reason for celebration. If it is the case that we expect that the potential will be realized, then of course we should celebrate, yet the reason for the celebration is not the potential gain but rather the fact that we expect an *actual* Pareto improvement. If, on the other hand, we do not expect

the potential to be realized, it is not clear why we should be happy that there has been a *potential* gain.

6. And there has been debate aplenty: see, for instance, Birdsall, Ross, and Sabot 1995; Deininger and Squire 1998; Atkinson 2005; Melchior 2001; Milanovich 2002; Wade 2004; Brandolini 2007.

7. See, for example, Melchior 2001; Cornia with Kiiski 2001; Milanovich 2002; Bourguignon and Morrisson 2002; Galbraith 2002; Naschold 2004; Sachs, 2005; Anand and Segal 2008. Some of these controversies on global inequality are mirrored in the discussion of global poverty; see, for instance, Ravallion and Chen 2007; Reddy and Minoiu 2007; Reddy and Pogge 2008.

8. The Gini coefficient is a sophisticated measure of inequality in a population. It takes values between 1 and 0, with 1 being the most unequal society, in which one person has it all, and with 0 being the most equal society, in which everybody has the same income. But over and above this, it takes the entire distribution of income of the population into account and not just the extremities, as would happen with simple indicators such as one that looks at the gap between the richest and poorest people. For a primer on the Gini coefficient, see Sen 1997.

9. There can also be increased unemployment among the unskilled. This is possible to explain theoretically once we recognize that employing each person entails some cost on the part of the employer (supervising, conflict mitigation with other employees, breakage of work instruments, and so on), and hence, unless the productivity of the worker is above a certain cutoff level, it is not worth employing the person even for a zero wage.

10. A simple adaptation of Atkinson's model (1995) could illustrate this.

11. Some recent studies seem to confirm at the level of India what I saw among the artisans of rural Gujarat. India's opening up in the 1990s, far from hurting the handicrafts sector, seems to have benefited it. Through the 1990s, the share of handicraft exports in the overall manufacturing exports of India rose from 2 to 5 percent (Leibl and Roy 2003).

12. We may maintain that "one must not kill a human being" is a basic value judgment. Then, seeing a friend suffering from acute pain because of a terminal condition, we may legitimately revise the basic value judgment to say that "one must not kill except to relieve a person in pain and in a terminal condition." Sen (1970) asserted that the possibility of having to revise what we think of as a basic value judgment will always be there.

13. This broad idea has been expressed by many, now and in classical times. Describing a conference held in New York, in October 2001, Peter Dougherty (2002, 189) mentions a comment made by a "prominent Keynesian economist" that "captured the purpose behind the entire, 200-year long modern economic enterprise. He talked about the plight of the people on a street in Gary, Indiana, the small de-industrialized and now dust-riddled working-class town in which he had grown up. In making this reference this great economist was echoing a sentiment stressed ages ago by Adam Smith, whose passion for the masses of people drove him to his obsessive preoccupation with what it took to stimulate the wealth of nations."

14. I put the word 'necessary' within quotes to highlight that this may itself be malleable. As societal organization changes, and our norms and preferences change, the inequality necessary to minimize poverty may itself change. In a long-run policy

exercise, one could try to change this parameter. For a recent discussion of the twin objectives of poverty mitigation and the control of inequality, see Daǧdeviren, van der Hoeven, and Weeks 2004.

15. An underlying general assumption that would lead to this conclusion is that the (pretax) income earned by the rich, $Y(t)$, when the tax is rate is t, has the following property. For all t less than or equal to three-tenths, $Y(t) = 1,000$, as already assumed, and for all t greater than three-tenths, $Y(t) = 1,900–3,000t$. It is easy to check, in this setting, if $t = \frac{1}{2}$ the person will work so as to have a (pretax) income of four hundred.

16. See Sen 1997.

17. That there *is* shrinkage in the policy space of the nation-state because of globalization is not an uncontested thesis. See, for instance, Krasner 2004. Stephen Krasner is right in emphasizing that globalization should not be treated as an exogenous force. It is itself a product of the interaction between nations. Yet this does not conflict with my claim, in this chapter and the next, that as this process persists, it erodes the space of each individual state's autonomy. As Peter Katzenstein (2004) points out, states are themselves situated within overarching structures—some domestic, and some transnational. What I am arguing is that these transnational forces are becoming more compelling over time.

18. Many of the references already cited in this chapter deal with this subject.

19. Provided, of course, the world that the law tries to bring about is already a potential self-enforcing equilibrium. This is the idea of the focal view of law that was developed in chapter 4.

20. This is derived from a recognition that what is popularly posed as a conflict between laborers in the developing nations and those in industrialized countries should more accurately be construed as a problem of global capital versus labor (Basu 2007d, chapter 11; Chau and Kanbur 2003).

Chapter 9. Globalization and the Retreat of Democracy

1. In an election, it seems reasonable to declare candidate x to be preferred to candidate y, if a majority of voters prefer x to y. This principle is often viewed as the staple of democracy. What Carroll discovered was that this widely respected rule has a problem. It can lead us to declare that candidate x is preferable to y, y is preferable to z, and z is preferable to x. This leads to the natural question of whether there are other reasonable voting rules that do not have this problem. Arrow tried to answer this question and, in the process, stumbled on one of the most original theorems to come out of the social sciences: the so-called Arrow impossibility theorem, which answers the question in the negative. A voting system that satisfies some elementary properties of democratic election is a *logical* impossibility.

2. Deborah Solomon, *New York Times Magazine*, March, 28, 2004, 15.

3. Much of what follows draws on Basu 2002.

4. Defining "rogue states" as "states that do not regard themselves as bound by international norms," Chomsky (2000, 1) goes on to point out in his inimitable way: "Logic suggests that most powerful states should tend to fall into [this] category unless internally constrained, an expectation that history confirms."

5. For a better-timed analysis of the same, see Cooper 1984.

6. For an analysis of dollarization see Bencivenga, Huybens, and Smith 2001.

7. Central bank autonomy is a large and complex topic. It is not axiomatic that a central bank should be autonomous. At least in democratic nations, the government is elected by the citizens, and so making the central bank autonomous from the government is to remove an important segment of national decision making from the reach of the citizenry. This has to be balanced against the fact that a central bank that is subservient to the government often ends up financing the irresponsible fiscal extravaganzas of the government.

8. See Rawls 1990; Nagel 2005.

9. Reported by Barbara Crossette in the *New York Times*, January 21, 2000, A1.

10. It is interesting that when I first wrote about this idea in 2002, it sounded like a pipe dream, but that is no longer so. Thanks to a growing chorus of intellectuals demanding such a change and, more important, the visible growth of China's power (witness the Chiang Mai Initiative), it now seems likely that even within the next three or four years we will see a further reapportioning of votes in the World Bank and the IMF that will increase the say of developing nations at the expense of some of the share that currently belongs to the United States and European nations. It will be better if these changes occur out of our sense of fairness and justice, and through debate and discussion, rather than as a reluctant response to the increasing power of emerging nations. The latter runs the risk that the unfairness of today will simply be restructured to another pattern of unfairness.

11. The quotes are from Basu 2002.

CHAPTER 10. WHAT IS TO BE DONE?

1. This disappointment, however, is in keeping with the original source from which the title of this chapter was taken—Nikolay Chernyshevsky's classic work, which being a novel, was also not a call to action. It is true that it ended up inspiring several revolutionary writers and may well have contributed to the overthrow of the czars. Interestingly, Chernyshevsky wrote *What Is to Be Done?* while in jail, serving a term for his essays, which were actual calls to action yet had little impact. As a prisoner, he had to have his writing cleared by the prison censor. It was then given to the censor of the journal *Sovremennik* and, once again, passed as an innocuous work of fiction. To add to the irony, the journal's editor left the manuscript in a taxi by mistake and the czar's police had to work hard to track it down. It was not for nothing that the publication of the book was described as "the most spectacular example of bureaucratic bungling ... during the reign of Alexander II" (Frank 1986, 285).

2. Kafka had begun writing *The Castle* in early 1926, in Spindermuhle, a snowy mountain village, much like the kind of place in which K found himself trying to reach the castle. He confided to his diary around the same time, on January 16, 1922: "Impossible to sleep, impossible to stay awake, impossible to endure life, or, more exactly, the course of life" (Diamant 2003, 151). Kafka died before finishing the novel. In fact the original draft ends, as befits the story line of the novel itself, in midsentence.

3. The fact that the popular anger against globalization reflects a misdirected but legitimate discontentment against other ills of the modern market economy, and that globalization in itself has a lot to offer, has been pointed out by several prominent economists (Sen 1999; Stiglitz 2002, 2006).

4. An important qualifying remark is needed here. In case there is an immutable law of nature that x number of people will be poor and y number rich, where x and y are unalterably fixed in the book of life, it is quite understandable for the currently poor to want a world in which *they* are the rich and the currently rich become the poor, and to want to use force, if necessary, to bring about such a world. But for an outside observer, there is no reason to recommend one of these worlds over another. I put this in abstract terms, but this is related to a question of considerable practical importance. As Martin Wolf (2008, 9) remarked in one of his recent columns, with the rise of populous nations such as China and India, the question of whether the world can support high living standards for so many people becomes inescapable. In case the answer is no, then it also becomes unavoidable that if China and India were to become developed nations, this can only happen with a concurrent rise in inequality within these nations. This raises momentous questions about political stability.

5. He says this in an interview with Fernanda Eberstadt (2007, 22).

6. Engels is the subject of a recent biography by Tristam Hunt (2009).

7. The fact of this being a hard-fought battle is evident from the strident resistance that the Stern Report, with its eminently reasonable emphasis on intergenerational equity, has had to face (Stern 2006).

8. This simple fact that "when [an] initial equilibrium is disturbed, everything that can change will change" (Solow 2009, 415), is often overlooked, and has caused many well-meaning interventions to flounder. Solow (2009) provides an elegant argument about how some popular demands for international environmental standards can end up hurting some of the very constituencies that we may want to help, unless these secondary repercussions are anticipated correctly.

9. Roemer's (1994) proposal for a system whereby each individual gets transient property rights in the nation's public firms and has these rights revert back to the state at the time of their death would have some of this property built into it.

10. The most prominent being the contribution of Rawls (1990), or what may be called Rawls II to distinguish it from Rawls I (1971) of the *Theory of Justice*, in which intercountry matters were not addressed; instead, there was a presumption of one closed economy. For other important contributions to this subject, see Miller 1998; Beitz 2000; Nagel 2005; Pogge 2005; Risse 2005; Buchanan and Keohane 2006; Trachtman 2006.

11. The idea of intercountry transfer is not fantasy. It has been discussed in the past, and effort has been made to work out the full mechanics. A good example is Jagdish Bhagwati's (1977) idea of a global tax and transfer scheme to compensate nations that suffer brain drain; this has been discussed at length. Moreover, in the area of pollution control and climate change, the world is close to actually putting schemes into action whereby polluting nations will transfer compensation to other countries.

12. This is discussed in Popescu 2005.

13. The subprime crisis in the U.S. mortgage market is an example of this. Banks and financial institutions sold mortgages to individuals, some of whom were unlikely to repay. These mortgages were then packaged into collections of risky and safe ones, and sold to investment banks, and then some of these mortgages were again repackaged and sold to holding companies. Beyond a certain point, the 'products' being traded were such complex bundles of contracts that their worth were virtually impossible to calculate.

14. Quoted in French 2007.

15. See Chau and Kanbur 2003; Basu 2007d, chapter 11.

16. In a somewhat different context and motivated by the stagflation of the 1970s, Martin Weitzman (1984) made a related recommendation. There have been others who have proposed systems for sharing a part of the aggregate profits occurring in society with all individuals in that society, and especially the poor, and in some cases, with the poor in other less-fortunate nations: see, for example, Roemer 1994; Pogge 2002; Hockett 2007b. Roemer's argument is constructed in the wake of the Soviet Union's fall and is an attempt to find other ways to better distribute incomes. It is possible to argue that systems of this kind can contribute not only to greater economic equality but also can potentially strengthen the functioning of democracy by giving the dispossessed a greater stake in society (Wright 1996).

17. I am aware that 'technically' is a loaded term. But we have to face up to the fact that an attempt to directly redistribute the current aggregate income will cause the aggregate income to collapse, and poverty will not be eradicated.

18. 'Twice born' refers to the rite of initiation or second birth that the members of upper-caste groups are expected to go through on reaching adulthood.

19. Alice Walker, *The Root*, available at http://www.theroot.com/id/45469/output/print.

REFERENCES

Agarwal, Bina. 1997. "'Bargaining' and Gender Relations: Within and Beyond the Household." *Feminist Economics* 3.

Akerlof, George. 1976. "The Economics of Caste and the Rat Race and Other Woeful Tales." *Quarterly Journal of Economics* 90.

Akerlof, George, and Rachel Kranton. 2000. "Economics and Identity." *Quarterly Journal of Economics* 105.

Aldashev, Gani, Imaane Chaara, Jean-Philippe Platteau, and Zaki Wahhaj. 2008. "Using Law to Change Custom." Mimeo, University of Namur, Belgium.

Alkire, Sabina. 2002). *Valuing Freedoms: Sen's Capability Approach and Poverty Reduction*. Oxford: Oxford University Press.

Ambady, Nalini, Margaret Shih, Amy Kim, and Todd Pittinsky. 2001. "Stereotype Susceptibility in Children: Effects of Identity Activation on Quantitative Performance." *Psychological Science* 12.

Anand, Sudhir, and Paul Segal. 2008. "What Do We Know about Global Income Inequality." *Journal of Economic Literature* 46.

Anderson, Siwan. 2007. "Some Economic Implications of Caste." Mimeo, University of British Columbia.

Andreoni, James, and Larry Samuelson. 2006. "Building Rational Cooperation." *Journal of Economic Theory* 127.

Aoki, Masahiko. 2001. *Toward a Comparative Institutional Analysis*. Cambridge, MA: MIT Press.

Appadurai, Arjun. 2004. "The Capacity to Aspire: Culture and the Terms of Recognition." In *Culture and Public Action*, ed. Vijayendra Rao and Michael Walton. Stanford, CA: Stanford University Press.

Appiah, Kwame Anthony. 2008. "Sen's Identities." In *Arguments for a Better World: Essays in Honor of Amartya Sen*, ed. Kaushik Basu and Ravi Kanbur. Oxford: Oxford University Press.

Aquinas, Thomas. [1265–74] 1911. *Summa Theologica*. Allen, TX: Christian Classics.

Arntzenius, Frank, Adam Elga, and John Hawthorne. 2004. "Bayesianism, Infinite Decisions, and Binding." *Mind* 113.

Arrow, Kenneth. 1951. *Social Choice and Individual Values*. New York: Wiley.

———. 1972. "Some Mathematical Models of Race Discrimination in the Labor Market." In *Racial and Discrimination in Economic Life*, ed. Anthony H. Pascal. Lexington, MA: D. C. Heath and Co.

———. 1994. "Methodological Individualism and Social Knowledge." *American Economic Review* 84.

Arrow, Kenneth. 2001. "A Note on Freedom and Flexibility." In *Choice, Welfare, and Development*, ed. Kaushik Basu, Prasanta Pattanaik, and Kotaro Suzumura. Oxford: Oxford University Press.

Arrow, Kenneth, and Frank Hahn. 1971. *General Competitive Equilibrium*. San Francisco: Holden Day.

Asheim, Geir, and Bertil Tungodden. 2004. "Resolving Distributional Conflicts between Generations." *Economic Theory* 24.

Atkinson, Anthony. 1995. "Capabilities, Exclusion, and the Supply of Goods." In *Choice, Welfare, and Development*, ed. Kaushik Basu, Prasanta Pattanaik, and Kotaro Suzumura. Oxford: Oxford University Press.

———. 2005. "Is Rising Inequality Inevitable? A Critique of the Transatlantic Consensus." In *Wider Perspectives on Global Development*, ed. Giovanni Andrea Cornia, Matti Pohjola, and Anthony Shorrocks. Basingstoke, UK: Palgrave Macmillan.

Baird, Douglas, Robert Gertner, and Randal Picker. 1995. *Game Theory and the Law*. Cambridge, MA: Harvard University Press.

Bakshi, Soham, and Pinaki Bose. 2007. "Harassment, Coercion, and the Inefficiency of Voluntary Contracts." Mimeo, Memphis University.

Baland, Jean-Marie, and Cedric Duprez. 2009. "Are Fair Trade Labels Effective against Child Labour?" *Journal of Public Economics*, forthcoming.

Baliga, Sandeep, and Tomas Sjostrom. 2004. "Arms Races and Negotiations." *Review of Economic Studies* 71.

Banerjee, Abhijit. 1992. "A Simple Model of Herd Behavior." *Quarterly Journal of Economics* 107.

———. 2005. "'New Development Economics' and the Challenge to Theory." *Economic and Political Weekly* 40 (October 1).

Banerjee, Abhijit, and Kaivan Munshi. 2004. "How Efficiently Is Capital Allocated? Evidence from the Knitted Garment Industry in Tirupur." *Review of Economic Studies* 71.

Banerjee, Abhijit, and Thomas Piketty. 2005. "Top Indian Incomes, 1956–2000." *World Bank Economic Review* 19.

Banerjee, Kuntal, and Tapan Mitra. 2007. "On the Impatience Implications of Paretian Social Welfare Functions." *Journal of Mathematical Economics* 43.

Banner, Stuart. 2005. *How the Indians Lost Their Land: Law and Power on the Frontier*. Cambridge, MA: Harvard University Press.

Bardhan, Pranab. 1997. "Method in the Madness? A Political-Economy Analysis of Ethnic Conflicts in Less Developed Countries." *World Development* 25.

———. 2005. "Theory or Empirics in Development Economics." *Economic and Political Weekly* 40 (October 1).

Barrett, Chris. 1999. "On Pluralistic Ethics and the Economics of Compassion." *Bulletin of the Association of Christian Economists* 33 (Spring).

Basu, Alaka. 1992. *Culture, the Status of Women, and Demographic Behavior*. Oxford: Clarendon Press.

Basu, Arnab, Nancy Chau, and Ulrike Grote. 2006. "Guaranteed Manufactured without Child Labor: The Economics of Consumer Boycotts, Social Labeling, and Trade Sanctions." *Review of Development Economics* 10.

Basu, Karna. 2009. "Time-Inconsistency in Informal Credit Markets: A Welfare Analysis." Mimeo, University of Chicago.

Basu, Kaushik. 1983. "On Why We Do Not Try to Walk Off without Paying after a Taxi Ride." *Economic and Political Weekly* 18 (November).

———. 1986. "One Kind of Power." *Oxford Economic Papers* 38.

———. 1987. "Monopoly, Quality Uncertainty, and 'Status Goods.'" *International Journal of Industrial Organization* 5.

———. 1989. "A Theory of Association: Social Status, Prices, and Markets." *Oxford Economic Papers* 41.

———. 1993. *Lectures in Industrial Organization Theory*. Oxford: Blackwell Publishers.

———. 1994a. "Group Rationality, Utilitarianism, and Escher's Waterfall." *Games and Economic Behavior* 7.

———. 1994b. "The Traveler's Dilemma: Paradoxes of Rationality in Game Theory." *American Economic Review, Papers and Proceedings* 71.

———. 1995. "Civil Institutions and Evolution: Concepts, Critique, and Models." *Journal of Development Economics* 46.

———. 2000. *Prelude to Political Economy: A Study of the Social and Political Foundations of Economics*. Oxford: Oxford University Press.

———. 2002. "The Retreat of Global Democracy." *Indicators: The Journal of Social Health* 1.

———. 2003a. "The Economics and Law of Sexual Harassment in the Workplace." *Journal of Economic Perspectives* 17.

———. 2003b. "Globalization and the Politics of International Finance: The Stiglitz Verdict." *Journal of Economic Literature* 41.

———. 2005a. "The New Empirical Development Economics: Remarks on Its Philosophical Foundations." *Economic and Political Weekly* 40 (October 1).

———. 2005b. "Racial Conflict and the Malignancy of Identity." *Journal of Economic Inequality* 3.

———. 2006a. "Gender and Say: A Model of Household Decision-Making with Endogenous Balance of Power." *Economic Journal* 116.

———. 2006b. "Globalization, Poverty, and Inequality: What Is the Relationship? What Can Be Done?" *World Development* 34.

———. 2006c. "Methodological Individualism." In *The New Palgrave Dictionary of Economics*, ed. Steven N. Durlauf and Lawrence E. Blume. Basingstoke, UK: Palgrave Macmillan.

———. 2007a. "Coercion, Conflict, and the Limits of the Market." *Social Choice and Welfare* 29.

———. 2007b. "Human Rights as Instruments of Emancipation and Economic Development." In *Economic Rights: Conceptual, Measurement, and Policy Issues*, ed. Shareen Hertel and Lanse Minkler. Cambridge: Cambridge University Press.

Basu, Kaushik. 2007c. "Participatory Equity, Identity, and Productivity: Policy Implications for Promoting Development." Mimeo, Cornell University.

———. 2007d. *The Retreat of Democracy and Other Itinerant Essays on Economics, Globalization, and India.* New Delhi: Permanent Black and London: Anthem Press.

———. 2010a. "A Marketing Scheme for Making Money Off Innocent People: A User's Manual." *Economics Letters.*

Basu, Kaushik. 2010b. "The Moral Basis of Prosperity and Oppression: Altruism, Other-Regarding Behavior, and Identity." *Economics and Philosophy.*

Basu, Kaushik, Sudipto Bhattacharya, and Ajit Mishra. 1992. "Notes on Bribery and the Control of Corruption." *Journal of Public Economics* 48.

Basu, Kaushik, and Amanda Felkey. 2008. "A Theory of Efficiency Wage with Multiple Unemployment Equilibria: How a Higher Minimum Wage Law Can Curb Unemployment." *Oxford Economic Papers* 61.

Basu, Kaushik, Gary Fields, and Shub Debgupta. 2008. "Labor Retrenchment Laws and Their Effect on Wages and Employment: A Theoretical Investigation." In *Development and Change*, ed. Bhaskar Dutta, Tridip Ray, and E. Somanathan. London: World Scientific Publishers.

Basu, Kaushik, Eric Jones, and Ekkehart Schlicht. 1987. "The Growth and Decay of Custom: The Role of the New Institutional Economics in Economic History." *Explorations in Economic History* 24.

Basu, Kaushik, and Tapan Mitra. 2003. "Aggregating Infinite Utility Streams with Intergenerational Equity." *Econometrica* 71.

———. 2007. "Utilitarianism and Infinite Utility Streams: A New Welfare Criterion and Its Axiomatic Characterization." *Journal of Economic Theory* 133.

Basu, Kaushik, and Pham Hoang Van. 1998. "The Economics of Child Labor." *American Economic Review.*

Basu, Kaushik, and Jörgen Weibull. 2003. "Punctuality: A Cultural Trait as Equilibrium." In *Economics for an Imperfect World: Essays in Honor of Joseph Stiglitz*, ed. Richard Arnott, Bruce Greenwald, Ravi Kanbur, and Barry Nalebuff. Cambridge, MA: MIT Press.

Basu, Kaushik, and Homa Zarghamee. 2008. "Is Product Boycott a Good Idea for Controlling Child Labor? A Theoretical Investigation." *Journal of Development Economics* 88.

Battigalli, Pierpaolo, and Martin Dufwenberg. 2005. "Dynamic Psychological Games." Mimeo, Bocconi University and the University of Arizona.

Becchetti, Leonardo and Furio Rosati. 2007. "Global Social Preferences and the Demand for Socially Responsible Products: Empirical Evidence from a Pilot Study on Fair Trade Consumers." *World Economy* 30.

Becker, Gary. 1968. "Crime and Punishment: An Economic Approach." *Journal of Political Economy* 76.

Beitz, Chuck. 2000. "Rawls's Law of Peoples." *Ethics* 110.

Benabou, Roland, and Jean Tirole. 2006. "Incentives and Prosocial Behavior." *American Economic Review* 96.

Bencivenga, Valerie, Elisabeth Huybens, and Bruce Smith. 2001. "Dollarization and the Integration of International Capital Markets." *Journal of Money, Credit, and Banking* 33.

Benjamin, Dan, James Choi, and A. Joshua Strickland. 2009. "Social Identity and Preferences." *American Economic Review*, forthcoming

Ben-Ner, Avner, and Louis Putterman. 2009. "Trust, Communication, and Contracts: An Experiment." *Journal of Economic Behavior and Organization* 70.

Benoit, Jean-Pierre, and Vijay Krishna. 1987. "Dynamic Duopoly: Prices and Quantities." *Review of Economic Studies* 54.

Bergson, Abraham. 1938. "A Reformulation of Certain Aspects of Welfare Economics." *Quarterly Journal of Economics* 52.

Berkowitz, Daniel, Katherina Pistor, and Jean-Francois Richard. 2003. "Economic Development, Legality, and the Transplant Effect." *European Economic Review* 47.

Bernard, Jessie. 1954. "The Theory of Games of Strategy as a Modern Sociology of Conflict." *American Sociological Review* 59.

Bertrand, Marianne, and Sendhil Mullainathan. 2004. "Are Emily and Greg More Employable Than Lakisha and Jamal?" *American Economic Review* 94.

Besley, Tim, and Steve Coate. 1992. "Understanding Welfare Stigma: Taxpayer Resentment and Statistical Discrimination." *Journal of Public Economics* 48.

Besley, Tim, and Maitreesh Ghatak. 2008. "Status Incentives." *American Economic Review* 98.

Beteille, Andre. 2006. *Ideology and Social Sciences*. New Delhi: Penguin Books.

Bevan, Edwyn. 1950. *Later Greek Religion*. Boston: Beacon Press.

Bhagwati, Jagdish. 1977. *Brain Drain and Income Taxation*. Oxford: Pergamon Press.

———. 2004. *In Defence of Globalization*. Oxford: Oxford University Press.

Bhargava, Rajeev. 1993. *Individualism in the Social Sciences: Forms and Limits of Methodology*. Oxford: Oxford University Press.

Bikhchandani, Sushil, David Hirschleifer, and Ivo Welch. 1992. "A Theory of Fads, Fashion, Custom, and Cultural Change as Informational Cascades." *Journal of Political Economy* 100.

Binmore, Ken. 1994. *Game Theory and the Social Contract: Volume 1: Playing Fair*. Cambridge, MA: MIT Press.

———. 1995. "The Game of Life: Comment." *Journal of Institutional and Theoretical Economics* 151.

———. 2005. *Natural Justice*. Oxford: Oxford University Press.

Birdsall, Nancy, David Ross, and Richard Sabot. 1995. "Inequality and Growth Reconsidered: Lessons from East Asia." *World Bank Economic Review* 9.

Blume, Lawrence. 2002. "Stigma and Social Control." Working paper, economics series no. 119, Institute for Advanced Studies, Vienna.

Bohnet, Iris, and Robert Cooter. 2001. "Expressive Law: Framing or Equilibrium Selection?" Mimeo, University of California at Berkeley.

Bourguignon, Francois, and Christian Morrisson. 2002. "Inequality among World Citizens: 1820–1992." *American Economic Review* 92.

Bowles, Sam. 2004. *Microeconomics: Behavior, Institutions, and Evolution.* Princeton, NJ: Princeton University Press.

Bowles, Sam, and Herb Gintis. 2005. "Can Self-interest Explain Cooperation?" *Evolutionary and Institutional Economics Review* 2.

Bowles, Sam, and Rajeev Sethi. 2006. "Persistent Group Inequality." Mimeo, Santa Fe Institute.

Brandolini, Andrea. 2007. "Inequality Patterns in Western-Type Democracies: Cross Country Differences and Times Changes." Mimeo, Bank of Italy, Rome.

Bruner, Jerome and Mary Potter. 1964. "Interference in Visual Recognition." *Science* 144 (April 24).

Bruni, Luigino, and Robert Sugden. 2007. "The Road Not Taken: How Psychology Was Removed from Economics and How It Might Be Brought Back." *Economic Journal* 117.

Buchanan, Allen, and Robert Keohane. 2006. "The Legitimacy of Global Governance Institutions." Mimeo, Duke University.

Buroway, Michael. 1979. *Manufacturing Consent: Changes in Labor Processes Under Monopoly Capitalism.* Chicago: Chicago University Press.

Burt, Ronald S. 1993. "The Social Structure of Competition." In *Explorations in Economic Sociology*, ed. Richard Swedberg. New York: Russell Sage Foundation.

Calasso, Roberto. 2005. *Ka.* Trans. from Italian by Geoffrey Brock. New York: Alfred Knopf.

Cantillon, Richard. [1755] 1964. *Essai Sur la Nature du Commerce en General* [Essay on the Nature of Trade in General]. Repr., New York: Augustus Kelley.

Capra, Monica, Jacob Goeree, Rosario Gomez, and Charles Holt. 1999. "Anomalous Behavior in a Traveler's Dilemma?" *American Economic Review* 89.

Carbonara, Emanuela, Francesco Parisi, and Georg won Wangenheim. 2008. "'Lawmakers as Norm Entrepreneurs." *Review of Law and Economics* 14, available at http://www.bepress.com/rle/vo14/iss3/art5.

Chang, Ha-Joon. 2002a. "Breaking the Mould: An Institutional Political Economy Alternative to the Neo-Liberal Theory of the Market and the State." *Cambridge Journal of Economics* 26.

———. 2002b. *Kicking Away the Ladder: Development Strategy in Historical Perspective.* London: Anthem Press.

Chang, Howard. 2000. "A Liberal Theory of Social Welfare: Fairness, Utility, and the Pareto Principle." *Yale Law Journal* 110.

Chatterjee, Partha. 2002. *A Princely Imposter? A Strange and Universal History of the Kumar of Bhawal.* Princeton, NJ: Princeton University Press.

Chattopadhyay, Raghabendra, and Esther Duflo. 2004. "Women as Policy Makers: Evidence from a Randomized Policy Experiment in India." *Econometrica* 72.

Chau, Nancy, and Ravi Kanbur. 2003. "Footloose Industries, Asymmetric Information, and Wage Bargaining." Mimeo, Cornell University.

Choi, Stephen, and Mitu Gulati. 2005. "Contract as Statute." *Michigan Law Review* 104.

Chomsky, Noam. 1991. *Media Control: The Spectacular Achievements of Propaganda.* New York: Seven Stories Press.

———. 2000. *Rogue States: The Role of Force in World Affairs.* New Delhi: India Research Press.

Cipriano, Marco, Paola Giuliano, and Olivier Jeanne. 2007. "The Transmission of Values from Parents to Children: Experimental Evidence from a Sample of African American and Hispanic Families." Mimeo, George Washington University.

Clingingsmith, David. 2009. "Language and Industrialization in Mid-20th Century India." Mimeo, Case Western Reserve University.

Clodfelter, Michael. 1995. *Vietnam in Military Statistics: A History of the Indochina Wars, 1772–1991.* Jefferson, NC: McFarland.

Coase, Ronald. 1991. "The Institutional Structure of Production." Nobel Prize lecture, Stockholm. Available at http://nobelprize.org/nobel_prizes/economics/laureates/1991/coase-lecture.html.

Coate, Stephen, and Glenn Loury. 1993. "Will Affirmative Action Policies Eliminate Negative Stereotypes?" *American Economic Review* 83.

Cohen, Gerald. 1986. "Self-Ownership, World-Ownership, and Equality." In *Justice and Equality Here and Now,* ed. Frank Lucash. Ithaca, NY: Cornell University Press.

———. 1987. "Are Disadvantaged Workers Who Take Hazardous Jobs Forced to Take Hazardous Jobs?" In *Moral Rights in the Workplace,* ed. Gertrude Ezorsky. Albany: State University of New York Press.

Coleman, James, and Mitu Gulati. 2006. "A Response to Professor Sander: Is It Really All about the Grades?" *North Carolina Law Review* 84.

Conlin, Michael, Michael Lynn, and Ted O'Donoghue. 2003. "The Norm of Restaurant Tipping." *Journal of Economic Behavior and Organization* 52.

Cooper, Richard. 1984. "A Monetary System for the Future." *Foreign Affairs* 63 (Fall).

Cooter, Robert. 1998. "Expressive Law and Economics." *Journal of Legal Studies* 27.

Cooter, Robert, and Melvin Eisenberg. 2001. "Fairness, Character, and Efficiency in Firms." *University of Pennsylvania Law Review* 149.

Cornia, Giovanni, with Sampsa Kiiski. 2001. "Trends in Income Distribution in the Post–World War II Period: Evidence and Interpretation." UNU-WIDER, Helsinki, discussion paper 2001/89.

Dağdeviren, Hülya, Rolph van der Hoeven, and John Weeks. 2004. "Redistribution Does Matter: Growth and Redistribution for Poverty Reduction." In *Growth, Inequality, and Poverty: Prospects for Pro-poor Economic Development,* ed. Anthony Shorrocks and Rolph van der Hoeven. Oxford: Oxford University Press.

Dahrendorf, Ralf. 1959. *Class and Class Conflict in Industrial Society.* Stanford, CA: Stanford University Press.

Darity, William, Patrick Mason, and James Stewart. 2006. "The Economics of Identity: The Origin and Persistence of Racial Identity Norms." *Journal of Economic Behavior and Organization* 60.

Dasgupta, Partha. 1990. "Trust as a Commodity." In *Trust: The Making and Breaking of Cooperative Relations*, ed. Diego Gambetta. Oxford: Blackwell.

Dasgupta, Partha, and Sanjeev Goyal. 2009. "Narrow Identities." Mimeo, University of Cambridge.

Davis, John. 2003. *The Theory of the Individual in Economics: Identity and Value*. London: Routledge.

Davis, Ronald. 2005. "Abstinence from Child Labor and Profit-Seeking." *Journal of Development Economics* 76.

Davis, Wade. 1997. *One River: Explorations and Discoveries in the Amazon Rain Forest*. New York: Touchstone.

Deininger, Klaus, and Lynn Squire. 1998. "New Ways of Looking at Old Issues: Inequality and Growth." *Journal of Development Economics* 57.

Desai, Kiran. 2006. *The Inheritance of Loss*. London: Penguin Books.

Desai, Sonalde, and Devaki Jain. 1994. "Maternal Employment and Family Dynamics: The Social Context of Women's Work in Rural South India." *Population and Development Review* 20.

Deshpande, Ashwini. 1999. "Loan Pushing and Triadic Relations." *Southern Economic Journal* 65.

———. 2000. "Does Caste Still Define Disparity? A Look at Inequality in Kerala, India." *American Economic Review* 90.

Diamant, Kathi. 2003. *Kafka's Last Love: The Mystery of Dora Diamant*. New York: Basic Books.

Dideon, Joan. 2005. *The Year of Magical Thinking*. New York: Alfred Knopf.

Dinopoulos, Elias, and Laixun Zhao. 2007. "Child Labor and Globalization." *Journal of Labor Economics* 25.

Dixit, Avinash. 2004. *Lawlessness and Economics: Alternative Modes of Governance*. Princeton, NJ: Princeton University Press.

———. 2009. "Governance Institutions and Economic Activity." *American Economic Review* 99.

Dougherty, Peter. 2002. *Who's Afraid of Adam Smith? How the Market Got Its Soul*. New York: Wiley.

Dreze, Jean. 2000. "Militarism, Development, and Democracy." *Economic and Political Weekly* 37 (April 1).

Dufwenberg, Martin, and Georg Kirchsteiger. 2004. "A Theory of Sequential Reciprocity." *Games and Economic Behavior* 47.

Durlauf, Steven. 2001. "The Memberships Theory of Poverty: The Role of Group Affiliations in Determining Socioeconomic Outcomes." In *Understanding Poverty in America*, ed. Sheldon H. Danziger and Robert H. Haveman. Cambridge, MA: Harvard University Press.

———. 2006. "Groups, Social Influences, and Inequality." In *Poverty Traps*, ed. Samuel Bowles, Steven Durlauf, and Karla Hoff. Princeton, NJ: Princeton University Press.

Dutta, Bhaskar. 2008. "Remarks on the Ranking of Infinite Utility Streams." In *Arguments for a Better World: Essays in Honor of Amartya Sen*, ed. Kaushik Basu and Ravi Kanbur. Oxford: Oxford University Press.

Dworkin, Ronald. 1986. *Law's Empire*. Cambridge, MA: Harvard University Press.

Eberstadt, Fernanda. 2007. "The Unexpected Fantasist." *New York Times Magazine*, August 26.

Eckel, Catherine, and Rick Wilson. 2002. "Conditional Trust: Sex, Race, and Facial Expressions in a Trust Game." Mimeo, Virginia Tech.

Einstein, Albert. 1949. "Why Socialism?" *Monthly Review* 1 (May).

Eisenberg, Melvin. 1999. "Corporate Law and Social Norms." *Columbia Law Review* 99.

Ellerman, David. 1995. *Property and Contract in Economics*. Cambridge, MA: Blackwell Publishers.

Ellickson, Robert. 1991. *Order without Law: How Neighbors Settle Disputes*. Cambridge, MA: Harvard University Press.

Ellingsen, Tore, and Magnus Johannesson. 2008. "Pride and Prejudice: The Human Side of Incentive Theory." *American Economic Review* 98.

Ellison, Glenn. 2005. "A Model of Add-on Pricing." *Quarterly Journal of Economics* 120.

Elster, Jon. 1982. "Marxism, Functionalism, and Game Theory." *Theory and Society* 11.

———. 1989. *The Cement of Society*. Cambridge, MA: Cambridge University Press.

Emerson, Patrick and Andre Portela Souza. 2003. "Is There a Child Labor Trap? Intergenerational Persistence of Child Labor in Brazil." *Economic Development and Cultural Change* 51.

Engerman, Stanley. 1973. "Some Considerations relating to Property Rights in Man." *Journal of Economic History* 33.

Ensminger, Jean. 2000. "Experimental Economics in the Bush: How Institutions Matter." In *Institutions and Organizations*, ed. Claude Ménard. London: Edward Elgar.

Esteban, Joan, and Debraj Ray. 2009. "A Model of Ethnic Conflict." Mimeo, New York University.

Evensky, Jerry. 2005a. *Adam Smith's Moral Philosophy: A Historical and Contemporary Perspective on Markets, Laws, Ethics, and Culture*. Cambridge: Cambridge University Press.

———. 2005b. "'Chicago Smith' and 'Kirkaldy Smith.'" *History of Political Economy* 37.

Fafchamps, Marcel. 1992. "Solidarity Networks in Pre-Industrial Societies." *Economic Development and Cultural Change* 41.

———. 2000. "Ethnicity and Credit in African Manufacturing." *Journal of Development Economics* 61.

Falk, Armin, Ernst Fehr, and Christian Zehnder. 2006. "Fairness Perceptions and Reservation Wages: The Behavioral Effects of Minimum Wage Laws." *Quarterly Journal of Economics* 121.

Farina, Francesco, Niall O'Higgins, and Patrizia Sbriglia. 2008. "Eliciting Motives for Trust and Reciprocity by Attitudinal and Behavioral Measures." LABSI working paper no. 21, University of Siena.

Fehr, Ernst, and Simon Gachter. 2000. "Fairness and Retaliation: The Economics of Reciprocity." *Journal of Economic Perspectives* 14.

Fershtman, Chaim, and Uri Gneezy. 2001. "Discrimination in a Segmented Society: An Experimental Approach." *Quarterly Journal of Economics* 116.

Field, Erica, and Patrick Nolen. 2005. "Race and Performance in Post-Apartheid South Africa." Mimeo, Cornell University.

Fish, Stanley. 1994. *There Is No Such Thing as Free Speech, and It's a Good Thing, Too.* New York: Oxford University Press.

Fishburn, Peter. 1970. "Intransitive Indifference in Preference Theory: A Survey." *Operations Research* 18.

Fisman, Ray, and Edward Miguel. 2007. "Corruption, Norms, and Legal Enforcement: Evidence from U.N. Diplomatic Parking Tickets." *Journal of Political Economy* 115.

Fiss, Owen. 1994. *The Irony of Free Speech.* Cambridge, MA: Harvard University Press.

Foley, Duncan. 2006. *Adam's Fallacy: A Guide to Economic Theology.* Cambridge, MA: Harvard University Press.

Foster, James. 2010. "Freedom, Opportunity and Wellbeing." In *Handbook of Social Choice and Welfare*, eds. Kenneth Arrow, Amartya Sen, Kotaro Suzumura. Amsterdam: Elsevier.

Francois, Patrick. 1998. "Gender Discrimination without Gender Difference: Theory and Policy Responses." *Journal of Public Economics* 68.

———. 2002. *Social Capital and Economic Development.* New York: Routledge.

Frank, Joseph. 1986. *Dostoyevsky: The Stir of Liberation, 1860–1865.* Princeton, NJ: Princeton University Press.

Frank, Robert. 1985. *Choosing the Right Pond: Human Behavior and the Quest for Status.* New York: Oxford University Press.

Frank, Robert, Tom Gilovich, and Dennis T. Regan. 1993. "Does Studying Economics Inhibit Cooperation?" *Journal of Economic Perspectives* 7.

Freeman, Richard, Douglas Kruse, and Joseph Blasi. 2004. "Worker Responses to Shirking under Shared Capitalism." National Bureau of Economic Research working paper no. W14227. Cambridge, MA: National Bureau of Economic Research.

French, Howard. 2007. "Fake Potter Books Flood China." *Times of India* (New Delhi), August 2 (from *New York Times News Service*).

Friedman, Milton. 1953. "The Methodology of Positive Economics." In *Essays in Positive Economics*, ed. Milton Friedman. Chicago: Chicago University Press.

———. 1962. *Capitalism and Freedom.* Chicago: University of Chicago Press.

Fryer, Roland, and Matt Jackson. 2008. "A Categorical Model of Cognition and Biased Decision-Making." *B. E. Journal of Theoretical Economics* 8.

Fukui, Yoshitaka. 2005. "What Distinguishes Accounting Harassment from Sexual One?" Mimeo, Aoyama Gakuin University, Tokyo.

Fukuyama, Francis. 1996. *Trust: The Social Virtues and the Creation of Prosperity*. New York: Free Press.

Gabaix, Xavier, and David Laibson. 2006. "Shrouded Attributes, Consumer Myopia, and Information Suppression in Competitive Markets." *Quarterly Journal of Economics* 121.

Gaertner, Wulf. 2008. "Individual Rights versus Economic Growth." *Journal of Human Development* 9.

Gaertner, Wulf, Prasanta Pattanaik, and Kotaro Suzumura. 1992. "Individual Rights Revisited." *Economica* 59.

Galbraith, James K. 2002. "A Perfect Crime: Inequality in the Age of Globalization." *Daedalus* 131.

Gallie, Walter. 1955. "Essentially Contested Concepts." *Proceedings of the Aristotelian Society* 56.

Gambetta, Diego, ed. 1990. *Trust: The Making and Breaking of Cooperative Relations*. Oxford: Blackwell.

Gans, Herbert. 1972. "The Positive Functions of Poverty." *American Journal of Sociology* 78.

Garoupa, Nuno. 1999. "Dishonesty and Libel Law: The Economics of the 'Chilling' Effect." *Journal of Institutional and Theoretical Economics* 155.

Genicot, Garance. 2002. "Bonded Labor and Serfdom: A Paradox of Voluntary Choice." *Journal of Development Economics* 67.

Gigerenzer, Gerd. 2007. *Gut Feelings: The Intelligence of the Unconscious*. New York: Viking Press.

Gintis, Herb. 2007. "Bayesian Rationality and Social Norms." Mimeo, Santa Fe Institute.

———. 2008. *Game Theory for Behavioral Scientists*. Princeton, NJ: Princeton University Press.

Glaeser, Edward, David Laibson, Jose Scheinkman, and Christine Souter. 2000. "Measuring Trust." *Quarterly Journal of Economics* 115.

Glueck, Grace. 2003a. "Relentless Seeker of the Authentic Jew: An Exhibition of a Photographer's Odyssey in Capturing Myriad Identities." *New York Times*, October 8, E1.

———. 2003b. "Seeking Out Jewish Faces Wherever They Might Be." *New York Times*, October 17, E38.

Goffman, Erving. 1959. *The Presentation of Self in Everyday Life*. New York: Double Day.

Granovetter, Mark. 1985. "Economic Action and Social Structure: The Problem of Embeddedness." *American Journal of Sociology* 91.

Granovetter, Mark, and R. Soong. 1983. "Threshold Models of Diffusion and Collective Behavior." *Journal of Mathematical Sociology* 9.

Gray, John. 2009. "The Appearance of Moderation: The Economics of Choosing Individual Identity." Mimeo, Cornell University.

Greif, Avner. 1998. "Self-Enforcing Political Systems and Economic Growth: Late Medieval Genoa." In *Analytic Narratives*, eds. Robert Bates, Avner Greif, Margaret Levi, Jean-Laurent Rosenthal, and Barry R. Weingast. Princeton, NJ: Princeton University Press.

Grossmann, Harald, and Jochen Michaelis. 2007. "Trade Sanctions and the Incidence of Child Labor." *Review of Development Economics* 11.

Guha, Ashok, and Brishti Guha. 2010. "Basu's Paradox or the Possibility of Honesty." Mimeo, Department of Economics, Singapore Management University.

Gussow, Mel. 1994. *Conversations with Harold Pinter*. New York: Grove Press.

Hahn, Frank. 1985. "In Praise of Economic Theory." In *Money, Growth, and Stability* by Frank Hahn. Oxford: Blackwell Publishers.

Halpern, Joseph, and Rafael Pass. 2009. "Iterated Regret Minimization: A More Realistic Solution Concept." *Proceedings of the 21st International Joint Conference on Artificial Intelligence*. Pasadena, CA: IJCAI.

Hardin, Russell. 1989. "Why a Constitution?" In *The Federalist Papers and the New Institutionalism*, ed. Bernard Grofman and Donald Wittman. New York: Agathon Press.

Harrington, Joseph. 1999. "Rigidity of Social Systems." *Journal of Political Economy* 107.

Hatlebakk, Magnus. 2002. "A New and Robust Subgame Perfect Equilibrium in a Model of Triadic Power Relations." *Journal of Development Economics* 68.

Havel, Václav. 1986. "The Power of the Powerless." In *Living in Truth*, ed. Jan Vadislav. London: Faber and Faber.

Hayashi, Andrew. 2008. "Review of *Economic Rights*." *Law and Politics Book Review* 18.

Heinrich, Joseph, Robert Boyd, Sam Bowles, Colin Camerer, Ernst Fehr, and Herb Gintis, eds. 2004. *Foundations of Human Sociality: Economic and Ethnographic Evidence from Fifteen Small-scale Societies*. Oxford: Oxford University Press.

Hockett, Robert. 2007a. "The Impossibility of a Prescriptive Paretian." Mimeo, Cornell University.

———. 2007b. "What Kinds of Stock Ownership Plans Should There Be? Of ESOPs, Other SOPs, and 'Ownership Societies,'" *Cornell Law Review* 92.

———. 2009. "Justice in Time." *George Washington Law Review* 77.

Hoff, Karla, Mayuresh Kshetramade, and Ernst Fehr. 2007. "Norm Enforcement under Social Discrimination: An Experimental Investigation in Village India." Mimeo: World Bank, Washington, DC.

Hoff, Karla, and Priyanka Pandey. 2005. "Persistent Effects of Discrimination and the Role of Social Identity." Mimeo, World Bank, Washington, DC.

———. 2006. "Discrimination, Social Identity, and Durable Inequalities." *American Economic Review* 96.

Hoff, Karla, and Joseph Stiglitz. 2008. "Exiting the Lawless State." *Economic Journal* 118.

Hoffman, Elizabeth, and Matthew Spitzer. 1982. "The Coase Theorem: Some Experimental Tests." *Journal of Law and Economics* 25.

Horst, Ulrich, Alan Kirman, and Miriam Teschl. 2006. "Changing Identity: The Emergence of Social Groups." Groupement de Recherche en Économie Quantitative working paper no. 2006-51.

Hume, David. [1739] 1969. *A Treatise of Human Nature*. Repr., London: Penguin.

———. [1758] 1987. "Of the First Principles of Government." In *Essays: Moral, Political, and Literary*. Repr., Indianapolis: Liberty Fund.

Hunt, Tristam. 2009. *Marx's General: The Revolutionary Life of Friedrich Engels*. New York: Metropolitan Books.

Huntington, Samuel. 1993. "The Clash of Civilizations." *Foreign Affairs* 72.

Hurwicz, Leo. 1960. "Optimality and Informational Efficiency in Resource Allocation Processes." In *Mathematical Methods in the Social Sciences*, ed. Kenneth J. Arrow, Samuel Karlin, and Patrick Suppes. Stanford, CA: Stanford University Press.

Iversen, Vegaard. 2004. "On Notions of Agency, Individual Heterogeneity, and the Existence, Size, and Composition of a Bonded Child." In *Globalization, Culture, and the Limits of the Market: Essays in Economics and Philosophy*, ed. Prasanta Pattanaik and Stephen Cullenberg. New York: Oxford University Press.

Iversen, Vegard, and P. S. Raghavendra. 2006. "What the Signboard Hides: Food, Caste, and Employability in Small South Indian Eating Places." *Contributions to Indian Sociology* 40.

Jencks, Christopher. 1994. *The Homeless*. Cambridge, MA: Harvard University Press.

Kafka, Franz. 1970. "The Problem of Our Laws" In *The Great Wall of China: Stories and Reflections*. New York: Schocken Books.

———. 1998. *The Trial*. New York: Schocken Books.

Kanbur, Ravi. 2004. "On Obnoxious Markets." In *Globalization, Culture, and the Limits of the Market: Essays in Economics and Philosophy*, ed. Prasanta Pattanaik and Stephen Cullenberg. New York: Oxford University Press.

———. 2005. "Goldilocks Development Economics: Not Too Theoretical, Not Too Empirical, But Watch Out for the Bears." *Economic and Political Weekly* 40 (October 1).

Kandori, Michihiro, George Mailath, and Rafael Rob. 1993. "Learning, Mutation, and Long-run Equilibria in Games." *Econometrica* 61.

Kaplow, Louis, and Steven Shavell. 2002. *Fairness and Welfare*. Cambridge, MA: Harvard University Press.

Karni, Edi, Tim Salmon, and Barry Sopher. 2007. "Individual Sense of Fairness: An Experimental Study." Mimeo, Johns Hopkins University.

Katzenstein, Peter. 2004. "Commentary: Globalization and State Power in World Politics." In *The Evolution of Political Knowledge: Democracy, Autonomy, and Conflict in Comparative and International Politics*, ed. Edward Mansfield and Richard Sisson. Columbus: Ohio State University Press.

Khan, M. Ali. 2002. "On Trust as a Commodity and on the Grammar of Trust." *Journal of Banking and Finance* 26.

Klasen, Stefan. 2004. "In Search of the Holy Grail: How to Achieve Pro-Poor Growth?" Mimeo, University of Munich.

Knack, Stephen, and Philip Keefer. 1997. "Does Social Capital Have an Economy Payoff? A Cross-country Investigation." *Quarterly Journal of Economics* 112.

Koestler, Arthur. 1972. *The Roots of Coincidence*. London: Hutchinson.

Kornblut, Anne. 2005. "He Says Yes to Legalized Torture." *New York Times*, December 11, sec. 4, 1, 4.

Korobkin, Russell. 2003. "Bounded Rationality, Standard Form Contracts, and Unconscionability." *University of Chicago Law Review* 70.

Kranton, Rachel, and Anand Swamy. 1999. "The Hazards of Piecemeal Reform: British Civil Courts and the Credit Market in Colonial India." *Journal of Development Economics* 58.

Krasner, Stephen. 2004. "Globalization, Power, and Authority." In *The Evolution of Political Knowledge: Democracy, Autonomy, and Conflict in Comparative and International Politics*, ed. Edward Mansfield and Richard Sisson. Columbus: Ohio State University Press.

Kremer, Michael, Kartik Muralidharan, Nazmul Chaudhury, Jeffrey Hammer, and F. Halsey Rogers. 2005. "Teacher Absence in India: A Snapshot." *Journal of European Economic Association* 3.

Kreps, David, and Jose Scheinkman. 1983. "Quantity Precommitment and Bertrand Competition Yield Cournot Outcomes." *Bell Journal of Economics* 14.

Ku, Hyejin, and Asaf Zussman. 2009. "Lingua Franca: The Role of English in International Trade." Mimeo, Florida State University.

Kuran, Timur. 1988. "Ethnic Norms and Their Transformation through Reputational Cascades." *Journal of Legal Studies* 27.

Laertius, Diogenes. 1925. *Lives of Eminent Philosophers, Volume II*, trans. Robert D. Hic. Cambridge, MA: Harvard University Press. (The original Greek text is usually dated to the third century AD.)

Landa, Janet Tai. 1995. *Trust, Ethnicity, and Identity: Beyond the New Institutional Economics of Ethnic Trading Networks, Contract Law, and Gift Exchange*. Ann Arbor: University of Michigan Press.

Leibenstein, Harvey. 1950. "Bandwagon, Snob, and Veblen Effects in the Theory of Consumers." *Quarterly Journal of Economics* 64.

Leibl, Maureen, and Tirthankar Roy. 2003. "Handmade in India: Preliminary Analysis of Crafts Producers and Crafts Production." *Economic and Political Weekly* 38 (December 27).

Levine, Robert V., Laurie J. West, and Harry T. Reis. 1980. "Perceptions of Time and Punctuality in the United States and Brazil." *Journal of Personality and Social Psychology* 38.

Li, James, David Dunning, Roy Malpass. 1998. "Cross-Racial Identification among European Americans: Basketball Fandom and the Contact Hypothesis." Mimeo, University of Texas.

Licht, Amir. 2007. "Social Norms and the Law: Why People Obey the Law." Mimeo, Radzyner Law School, Herzliva.

Lilienfeld-Toal, Ulf von, and Dilip Mookherjee. 2008. "The Political Economy of Debt Bondage." Mimeo, Boston University.

Lin, Ann Chih, and David Harris. 2008. "Why Is American Poverty Still Colored in the 21st Century?" In *The Colors of Poverty: Why Racial and Ethnic Disparities Persist*, ed. Ann Chih Lin and David Harris. New York: Russell Sage Foundation.

Lin, Justin Yifu. 2009. *Economic Development and Transition: Thought, Strategy, and Viability*. Cambridge: Cambridge University Press.

Lindbeck, Assar, Stefan Nyberg, and Jörgen Weibull. 1999. "Social Norms and Economic Incentives in the Welfare State." *Quarterly Journal of Economics* 114.

Lindqvist, Erik, and Robert Ostling. 2007. "Identity and Redistribution." Mimeo, Stockholm School of Economics.

López-Calva, Luis-Felipe. 2003. "Social Norms, Coordination, and Policy Issues in the Fight against Child Labor." In *International Labor Standards*, ed. Kaushik Basu, Henrik Horn, Lisa Román, and Judith Shapiro. Oxford: Blackwell Publishing.

Lopucki, Lynn, and Walter Weyrauch. 2000. "A Theory of Legal Strategy." *Duke Law Journal* 49.

Loury, Glenn. 2002. *The Anatomy of Racial Inequality*. Cambridge, MA: Harvard University Press.

Luhman, Niklas. 1979. *Trust and Power*. Chichester, UK: Wiley.

Lundberg, Shelly, Robert Pollak, and Terence Wales. 1997. "Do Husbands and Wives Pool Their Resources? Evidence from the United Kingdom Child Benefit." *Journal of Human Resources* 32.

Luttmer, Erzo. 2001. "Group Loyalty and the Taste for Redistribution." *Journal of Political Economy* 109.

Mackie, Gerry. 1996. "Ending Footbinding and Infibulation: A Convention Account." *American Sociological Review* 61.

Macpherson, Crawford. 1973. *Democratic Theory: Essays in Retrieval*. Oxford: Clarendon Press.

Madison, Angus. 2001. *The World Economy: A Millennial Perspective*. Paris: Organization for Economic Cooperation and Development.

Mailath, George, Stephen Morris, and Andrew Postlewaite. 2001. "Laws and Authority." Mimeo, University of Pennsylvania.

Majumdar, Tapas. 1958. *The Measurement of Utility*. London: Macmillan.

Mansuri, Ghazala, and Vijayendra Rao. 2004. "Community Based (and Driven) Development: A Critical Review." *World Bank Research Observer* 19.

Marshall, Alfred. 1890. *Principles of Economics*. London: Macmillan.

Marx, Karl. [1875] 1959. *Critique of the Gotha Programme*. Repr., Moscow: Foreign Languages Publishing House.

Maskin, Eric, and Thomas Sjöström. 2002. "Implementation Theory." In *Handbook of Social Choice Theory and Welfare*, ed. Kenneth J. Arrow, Amartya K. Sen, and Kotaro Suzumura. Amsterdam: Elsevier.

McAdams, Richard. 2000. "A Focal Point Theory of Expressive Law." *Virginia Law Review* 86.

Medema, Steven. 2009. *The Hesitant Hand: Taming Self-interest in the History of Ideas.* Princeton, NJ: Princeton University Press.

Meissner, Christian, and John Brigham. 2001. "Thirty Years of Investigating the Own-Race Bias in Memory for Faces: A Meta-Analytic Review." *Psychology, Public Policy, and Law* 7.

Melchior, Arne. 2001. "Global Income Inequality: Beliefs, Facts, and Unresolved Issues." *World Economics* 2.

Melchior, Arne, Kjetil Telle, and Henrik Wiig. 2000. *Globalization and Inequality—World Income Distribution and Living Standards, 1960–1998.* Oslo: Royal Norwegian Ministry of Foreign Affairs, Studies on Foreign Policy Issues, no. 6b.

Menger, Carl. [1883] 1986. *Investigations into the Method of the Social Sciences with Special Reference to Economics.* Repr., New York: New York University Press.

Mercuro, Nicholas, and Steven Medema. 1997. *Economics and the Law: From Posner to Post-Modernism.* Princeton, NJ: Princeton University Press.

Messer, Kent, Homa Zarghamee, Harry Kaiser, and William Schulze. 2007. "New Hope for the Voluntary Contributions Mechanism." *Journal of Public Economics* 99.

Miguel, Edward, and Gerard Roland. 2005. "The Long Run Impact of Vietnam Bombing." Mimeo, University of California at Berkeley.

Milanovich, Branko. 2002. "True World Income Distribution, 1988 and 1993: First Calculation Based on Household Surveys Alone." *Economic Journal* 112.

Mill, John Stuart. [1848] 1970. *Principles of Political Economy.* Repr., Harmondsworth, UK: Penguin.

———. [1859] 1971. *On Liberty.* Repr., London: Dent and Sons.

Miller, Richard. 1998. "Cosmopolitan Respect and Patriotic Concerns." *Philosophy and Public Affairs* 27.

Minkler, Lanse. 2004. "Shirking and Motivations in Firms: Survey Evidence on Worker Attitudes." *International Journal of Industrial Organization* 22.

Minkler, Lanse, and Thomas Miceli. 2004. "Lying, Integrity, and Cooperation." *Review of Social Economy* 57.

Mishra, Ajit. 2002. "Hierarchies, Incentives, and Collusion in a Model of Enforcement." *Journal of Economic Behavior and Organization* 47.

Mookherjee, Dilip. 2005. "Is There Too Little Theory in Development Economics Today?" *Economic and Political Weekly* 40 (October 1).

Myerson, Roger. 1983. "Mechanism Design by an Informed Principal." *Econometrica* 51.

———. 2004. "Justice, Institutions, and Multiple Equilibria." *Chicago Journal of International Law* 5.

———. 2008. "The Autocrat's Credibility Problem and Foundations of the Constitutional State." *American Political Science Review* 102.

Nagel, Thomas. 2005. "The Problem of Global Justice." *Philosophy and Public Affairs* 33.

Naqvi, Nadeem, and Frederick Wemhoner. 1995. "Power, Coercion, and the Games That Landlords Play." *Journal of Development Economics* 47.

Naschold, Felix. 2004. "Growth, Redistribution, and Poverty Reduction: LDCs Are Falling Behind." In *Growth, Inequality, and Poverty: Prospects for Pro-Poor Economic Development*, ed. Anthony Shorrocks and Rolph van der Hoeven. Oxford: Oxford University Press.

Neeman, Zvika. 1999. "The Freedom to Contract and the Free-Rider Problem." *Journal of Law, Economics, and Organization* 15.

Nozick, Robert. 1969. "Coercion." In *Philosophy, Science, and Method: Essays in Honor of Ernest Nagel*, ed. Sidney Morgenbesser, Patrick Suppes, and Morton White. New York: St. Martin's Press.

———. 1974. *Anarchy, Utopia, and State*. Oxford: Blackwell Publishers.

Nussbaum, Martha. 2008. "Toward a Globally Sensitive Patriotism." *Daedalus* 137 (Summer).

Nussbaum, Martha, and Joshua Cohen. 1996. *For Love of Country*. Boston: Beacon Press.

O'Brien, Dennis. 1975. *The Classical Economists*. Oxford: Clarendon Press.

O'Donoghue, Ted, and Mathew Rabin. 2001. "Choice and Procrastination." *Quarterly Journal of Economics* 116.

O'Flaherty, Brendan. 1996. *Making Room: The Economics of Homelessness*. Cambridge, MA: Harvard University Press.

Ostrom, Elinor. 1990. *Governing the Commons: The Evolution of Institutions for Collective Action*. New York: Cambridge University Press.

Otsuka, Michael. 1998. "Self-Ownership and Equality: A Lockean Reconciliation." *Philosophy and Public Affairs* 27.

Pagano, Ugo. 2007. "Bounded Rationality, Institutionalism, and the Diversity of Economic Institutions." In *Is Economics an Evolutionary Science? The Legacy of Thorstein Veblen*, ed. Francisco Louçã and Mark Perlman. Cheltenham, UK: Edward Elgar.

Parfit, Derek. 1984. *Reasons and Persons*. Oxford: Clarendon Press.

Pattanaik, Prasanta. 1970. "On Social Choice with Quasi-Transitive Individual Preferences." *Journal of Economic Theory* 2.

Pattanaik, Prasanta, and Yongsheng Xu. 1990. "On Ranking Opportunity Sets in Terms of Freedom of Choice." *Researches Economiques de Louvain* 56.

Perez, Wilson. 2007. "Divide and Conquer: Distorted Communication in Networks, Power, and Wealth Distribution." Mimeo, Banco Central del Ecuador.

Phelps, Edmund. 1972. "The Statistical Theory of Racism and Sexism." *American Economic Review* 62.

Platteau, Jean-Philippe. 1994. "Behind the Market Stage Where Real Societies Exist, II: The Role of Moral Norms." *Journal of Development Studies* 30.

———. 2000. *Institutions, Social Norms, and Economic Development*. Amsterdam: Harwood Academic Publishers.

Pogge, Thomas. 2002. *World Poverty and Human Rights: Cosmopolitan Responsibilities and Reforms*. Cambridge, UK: Polity Press.

Pogge, Thomas. 2005. "Recognized and Violated International Law: The Human Rights of the Global Poor." *Leiden Journal of International Law* 18.

Polanyi, Karl. [1944] 1957. *The Great Transformation: The Political and Economic Origins of Our Time*. Boston: Beacon Paperback.

Popescu, Oxana. 2005. "Taking a Gamble on Human Capital." *International Herald Tribune*, June 18–19, 16.

Posner, Eric. 2000. "Law and Social Norms: The Case of Tax Compliance." *Virginia Law Review* 86.

Pritchett, Lant. 1997. "Divergence, Big Time." *Journal of Economic Perspectives* 11.

PROBE. 1999. *Public Report on Basic Education in India*. New Delhi: Oxford University Press.

Rabin, Matt, and Joel Shrag. 1999. "First Impressions Matter: A Model of Confirmatory Bias." *Quarterly Journal of Economics* 114.

Rae, John. 1895. *The Life of Adam Smith*. London: Macmillan.

Ravallion, Martin, and Shaohua Chen. 2007. "Absolute Poverty Measures for the Developing World, 1981–2004." Policy Research working paper no. 4211, World Bank, Washington, DC.

Rawls, John. 1971. *A Theory of Justice*. Cambridge, MA: Harvard University Press.

———. 1990. *The Law of Peoples*. Cambridge, MA: Harvard University Press.

Raynauld, Andre, and Jean-Pierre Vidal. 1998. *Labor Standards and International Competitiveness*. Northhampton, MA: Edward Elgar.

Raz, Joseph. 1980. *The Concept of a Legal System*. Oxford: Clarendon Press.

Reddy, Sanjay, and Camelia Minoiu. 2007. "Has World Poverty Really Fallen?" *Review of Income and Wealth* 53.

Reddy, Sanjay, and Thomas Pogge. 2008. "How Not to Count the Poor." In *Debates in the Measurement of Poverty*, ed. Sudhir Anand, Paul Segal, and Joseph E. Stiglitz. Oxford: Oxford University Press.

Risse, Matthias. 2005. "How Does the Global Order Harm the Poor?" *Philosophy and Public Affairs* 33.

Robertson, Lindsay. 2005. *Conquest by Law: How the Discovery of America Disposed Indigenous Peoples of Their Lands*. Oxford: Oxford University Press.

Robinson, Joan. 1979. *Collected Economic Papers, Volume 5*. Oxford: Blackwell Publishers.

Robson, Arthur. 1990. "Efficiency in Evolutionary Games: Darwin, Nash, and the Secret Handshake." *Journal of Theoretical Biology* 144.

Rodrik, Dani. 2008. "The New Development Economics: We Shall Experiment but How Shall We Learn." Mimeo, Harvard University.

Roemer, John. 1981. *Analytical Foundations of Marxian Economic Theory*. Cambridge: Cambridge University Press.

———. 1994. *A Future for Socialism*. Cambridge, MA: Harvard University Press.

Rosenthal, Robert. 1981. "Games of Perfect Information, Predatory Pricing, and the Chain Store Paradox. *Journal of Economic Theory* 25.

Ross, Lee, and Andrew Ward. 1996. "Naive Realism in Everyday Life: Implications for Social Conflict and Misunderstanding." In *Values and Knowledge*, ed. Edward S. Reed, Elliot Turiel, and Terrance Brown. Hillsdale, NJ: Erlbaum.

Rothschild, Emma. 2001. *Economic Sentiments: Adam Smith, Condorcet, and the Enlightenment*. Cambridge MA: Harvard University Press.

Rubinstein, Ariel. 1998. *Modeling Bounded Rationality*. Cambridge, MA: MIT Press.

———. 2006a. "Dilemmas of an Economic Theorist." *Econometrica* 74.

———. 2006b. "A Skeptic's Comment on the Study of Economics." *Economic Journal* 116.

———. 2008. "Comments on 'Behavioral Economics.'" Mimeo, Tel Aviv University.

Rush, Norman. 1991. *Mating*. New York: Alfred Knopf.

Sacconi, Lorenzo. 2000. *The Social Contract of the Firm: Economics, Ethics, and Organisation*. Heidelberg: Springer.

Sachs, Jeffrey. 2005. *The End of Poverty: Economic Possibilities for our Time*. New York: Penguin.

Salles, Maurice. 1999. "Fuzzy Utility." In *Handbook of Utility Theory*, ed. Salvador Barberà, P. J. Hammond, and Christian Seidl. Dordrecht: Kluwer.

Samuelson, Paul. 1947. *Foundations of Economic Analysis*. Cambridge, MA: Harvard University Press.

Sander, Richard. 2006. "The Racial Paradox of the Corporate Law Firm." *North Carolina Law Review* 84.

Satz, Debra. 2003. "Child Labor: A Normative Perspective." *World Bank Economic Review* 17.

———. 2004. "Noxious Markets: Why Should Some Things Not Be for Sale?" In *Globalization, Culture, and the Limits of the Market: Essays in Economics and Philosophy*, ed. Prasanta Pattanaik and Stephen Cullenberg. New York: Oxford University Press.

Saxenian, AnnaLee. 2000. "The Origins and Dynamics of Production Networks in Silicon Valley." In *Entrepreneurship: The Social Science View*, ed. Richard Swedberg. Oxford: Oxford University Press.

Schelling, Thomas. 1960. *The Strategy of Conflict*. Cambridge, MA: Harvard University Press.

———. 1985. "Enforcing Rules on Oneself." *Journal of Law, Economics, and Organization* 1.

Schlicht, Ekkehart. 1998. *On Custom in the Economy*. Oxford: Clarendon Press.

Schott, Jeffrey, and Jayashree Watal. 2000. "Decision Making in the WTO." In *The WTO after Seattle*, ed. Jeffrey Schott. Washington, DC: Institute for International Economics.

Schumpeter, Joseph. 1909. "On the Concept of Social Value." *Quarterly Journal of Economics* 23.

Seabright, Paul. 2004a. "Blood and Bribes: Ethical Restraints to Trade." In *Globalization, Culture, and the Limits of the Market: Essays in Economics and Philosophy*, ed. Prasanta Pattanaik and Stephen Cullenberg. New York: Oxford University Press.

———. 2004b. *The Company of Strangers: A Natural History of Economic Life*. Princeton, NJ: Princeton University Press.

Selten, Reinhart. 1978. "The Chain Store Paradox." *Theory and Decision* 9.

Sen, Amartya. 1967. "Isolation, Assurance, and the Social Rate of Discount." *Quarterly Journal of Economics* 81.

———. 1970. *Collective Choice and Social Welfare*. San Francisco: Holden Day.

Sen, Amartya. 1997. *On Economic Inequality*. Oxford: Clarendon Books.

———. 1999. *Development as Freedom*. New York: Alfred Knopf.

———. 2006. *Identity and Violence*. New York: Alfred Knopf.

Sen, Amartya, and Prasanta Pattanaik. 1969. "Necessary and Sufficient Conditions for Rational Choice under Majority Decision." *Journal of Economic Theory* 1.

Sen, Arunava. 2007. "The Theory of Mechanism Design: An Overview." *Economic and Political Weekly* 42 (December 8).

Sheard, Michael, David Astrachan, and Michael Davis. 1975. "Effect of Noise on Shock-Elicited Aggression in Rats." *Nature* 257.

Shell, Karl. 1971. "Notes on the Economics of Infinity." *Journal of Political Economy* 79.

Siddique, Zahra. 2008. "Caste-Based Discrimination: Evidence and Policy." Mimeo, Northwestern University.

Simmel, Georg. 1950. *The Sociology of Georg Simmel*. Ed. Kurt H. Wolff. New York: Free Press.

Singh, Jaivir. 2009. "Labour Laws and Special Economic Zones in India." *Pragati: The Indian National Interest Review* 29, available at http://pragati.nationalinterest.in/2009/08/labour-law-and-special-economic-zones-in-india/.

Singh, Nirvikar. 2003. "The Impact of International Labor Standards: A Survey of Economic Theory." In *International Labor Standards*, ed. Kaushik Basu, Henrik Horn, Lisa Román, and Judith Shapiro. Oxford: Blackwell Publishers.

Smead, Rory. 2008. "The Evolution of Cooperation in the Centipede Game with Finite Populations." *Philosophy of Science* 75.

Smith, Adam. 1759. *The Theory of Moral Sentiments*. London: A. Millar.

———. [1776] 1937. *An Inquiry into the Nature and Causes of the Wealth of Nations*. Repr., New York: Random House, Inc.

Solow, Robert. 1995. "Mass Unemployment as a Social Problem." In *Choice, Welfare, and Development: A Festschrift in Honor of Amartya K. Sen*, ed. Kaushik Basu, Prasanta Pattanaik, and Kotaro Suzumura. Oxford: Oxford University Press.

———. 2006. "How to Understand the Economy." *New York Review of Books* 53 (November 16).

———. 2009. "Imposed Environmental Standards and International Trade." In *Arguments for a Better World: Essays in Honor of Amartya Sen*, ed. Kaushik Basu and Ravi Kanbur. Oxford: Oxford University Press.

Spence, A. Michael. 1974. *Market Signaling: Information Transfer in Hiring and Related Screening Processes*. Cambridge, MA: Harvard University Press.

Sporer, Siegfried. 2001. "Recognizing Faces of Other Ethnic Groups: An Integration of Theories." *Psychology, Public Policy, and Law* 7.

Srinivas, M. N. 1955. "The Social System of a Mysore Village." In *Village India: Studies in the Little Community*, ed. McKim Marriott. Chicago: University of Chicago Press.

Steele, Claude, and Joshua Aronson. 1995. "Stereotype Threat and the Intellectual Test Performance of African Americans." *Journal of Personality and Social Psychology* 69.

Steiner, Hillel. 1994. *An Essay on Rights*. Oxford: Blackwell Publishers.

Stern, Nicholas. 2006. *The Economics of Climate Change: The Stern Review*. Cambridge: Cambridge University Press.

Stewart, Rory. 2006. *The Prince of the Marshes and Other Occupational Hazards of a Year in Iraq*. New York: Harcourt.

Stiglitz, Joseph. 1974. "Theories of Discrimination and Economic Policy." In *Patterns of Racial Discrimination*, ed. George M. von Furstenberg. Lexington, MA: D. C. Heath and Co.

———. 2002. *Globalization and Its Discontents*. New York: Alfred Knopf.

———. 2006. *Making Globalization Work*. New York: W. W. Norton.

Subramanian, S. 2006. "Introduction: The Measurement of Inequality and Poverty." In *Measurement of Inequality and Poverty* by S. Subramanian. New Delhi: Oxford University Press.

———. 2007. "Social Groups and Economic Poverty: A Problem in Measurement." In *Inequality, Poverty, and Well-being*, ed. Mark McGillivray. Basingstoke, UK: Palgrave Macmillan.

Sugden, Robert. 1989. "Spontaneous Order." *Journal of Economic Perspectives* 3.

———. 2000. "Team Preference." *Economics and Philosophy* 16.

Sunstein, Cass. 1996. "On the Expressive Function of the Law." *University of Pennsylvania Law Review* 144.

———. 1997. *Free Markets and Social Justice*. Oxford: Oxford University Press.

Suzumura, Kotaro. 1983. *Rational Choice, Collective Decisions, and Social Welfare*. Cambridge, UK: Cambridge University Press.

Swedberg, Richard. 2001. "Sociology and Game Theory: Contemporary and Historical Perspectives." *Theory and Society* 30.

———. 2003. *Principles of Economic Sociology*. Princeton, NJ: Princeton University Press.

———. 2005. *Interest*. New York: Open University Press.

Swidler, Ann. 1986. "Culture in Action: Symbols and Strategies." *American Sociological Review* 51.

Tajfel, Henri. 1974. "Social Identity and Intergroup Behavior." *Social Science Information* 13.

Taylor, Charles. 1994. "The Politics of Recognition." In *Multiculturalism*, ed. Amy Gutmann. Princeton, NJ: Princeton University Press.

Thaler, Richard. 1992. *The Winner's Curse: Paradoxes and Anomalies of Economic Life.* Princeton, NJ: Princeton University Press.

Trachtman, Joel. 2006. "Welcome to Cosmopolis, World of Boundless Opportunity." Mimeo, Tufts University.

Trebilcock, Michael. 1993. *The Limits of Freedom of Contract.* Cambridge, MA: Harvard University Press.

Troyer, Lisa, and C. Wesley Younts. 1997. "Whose Expectations Matter? The Relative Power of First- and Second-Order Expectations in Determining Social Influence." *American Journal of Sociology* 103.

Turner, John C. 1999. "Some Current Issues in Research on Social Identity and Self-Categorization Theories. In *Social Identity*, ed. Naomi Ellemers, Russell Spears, and Bertjan Doosje. Oxford: Blackwell Publishers.

Tversky, Amos, and Daniel Kahneman. 1971. "Belief in the Law of Small Numbers." *Psychological Bulletin* 2.

Vallentyne, Peter. 2000. "Introduction: Left-Libertarianism—A Primer." In *Left-Libertarianism and Its Critics: The Contemporary Debate*, ed. Peter Vallentyne and Hillel Steiner. New York: Palgrave.

Varian, Hal. 1975. "Distributive Justice, Welfare Economics, and the Theory of Fairness." *Philosophy and Public Affairs* 4.

Varshney, Ashutosh. 2002. *Ethnic Conflict and Civic Life: Hindus and Muslims in India.* New Haven, CT: Yale University Press.

Veblen, Thorstein. 1899. *The Theory of the Leisure Class.* London: Macmillan.

Villanger, Espen. 2004. "Company Influence on Foreign Aid Disbursement: Is Conditionality Credible with Donors Having Mixed Motives?" *Southern Economic Journal* 70.

————. 2005. "Company Interests and Foreign Aid Policy: Playing Donors Out against Each Other." *European Economic Review* 49.

Viner, Jacob. 1927. "Adam Smith and Laissez Faire." *Journal of Political Economy* 35.

Voorneveld, Mark. 2009. "The Possibility of Impossible Stairways: Tail Events and Countable Player Sets." *Games and Economic Behavior.*

Wade, Roert. 2004. "Is Globalization Reducing Poverty and Inequality?" *World Development* 32.

Warneryd, Karl. 1990. *Economic Conventions: Essays in Institutional Evolution.* Stockholm: Stockholm School of Economics.

Watkins, John. 1952. "The Principle of Methodological Individualism." *British Journal for the Philosophy of Science* 3.

Weber, Max. [1922] 1968. *Economy and Society.* Vol. 1. Repr., New York: Bedminster Press.

Weibull, Jörgen. 1995. *Evolutionary Game Theory.* Cambridge, MA: MIT Press.

————. 2004. "Testing Game Theory." In *Advances in Understanding Strategic Behaviour: Game Theory, Experiments and Bounded Rationality*, ed. Steffen Huck. New York: Palgrove.

Weise, Kristian. 2007. "Corporate Tax Warning." *OECD Observer* 261 (May).

Weitzman, Martin. 1984. *The Share Economy: Conquering Stagflation*. Cambridge, MA: Harvard University Press.

Wertheimer, Alan. 1996. *Exploitation*. Princeton, NJ: Princeton University Press.

Williamson, Jeffrey. 2002. "Winners and Losers over Two Centuries of Globalization." WIDER annual lecture 6, WIDER, Helsinki.

Wilson, William Julius. 1987. *The Truly Disadvantaged: The Inner City, the Underclass, and Public Policy*. Chicago: University of Chicago Press.

Wolf, Martin. 2008. "Sustaining Growth Is the 21st Century's Big Challenge." *Financial Times*, June 11.

World Bank. 2001. *World Development Report 2000–1*. New York: Oxford University Press.

———. 2005. *World Development Indicators 2005*. Washington, DC: World Bank.

———. 2007. *World Development Indicators 2007*. Washington, DC: World Bank.

———. 2008. *World Development Indicators 2007*. Washington, DC: World Bank.

Wright, Erik Olin. 1996. "Political Power, Democracy, and Coupon Socialism." In *Equal Shares: Making Market Socialism Work*, ed. Erik Olin Wright. London: Verso.

Young, Allyn. 1928. "Increasing Returns and Economic Progress." *Economic Journal* 38.

Young, Peyton. 1998. *Individual Strategy and Social Structure: An Evolutionary Theory of Institutions*. Princeton, NJ: Princeton University Press.

Zambrano, Eduardo. 2004. "Counterfactual Reasoning and Common Knowledge of Rationality in Normal Form Games." *Topics in Theoretical Economics* 4.

Zelizer, Viviana. 2005. *The Purchase of Intimacy*. Princeton, NJ: Princeton University Press.

Ziesemer, Thomas. 1997. "From Loan Pushing to Credit Rationing: A Brief Note on Interest Shocks in a Model by Basu." *Journal of Institutional and Theoretical Economics* 153.

Zimmerman, David. 1981. "Coercive Wage Offers." *Philosophy and Public Affairs* 10.

Zinn, Howard. 2003. *A People's History of the United States, 1492–Present*. New York: HarperCollins.

INDEX

Milton Keynes UK
Ingram Content Group UK Ltd.
UKHW031307310824
447656UK00015B/129